Chronicle
of the Year
1989

Chronicle of the Year 1989

Has been conceived and published by Jacques Legrand

Editorial Director: **Clifton Daniel**

Managing Editor: **Tod Olson**
Editor in Chief: E. Curtiss Pierson

Staff Writers: Elizabeth Abbott, Tom Anderson, Susan Breen, Benton Boggs, Michael D'Arcy, Kevin Delaney, Vincent DeSomma, Philip Farber, James Forsht, Arthur Holch, Catherine Hulbert, Marguerite Jones, John Kirshon, Susan Merrill, Erik Migdail, Louis M. Nevin Jr., Noel Rae, Karen Rohan, Marianne Ruuth, Burt Solomon, Sam Tanenhaus, Steve Taylor, William Teague, Ken Weinstock, Marianne Yurchuk

Copy Editor: Ralph Berens

Editorial Research: Vincent DeSomma *(Editor)*
Carolyn Welch
Laura Williams
Jesse Stone *(Index)*

Photo Research: Erik Migdail *(Editor)*
Christian Danger *(Editions Chronique, Paris)*
Peter Dervis *(The Bettmann Archive)*
Veronique de Saint Andre *(SIPA)*
Kathy Bonomi

Production: Jean O'Neill
Henri Marganne and Alan Turpin *(Editions Chronique, Paris)*

Administration: Rose Ann Caris *(Manager)*
Georgine Santiago

Systems: Catherine Balouet *(Manager)*
Dominique Klutz *(Software Engineer)*
Darin Hamilton *(DPC)*

Marketing: Christine Remonte *(Manager)*

© 1989, Jacques Legrand s.a. International Publishing, Paris for World English rights.

© 1989, Ecam Publications, Inc., 105 South Bedford Road, Mount Kisco, N.Y. 10549; (914) 666-7668, for North American edition.

© Harenberg Kommunikation, Dortmund for Chronicle System.

ISBN 013 133 430-1
Printed and bound in the United States of America
Typesetting: Digital Prepress Center (DPC)
7 Odell Plaza, Yonkers, N.Y. 10701.
Quality Printing & Binding: Ringier America, Inc.,
12821 West Blue Mound Road, Brookfield, Wis. 53005.

Distributed in the United States of America by:
Prentice Hall Trade
A division of Simon & Schuster, Inc.
15 Columbus Circle
New York, N.Y. 10023

Distributed in Canada by:
Raincoast Books Ltd.
112 East 3rd Avenue
Vancouver
British Columbia V5T 1C8

Chronicle
of the Year
1989

Ecam
Publications

Mount Kisco, N.Y.

Su	Mo	Tu	We	Th	Fr	Sa
1	2	3	4	5	6	7
8	9	10	11	12	13	14
15	16	17	18	19	20	21
22	23	24	25	26	27	28
29	30	31				

1. Rio de Janeiro: New Year's Eve party boat capsizes in bay, killing 51; many missing.

1. Moscow: Soviets announce curbs on export of scarce products to combat shortage of consumer goods (→ 30).

2. Tempe, Ariz.: Notre Dame beats West Virginia 34-21 in Fiesta Bowl to finish undefeated season at top of college football rankings.

2. Pasadena, Calif.: Michigan beats U.S.C. 22-14 in Rose Bowl.

3. Washington, D.C.: U.S. accuses Libya of transporting chemicals for weapons from storage area to factory (→ 8).

3. Boston: Michael Dukakis announces he will not seek re-election as governor of Massachusetts.

4. Washington, D.C.: George Bush, as vice president, is first to proclaim his own presidential victory in Congress since Martin Van Buren (→ 20).

6. Boston: Sixteen Polish seamen jump ship and ask for political asylum in U.S.

6. Washington, D.C.: Federal grand jury returns first indictments for fraud in military contracting scandal, to Teledyne Industries.

6. New Delhi: Executions of two Sikhs for murder of Indira Gandhi spark protests.

6. Wilkes-Barre, Pa.: Larry and Leona Cottam charged with homicide for allowing 14-year-old son to starve to death; they claim money was being saved for God.

6. Bischofshofen, Austria: Mike Holland becomes first American to win four-hill ski jumping tournament in its 37-year history.

7. Cuba: It is revealed that Fidel Castro has a small malignancy on his lung, hence absence of trademark cigar since 1985.

DEATH

2. Eddie Heywood, jazz pianist and composer, leader of one of most popular bands of 1940s (*Dec. 4, 1915).

U.S. downs 2 Libyan jets

Vernon Walters, U.S. envoy to the U.N., displays a missile-carrying MiG.

Jan 4. Two U.S. Navy fighter planes shot down two Libyan warplanes early today in a skirmish over international waters 70 miles off the coast of Libya. According to Defense Secretary Frank C. Carlucci, the U.S. planes — F-14s on patrol from the carrier John F. Kennedy — acted defensively in response to the "clear hostile intent" of the Libyan planes. Libya claims, however, that its planes were on routine maneuvers and were not armed. Libya's leader, Col. Muammar el-Qaddafi, charges that "official U.S. terrorism" is responsible for the confrontation.

The Reagan administration has denied any connection between today's incident and U.S. attempts to stop construction of a Libyan plant that the administration says will produce chemical weapons. Last month, President Reagan himself implied that a military strike against the chemical plant was not out of the question.

This is one of several military clashes that have taken place between the two countries during the Reagan administration. The first, remarkably similar to today's encounter, occurred in 1981 when two F-14s shot down two Libyan warplanes near the Gulf of Sidra.

The latest conflict comes as the two countries are about to join some 140 other nations in Paris to discuss chemical weapons, including the suspect Libyan plant (→ 11).

Soviet-made MiG-23: missile-bearing warplane with "hostile intent"?

Nuclear cleanup to cost $92 billion

Jan 4. The legacy of America's unwaning dependence on nuclear technology is just a bit clearer today. The Energy Department has announced it will cost $92 billion to clean up after nuclear weapons manufacturers and other installations under its control. The study, prompted by several nuclear mishaps last year, is the first of its kind conducted by the government.

The Reagan Administration has budgeted $1.3 billion for the cleanup, a figure that represents 75 percent of the amount needed to run all the facilities next year. But Sen. John Glenn (D-Ohio), who released the report, feels the amount is not large enough. Without proper cleanup efforts, he says, the long-term costs to the environment will be far higher.

Salvadorans resign in wake of threats

Local leaders in El Salvador are resigning en masse as murders and threats have made officeholding a risky occupation. In a month, 35 mayors have quit and eight others have been killed by opposition forces fighting the U.S.-backed government. The revolutionary Farabundo Marti National Liberation Front has left 40 percent of the country's towns without mayors, dealing a severe blow to U.S. attempts at extending central control into the countryside. The 10-year war has killed 70,000 (→ Mar 12).

Europe to be linked by super-fast trains

London to Paris in 2 hours 40 minutes? That is the plan for 1993, when railroad visionaries hope to inaugurate the Channel tunnel with a ride on a 180-mph train. Seven European nations, in fact, hope to build extensive high-speed lines by 1995. Cost estimates run about $50 billion. But potential gains in lowered air fares and easier travel are great. The high-speed train, says one French executive, "is not a gadget. It earns its keep right away."

Japan's Emperor Hirohito dies at 87

North prosecutor seeking dismissals

Jan 5. The independent prosecutor in the "Irangate" case has asked a federal court to dismiss the two main criminal charges against Lt. Col. Oliver North. Lawrence Walsh says he cannot obtain the documents needed to prove that North defrauded the government by taking money from arms sales to Iran in order to aid the Nicaraguan contras. The Reagan administration contends that disclosing the records would jeopardize national security. North's lawyers, however, insist that high officials are simply covering up their own involvement in the conspiracy.

North still faces charges of illegal use of funds and lying to Congress. If convicted, he could face up to 65 years in jail and $2 million in fines (→ 13).

Students in China clash in race riots

Jan 5. Racial violence is smoldering in Chinese cities. Clashes between African and Chinese students were kindled Dec. 24 in a brawl in the eastern city of Nanjing, and sizzled again Sunday over an alleged attack on a Chinese woman by an African student at Beijing University. African students are preparing to leave the country, claiming their leaders are being arrested and tortured by police, and that China is "unsafe" for Africans.

Jan 7. The flower of the Japanese Chrysanthemum Throne has wilted and finally expired, and a mourning nation has discovered to its sorrow that even a man once regarded as a living god can die. Emperor Hirohito, the 124th monarch of the world's oldest dynasty and the longest holder of that title, has passed into history at the age of 87. Although Hirohito had renounced his divinity after Japan's defeat in World War II, he remained an object of deep reverence for many Japanese. Soon after his death ended the "Era of Enlightened Peace," his son, Prince Akihito, ascended the throne to usher in the "Era of Achieving Peace."

As befits the passing of a figure who once held so strong an influence on the Japanese national psyche, a six-day mourning period was mandated by the Cabinet. Government agencies were requested to refrain from joyous dancing and singing and to display flags in the Emperor's honor. Private citizens were asked to observe a two-day mourning period and also to fly flags.

It seems, however, that no orders are needed. Many citizens, having prepared themselves for this moment during the monarch's long illness (they were informed only that duodenal cancer was the cause of his demise), wept openly. Radio stations played quiet classical music, and a tide of mourners made their

A Buddhist monk kneels in sorrow before the Imperial Palace. The loss of Japan's once-divine ruler has sparked expressions of grief in all walks of life.

pilgrimage to the Imperial Palace to offer prayers. American servicemen stationed in Japan were ordered to refrain from saying anything disrespectful about the man against whom their predecessors had fought so passionately in the Second World War.

The altered role of the monarchy during Hirohito's reign is symbolic in many ways of the changes that have brought Japanese society in tune with modern Western sensibilities. While the head of an ancient Oriental dynasty, the diminutive ruler nonetheless adopted many

Western styles and devoted himself fervently to marine biology, becoming an authority on jellyfish. Under the direction of Gen. Douglas MacArthur, head of the postwar military occupation, the Emperor gave up his power, the peerage was abolished and Parliament placed in control of the Cabinet.

His funeral also will be a break with tradition, not following the Shinto ritual that was customary before the war. Hirohito's son, Akihito, however, will be installed with the same rites and symbols as his 124 predecessors.

The life of a once-divine ruler: symbol of a transforming nation

Students read anti-African posters.

Jan 7. As the longest reigning monarch on earth, an embodiment of the Japanese nation, Hirohito symbolized one of the most tumultuous periods in the country's history.

Under his divine name, Japanese generals launched a bid for control of Asia. And through the painful renunciation of his divinity after the war, a defeated nation was brought into the modern world.

Even before the great upheaval, however, Hirohito reflected his country's growing fascination with the West. In 1921, a visit to Europe made him the first member of the royal family ever to leave Japan. A Paris subway ticket forever remained a treasured possession. In 1975, on the eve of Japan's ascen-

dance as the world's premier economic power, he visited the United States, returning with a Mickey Mouse watch for the royal wrist.

When he assumed the throne on Dec. 25, 1926, he was one of the world's few remaining divine monarchs. The very sight of his face was said to be blinding to children. By the end of his reign, he was little more than a figurehead. As a man, Hirohito was quiet and unassuming, more taken with marine biology than the affairs of state. As the postwar decades slipped by and the values of democracy and capitalism took over, he faded into benign obscurity. From Hiroshima until his death, he was respected, yet something of an anachronism.

Emperor Hirohito as a younger man.

Su	Mo	Tu	We	Th	Fr	Sa
1	2	3	4	5	6	7
8	9	10	11	12	13	14
15	16	17	18	19	20	21
22	23	24	25	26	27	28
29	30	31				

8. Detroit: Edmund Cardinal Szoka, Roman Catholic Bishop of Detroit, orders 30 lower-income parishes to close, despite widespread local opposition.

8. Paris: Soviet Union announces, at international talks on chemical weapons, it will begin to destroy chemical weapons stockpiles (→ 10).

9. Quebec: Two Indian nations sign free-trade agreement to set up Cree-Mohawk Trade Authority in what is apparently first such arrangement between two North American native groups.

9. Atlanta: Four KKK members plead guilty to charges stemming from May 1979 attack on civil rights marchers in Decatur, Ga. (→ July 26).

9. Cooperstown, N.Y.: Johnny Bench, Carl Yastrzemski voted into Baseball Hall of Fame in first year of eligibility.

10. Bonn: West Germany announces it will curb exports of nuclear and chemical materials that can be used in making weapons (→ 12).

11. Washington, D.C.: President Reagan raises quota of Soviet refugees allowed into U.S. by lowering quota for Asians.

11. Washington, D.C.: President-elect Bush nominates James D. Watkins for energy secretary, last Cabinet post.

11. United Nations: U.S., Britain and France veto resolution condemning downing of two Libyan fighters by U.S.

11. Washington, D.C.: Poll by NAACP finds most whites think blacks are treated fairly by society, while most blacks disagree.

12. Paris: French police arrest Jose Antonio Urrutikoetxea, Basque separarist leader. It is major blow to movement.

12. Newark, N.J.: Customs Service agents arrest businessman Juwhan Yun for attempting to acquire 125 tons of U.S. nerve gas (→ 12).

13. Washington, D.C.: Judge agrees to drop two main charges against Lt. Col. North due to lack of evidence (→ Feb 13).

Cuban forces finally begin to leave Angola

Bringing the boys back home: Cubans leave after long sojourn across the sea.

Jan 10. To the rhythmic beat of a brass band, an honor guard today bore a faded Cuban flag aboard a Caribbean-bound, Soviet-built jet in Luanda. The ceremony marks the beginning of Cuba's withdrawal from revolutionary Angola.

The flag had arrived with the first Cuban troops 13 years earlier, shortly after Portugal ended its 500-year reign as master of the oil-rich African land. In the civil war that followed independence, Angola's Marxists gained control of the government, propped up by Soviet financial support. Soon after, they called for Cuban help in fighting off guerrilla rivals backed by the United States and South Africa.

Now that the major powers have better use for their money, an eight-year-old U.S. mediation effort has paid off. South Africa has agreed to pull out of the newly independent neighboring nation of Namibia as a condition for Cuba's withdrawal.

As a Czechoslovakian army major with the U.N. observer team counted the first planeload of 150 Cubans, the commander declared, "Mission accomplished." But some 50,000 more troops wait their turn. And Cuba warns that if South Africa fails to leave, the Communist forces will "remain on guard in their trenches, and maintain their fighting stance to the last man, to the last day of Cuba's internationalist mission in Angola" (→ June 22).

Jan 8. *At least 30 are dead in the wreckage of a British airliner that crashed today near a major highway in central England.*

Chinese are treated to nude art exhibit

Jan 8. A visitor might have guessed the artwork was displayed on the floor, judging by how many onlookers kept their eyes downcast. The nature of the art — 120 oil and mixed media portraits of nudes — and the place — Beijing, China — explain such seemingly odd behavior. From the days of Confucius, the naked human figure has been excluded from Chinese art. And not all of the 180,000 who attended the 18-day exhibit at the Beijing Art Gallery were quite ready to face the bare facts of Western-influenced painting. The show closed today, to the blushing relief of many.

Belgian arrested in chemical scandal

Jan 12. The arrest today of a Belgian shipping agent provides a direct link between a West German chemical company and a plant in Libya that is allegedly being built to produce chemical weapons. The Bonn government of Helmut Kohl has finally conceded there are "indications" that U.S. allegations of West German participation in the Libyan project may be true. The shipping agent, Jozef Gedopt, has been charged with falsifying documents for chemicals supposedly sent from Hamburg to Hong Kong, but actually routed to Libya. The Libyans claim the factory will produce pharmaceuticals (→ July 17).

Pentagon plans for helium radar blimp

Jan 8. For most Americans a blimp is a giant sausage that floats over a football stadium advertising tires. Now, 25 years after the Navy scrapped its last blimp, it is building the YEZ-2A, a 425-foot ship containing 2.5 milllon cubic feet of helium. The Coast Guard and the Navy plan to use its powerful radar to protect the shores of the United States from cruise missiles and drug smugglers. The enormous airship is being developed by Westinghouse-Airship Industries, a British-American consortium.

Long-running show closes on Broadway

Jan 8. The musical *42nd Street* had an inauspicious start, opening the night that its director, Gower Champion, died. Tonight, however, the show about a small-town hoofer who makes it to the big time lowered its last curtain on a high note. Nostalgic cheers broke into the performance after the line "think of musical comedy — the most glorious words in the English language." The show's 3,486 performances make it the second-most-durable Broadway musical (after *A Chorus Line*). Producer David Merrick noted happily that 10 million people have seen *42nd Street*.

S&L crisis is laid to regulatory policy

Jan 10. Blame for the crisis that has engulfed the country's savings and loan institutions should be laid at the door of government regulatory policies, according to the 1990 President's Economic Report. "We got a mess," said Beryl W. Sprinkel, chairman of the Council of Economic Advisers and main author of the report. Despite its anti-deregulation stance, the council criticized the recent flurry of government-engineered takeovers of insolvent savings and loans. Rather than rely on healthy members to save it, the system will probably have to look to the taxpayer for the $50 to $100 billion needed to bail it out (→ Feb 6).

80 die in renewed Beirut civil conflict

Jan 9. Police in southern Lebanon have reported 80 people killed and 200 wounded as fierce fighting continues to rage between rival Shiite Muslim militia groups. Thousands of civilians have fled north, leaving the streets of the Iqlim al Toffah district dotted with black-robed women searching for the bodies of their sons. The fighting is a direct result of the prolonged rivalry between the pro-Syrian Amal militia and the fundamentalist Hizballah, or Party of God, which is supported by Iran (→ Feb 28).

Veterans of divorce avoid remarriage

Jan 9. "Never again" seems to be the refrain being echoed across the country by the battle-scarred veterans of divorce. According to a report by the National Center for Health Statistics, "only 9 percent of divorced women and 14 percent of divorced men remarried in 1983, compared with 12 percent of divorced women and 20 percent of divorced men in 1970." Divorce, however, is ever popular; one of every three newlyweds is trying for at least the second time. And, searching for that shared experience, most divorced men marry divorced women.

Reagan says goodbye in last address

In spring of '84, Reagan the candidate strives for that strong, youthful look.

A familiar sight for reporters.

In July '87, the President shows a group of Right-to-Lifers his latest problem — a patch of skin cancer.

Jan 11. President Ronald Reagan bid farewell to the American people tonight in his final address to the nation. Following a 200-year-old custom, he gave a report on the state of America — and a warning.

While lauding the nation's restored sense of patriotism, the President cautioned that failing to understand history "could result . . . in an erosion of the American spirit." But he also praised his two terms in office, comparing America today to the "City on the Hill" described in 1630 by John Winthrop, the first governor of Massachusetts. "My friends, we did it," he said. "We weren't just marking time . . . We made the city stronger — we made the city freer — and we left her in good hands. All in all, not bad. Not bad at all" (→ 20).

Pop culture in the White House: Mr. T, veteran of the "Just Say No" campaign," visits Nancy, Christmas '83.

In California, just before the first inauguration, breaking in a present from the President of Mexico.

Crowning achievement: Led by Gorbachev's gentle tug, the U.S.S.R. transformed in the presidential mind from "evil empire" to partner in arms control.

7

Su	Mo	Tu	We	Th	Fr	Sa
1	2	3	4	5	6	7
8	9	10	11	12	13	14
15	16	17	18	19	20	21
22	23	24	25	26	27	28
29	30	31				

15. Prague: Police brutally crush a crowd of nearly 1,000 demonstrators marching in honor of dead "Prague Spring" leader Jan Palach (→ Feb 21).

16. Vienna: New East-West human rights agreement is signed by 35 nations, United States, Soviet Union and Canada included.

16. Dhaka, Bangladesh: Seventy people are killed in country's worst train disaster.

18. Canada: Molson and Carling-O'Keefe breweries merge into a $1.5 billion firm designed to break into the U.S. beer market.

18. Washington, D.C.: Supreme Court upholds constitutionality of new seven-member commission endowed with power to revise most federal criminal sentences.

18. New York City: Rock and Roll Hall of Fame inducts Rolling Stones, Otis Redding, Stevie Wonder, The Temptations and Dion.

18. Washington, D.C.: Lee Atwater, Bush's '88 campaign manager, is elected chairman of Republican Party.

19. Belgrade, Yugoslavia: Economic reformer Ante Markovic is appointed Yugoslavia's new Prime Minister.

19. Washington, D.C.: Outgoing President Ronald Reagan pardons Yankees owner George Steinbrenner, convicted of illegally contributing to Nixon's 1972 campaign.

20. Moscow: Physicist and human rights activist Andrei Sakharov nominated for a seat in the new National Congress of Deputies (→ March 26).

20. Chicago: A Piedmont airliner loses one of its engines taking off from O'Hare.

DEATHS

20. Lord Harding, British commander of Desert Rats in North Africa during World War II (*1896).

21. Carl Furillo, baseball star for Brooklyn Dodgers; immortalized in Roger Kahns' *The Boys of Summer* (*March 8, 1922).

George Bush becomes 41st President

Jan 20. Calling for an end to interparty hostility and the formation of a bipartisan coalition to fight social ills, George Bush today became the nation's 41st President. Dan Quayle was sworn in as vice president. Bush took the oath exactly 200 years after the swearing in of America's first President, George Washington. Organizers have thus named this the "George to George" inauguration.

In his inaugural address, the former vice president announced that "We live in a peaceful and prosperous time, but we can make it better." In keeping with his campaign promise to bring about a "kinder and gentler America," he said he would seek "to celebrate the quieter, deeper successes that are made not of gold and silk but of better hearts and finer souls." While thanking Ronald Reagan for eight years of service, Bush also called for change, returning again and again to a single refrain: "A new breeze is blowing."

Using the terminology of James Barber, a presidential scholar, George Bush is expected to be a "positive/passive" president, that is, positive about the office of the presidency and passive about shaking the political tree. Some analysts are already comparing him to President Dwight D. Eisenhower.

He is certainly excited about his

A "kinder, gentler" President: George Herbert Walker Bush IV.

new job. His brother Jonathan described Bush's enthusiasm: "It is as if you took a bottle of soda water, shook it up and down, and then took the cork out, and boom goes the spray all over the room."

It was champagne spraying the room, however, at tonight's inaugural ball, where the President and his wife, Barbara, basked in the glory as only the First Couple can. A gala dinner was held at Union Station last week, where across the street homeless people protested the multimillion dollar inauguration. While most Americans give Bush their best wishes for a smooth and successful start, many too are anxious to see Bush's "1,000 points of light" shed on those in need.

Flying off into the sunset, Reagan bids a final farewell to the Capitol.

Japan is world's top foreign lender

Jan 19. The latest sign of Japan's growing global role is the fact that it has displaced the United States as the world's No. 1 donor and lender of foreign aid. News of the historic change came as the government made public its 1989 budget of $491 billion. More than $10 billion of that figure will be allocated to foreign aid, including a 6 percent increase in outright grants to foreign nations. Last year, the U.S. foreign aid budget was about $9 billion, an amount that is expected to decline. Japan also plans to push its military spending to $31.6 billion, an increase of 5.2 percent.

NCAA ruling called racist by opponents

Jan 18. Tough new NCAA curbs on scholarships for athletes with poor grades have provoked a one-man strike at Georgetown University. That one man is John Thompson, coach of the nation's second-ranked college basketball team. On Saturday, when he walked off the court before the Hoyas' game against Boston College, problems of class, race and sports were thrown into national focus. The new requirements, Thompson says, discriminate against students from culturally and economically disadvantaged backgrounds, many of whom gain opportunity through athletics.

Idi Amin has turned up in Zaire under a false passport, perhaps on a mission to terrorize Uganda as he did before his exile in 1979.

Black's death sparks race riots in Miami

Jan 18. Blacks in Miami took to the streets during the past two days, rioting, looting and burning stores in anger over the death of a black man in a police chase. Six people have been shot and 250 arrested in the disturbances.

The mute cause of the turmoil was one Clement Lloyd, whose erratic motorcycle driving attracted attention two nights ago. Unarmed, he was shot by police during the ensuing chase.

Riots began after Miami Mayor Xavier Suarez arrived at the scene and urged police to allow Lloyd's family to see the body. When the sheet was lifted from the victim, two dozen angry blacks began shouting and throwing bottles be-

fore police moved in to push back the crowd, setting off further rioting. Suarez apologized to the police for his handling of the incident.

As the clashes continued last night, 250 people were arrested, most charged with prowling or inciting to riot. Dozens of instances of looting and arson were reported, and 27 buildings had been set afire.

The City Commission voted to set up a citizens review panel to investigate the shooting. Black citizens have charged that Hispanic immigrants receive special treatment, while blacks have been the victims of police brutality. Suarez, a Cuban immigrant, has visited black neighborhoods hoping to ease some of the tension.

Ravaged by rampant looting and arson, Miami deals with the damage.

Crazed gunman kills five school children

Jan 17. Five Asian children, ages 6 to 9, died just before noon today at a Stockton, Calif., elementary school at the hands of a crazed unemployed welder. Thirty others, including a teacher, were wounded when the gunman approached the Cleveland School playground during recess and scattered at least 106 rounds from an AK-47 military assault rifle before shooting himself in the head with a pistol.

Police say the gunman, Patrick Edward Purdy, who was in his 20s, left no motive for the bloody rampage except an obsession with warfare and guns. He had been a student at the school, which now serves mostly Vietnamese and Cambodian refugees (→ March 2).

In the aftermath, succor is given to injured and uninjured alike.

Managua collapsing under weight of war

"Managua, Nicaragua, what a wonderful spot / Coffee and bananas and the temperature's hot / So take the trip / Get on a ship / Go sailing away / To Managua, Nicaragua, Nicaragua. Ole!"

The old song that depicts this city as a thriving Latino resort paradise holds little relevance now. Ten years of war, a 1972 earthquake from which residents have yet to recover, and a deep depression have made this once majestic city a shell of ruin and collapse. Often visitors are shocked to see the nation's capital, particularly the ghostly downtown, in such a state. But locals and

regional experts are fully aware of the devastation wrought by the protracted war against the U.S.-backed contra rebels, and by the American trade embargo imposed after the Sandinistas came to power in 1979.

Visitors are also surprised that inhabitants are so congenial in a city where water shuts off without notice and necessities can be impossible to get. As one tourist said, "In Manhattan, a city strike brings violence and looting. Here, the most dire conditions are met with strong will and a smile, even to those of us from the enemy nation" (→ Feb 14).

Junk food malls rise across nation

In the parlance of the fast food industry, more has always been better. Now some entrepreneurs are taking the concept a step further by combining several junk food outlets under one roof, creating what are variously called treat centers, food courts or cluster restaurants. Thus, prefab food connoisseurs from Minnesota to Manhattan are dazzled simultaneously by the glaring neon of Taco Bell, Burger King or Le Croissant, creating an ever more complex set of choices. Said one eager food executive: "You have to have a name, and five names are better than one."

Specter of AIDS haunts drug users

Education has become an important tool in the fight against AIDS, but unfortunately not everyone hears the message. While new cases of AIDS are reported to be declining in gay communities, the number of intravenous drug users testing positive is on the rise. In some gay communities, where the emphasis has been on changing sex habits, new cases have fallen 15 percent in the last few years. The opposite appears to be true for drug addicts. In New York State alone, 3,500 new cases of AIDS are expected among users this year, compared to 2,700 among gays (→ 29).

These proud beasts in India fare better than their cousins in Saudi Arabia, where camels, once an integral part of Saudi life, have given way to Toyotas and BMWs, surviving only as a food source or racing animal.

JANUARY
1989

Su	Mo	Tu	We	Th	Fr	Sa
1	2	3	4	5	6	7
8	9	10	11	12	13	14
15	16	17	18	19	20	21
22	23	24	25	26	27	28
29	30	31				

22. South Carolina: An octogenarian couple is rescued from a deserted island off the coast of South Carolina four days after shipwreck.

23. U.S.S.R.: An earthquake in Soviet Central Asia sets off a landslide, killing an estimated 1,000 people.

24. New York City: U.S. government files a range of illegal trading charges against Drexel Burnham Lambert (→ March 29).

25. Washington, D.C.: U.S. announces plans to construct four-mile-long ditch along Mexican-American border in attempt to stem flow of drugs.

26. Moscow: Recently declassified documents show U.S. drew up plan to oust Cuban government in 1962.

27. The Hague: Dutch parliament pardons two convicted Nazi war criminals after they spent 43 years in prison for the deaths of 10,000 Jews.

28. Moscow: Soviet representatives at conference on Cuban Missile Crisis admit that Soviet warheads were in Cuba and ready for launch in 1962.

28. Arcadia, Calif.: Alysheba, biggest money-making Thoroughbred ever, is named Race Horse of the Year for 1988.

28. Washington, D.C.: Justice Department releases report citing misdoings of former Attorney General Ed Meese.

29. Washington, D.C.: President Bush requests $1.4 billion for AIDS research, far below what Congress has called for (→ Feb 2).

30. Washington, D.C.: Vice President Dan Quayle, in speech to meeting of National Religious Broadcasters, says that ''hatred of God'' is at root of Soviet Union's misfortunes.

DEATHS

27. Sir Thomas Sopwith, inventor of Sopwith Camel, in which he was shot down in World War I by Red Baron (*1888).

31. William Stephenson, British spy known as Intrepid (*Jan. 11, 1896).

Dali, master of the bizarre, is dead

The artist or the art, who can tell?

Jan 23. Salvador Dali closed the circle of his life today in the town where it began, Figueras, Spain. He was 84 years old. His name will be forever synonymous with Surrealism, as the art world is left to puzzle over the compelling compositions that defined the genre. There is a magic to Dali's work — dreams captured on canvas. Yet he reached beyond painting into sculpture, writing and film making. His vision teased the eye and delighted the imagination, playing always with the line between what is and what could never be. At age 25 he had his first exhibition, in Paris, and his career remained not only controversial but also fantastically successful throughout his lifetime.

Extremist LaRouche sentenced for fraud

Jan 27. Lyndon R. LaRouche, who for years launched bombastic pronouncements from the political fringe, was sentenced today to 15 years in prison for tax fraud and defaulting on loans of $30 million. A presidential candidate who ran on a ticket named after himself, LaRouche said he was the victim of a government plot. Federal Judge Albert Bryan called that ''nonsense.'' As a soapbox speaker, LaRouche has accused former Vice President Walter Mondale of espionage and the Vatican of drug-running.

Supreme Court limits affirmative action

Jan 23. A number of government programs designed to provide jobs for minorities are in jeopardy following the Supreme Court's ruling on a Richmond, Va., law that directed 30 percent of public works funds to minority-owned construction companies. In a 6-3 decision, the court ruled that the Richmond ordinance denies white contractors their constitutional right to equal protection under the law.

Justice Sandra Day O'Connor, in the majority opinion, insisted that discrimination based on race could never be ''benign,'' no matter how laudable its purpose. Programs such as Richmond's, she wrote, were invalid unless they served the ''compelling state interest'' of redressing ''identified discrimination'' by the government or private parties. Many affirmative action programs, including similar minority set-aside programs in 36 states, fail to meet this standard.

In his dissenting opinion, Justice Thurgood Marshall said the court's decision ''sounds a full-scale retreat from the court's long-standing solicitude to race-conscious remedial efforts directed toward deliverance of the century-old promise of equality of economic opportunity.'' The ruling moved Justice Harry A. Blackmun to refer to the court as a ''supposed bastion of equality'' (→ June 5).

Kremlin admits 43 million live in poverty

In Azerbaijan, residents surround a vendor, competing for scarce biscuits.

Jan 30. The poor are the Soviet Union's invisible citizens. They are rarely seen begging on street corners or sleeping in terminals. So well hidden are they that for many years Soviet officials proclaimed poverty solely an evil of capitalism.

But recently, the government has been forced to acknowledge that some 20 percent of the population lives in poverty, as compared to 14 percent in the U.S. ''poverty is a reality, our national tragedy,'' one Soviet newspaper reported.

Soviet authorities say a person needs about 75 rubles, or $124, a month to maintain ''minimum material security.'' An estimated 43 million Russians live below that line, one-third of them retirees.

For example, Valeriya Ionava receives a pension of less than 36 rubles a month. After paying rent, she has eight rubles left to live on.

Ironically, the very reforms that have made the discussion of poverty possible have made the plight of the poor more difficult. Soviet leader Mikhail Gorbachev's perestroika, so far, has led to higher prices and greater shortages.

What do the Soviets plan to do for those living in what officials call a state of ''underprovisioning''? There are no programs yet, but one thing they will not have is soup kitchens. Says one Soviet official, ''We are opposed to this system used in the United States where people get free dinner'' (→ March 16).

Ted Bundy is executed as crowd cheers

Argentina quells yet another rebellion

Ted Bundy, who claims that pornography in media fueled his violent fantasies, glares from a TV monitor on the grass at the Florida state prison.

Peering over a covering wall, the defense rests while looking for an opening to assist in the repulsion of the rebels' early morning coup attempt.

Jan 24. Some 200 persons outside the Florida State Prison at Starke let out cheers today when they got the news that serial killer Ted Bundy had died in "Ol' Sparky," the prison's electric chair. As the end of his life neared, Bundy lost his smug, superior demeanor and tried to stall the inevitable by confessing to the murders of young women across the country. But the governor turned a deaf ear.

Bundy's killing spree began in Seattle in February 1974 and soon spread throughout the Northwest, then to Colorado and Utah. He was arrested twice, but escaped both times, ending up finally in Florida. There he was charged with the slaying of 12-year-old Kimberly Leach of Lake City, whose mutilated body was found in an animal pen, and the bludgeoning and strangling murders of two Chi Omega sorority sisters at Florida State University. Those crimes occurred three weeks apart in late 1978 and early 1979. Bundy's six years on the loose produced a string of victims estimated to number between 30 and 100.

Jan 24. Argentina is caught between right and left. After warding off three recent army rebellions by right-wing officers, the shaky government of President Raul Alfonsin today fought off a blow from the left. An armed civilian attack on an army barracks outside Buenos Aires has killed at least 21 and wounded many on both sides. Six soldiers and policemen were among those killed during a counterattack on snipers who were dug into bunkers. More than 20 rebels were captured.

Some believe foreigners were involved, but the alleged agitators have not been identified. Officials say the civilians used Soviet- and Chinese-made machine guns. Sporadic gunfire continued during a visit to the captial by President Alfonsin, whose supporters said the raiders are remnants of a guerrilla group believed destroyed by harsh military repression during the 1970s. The president's press secretary told reporters that soldiers have captured pamphlets warning of a military coup and calling for support to oppose it (→ May 30).

Steinberg is guilty of manslaughter

Jan 30. One of New York's most sensational murder trials ended tonight when a Manhattan jury convicted Joel B. Steinberg, a 47-year-old disbarred lawyer, of first-degree manslaughter. Steinberg, the jury decided, inflicted the blows to the head that killed Lisa, the 6-year-old child he and his companion, Hedda Nussbaum, were raising in their Greenwich Village apartment. The conviction carries a maximum sentence of 25 years.

The case has focussed national attention on a sordid tale of physical and emotional brutality. Nussbaum, the jury determined, was so incapacitated by Steinberg's beatings that she was incapable of murdering Lisa (→ March 24).

Jan 22. *Icky Woods avoided Kevin Fagan's tackle, but the Bengals could not avoid a 20-16 defeat by the San Francisco 49ers in Super Bowl XXIII.*

Extreme rightists gain in West Berlin

Jan 29. Shades of a shameful past emerged in West Berlin today as election returns showed a shocking surge of support for the Republican Citizens Party, a far-right group headed by ex-Nazi Franz Schonhuber. His call for "purified patriotism" — a dig against Turks, Poles and other foreign job-seekers who are often blamed for a local housing shortage — garnered the rightist party 8 percent of the vote and gave them their first seats (11 out of 144) in the city's legislature. Not to worry, say pundits: though it will wreck the centrist coalition formed by the Christian Democrats, the vote is tied to particular issues and does not augur a broad-based shift toward fascism (→ Feb 9).

Su	Mo	Tu	We	Th	Fr	Sa
			1	2	3	4
5	6	7	8	9	10	11
12	13	14	15	16	17	18
19	20	21	22	23	24	25
26	27	28				

1. Seoul, South Korea: North and South Korea agree to a joint project for construction of resort in North.

1. New York City: Diana, Princess of Wales, arrives for a three-day visit.

1. Soviet Union: Results of poll conducted by Soviet press agency Tass show Leonid Brezhnev slightly less popular with Soviet citizens than Josef Stalin (→ 3).

1. Middle East: PLO rejects Israel's offer to withdraw troops from occupied territories if PLO will settle for limited autonomy (→ 4).

2. Caracas, Venezuela: Dan Quayle criticizes ex-President Carter for meeting with Nicaraguan President Daniel Ortega (→ 4).

2. Washington, D.C.: Without full testing, FDA announces it will permit sale of anti-AIDS drug aerosol pentamidine (→ March 14).

2. Washington, D.C.: Senate votes down 50 percent congressional pay raise, leaving ball in House's court (→ 7).

2. Honolulu: Vice President Salvador Laurel of the Philippines visits former President Ferdinand Marcos as a "humanitarian" gesture.

2. Leningrad: Natalya Makarova returns to dance at the Kirov 18 years after seeking asylum in the West.

2. Vail, Colo.: Tamara McKinney wins Gold Medal at the world Alpine Championships, ending four-year American medal drought.

2. New York City: It is revealed that Diane Sawyer of CBS's *60 Minutes* has signed a contract with ABC News for $1.3 million per year.

2. United States: Anxiety drug Xanax has become most commonly prescribed drug in U.S.

4. Israel: Two Arabs and a Red Cross worker are killed by Israeli troops (→ March 1).

DEATH

3. John Cassavetes, film actor/director (*Dec. 9, 1929).

Vice President Quayle practices diplomacy

Quayle in Caracas, sampling the exotic foods from far away places.

Feb 4. In his first trip abroad since rising to America's second-highest office, Vice President Dan Quayle has joined dignitaries of 22 nations in Caracas for the inauguration of Venezuela's newly elected President Carlos Andres Perez. And many fellow Republicans are holding their breath for fear the neophyte diplomat might stumble. With minor exceptions, Quayle has avoided any major pitfalls.

In off-the-cuff remarks, however, he did berate former President Carter for trying to negotiate with the Nicaraguan Sandinistas, and unintentionally suggested that President Reagan used excuses to bow out of press conferences.

But for the most part, Quayle has managed to fulfill without event the typical, ceremonial functions of the vice presidency. He was directed not to articulate the foreign policy of the Bush administration — some say because policy has yet to be formulated. He will meet with several Latin America representatives on an exploratory level when he visits El Salvador tomorrow.

The gathering of so many Latin American leaders has brought some substantive issues to the fore. Nicaraguan President Daniel Ortega has told of plans to repatriate members of the opposition forces. Discussions were also held on the Latin nations' debts to the first world, drug trafficking and widespread unrest in Panama (→ June 26).

Bill White is first black NL president

Feb 3. Bill White, a one-time slick-fielding first baseman who proved equally smooth during an 18-year stint as the voice of the New York Yankees, has been named the president of baseball's National League. White, 55, was the unanimous choice of the 12 league owners and will become the highest-ranking black executive in professional sports. The ex-San Francisco Giant and St. Louis Cardinal power hitter broke into baseball in 1956, less than a decade after Jackie Robinson shattered the racial barrier. Downplaying the symbolism of his new job, White said blacks "should be judged on how we do the job."

Bill White, ex-player, announcer.

Soviets finally admit 20 million citizens died under Stalin

Josef Stalin, the Georgian butcher.

Feb 3. No country lost more people during World War II than the Soviet Union. But today the Soviets acknowledged an even more horrible statistic: an equal number of its citizens died between 1927 and 1953 as victims of Josef Stalin.

Some 20 million Russians died in executions, labor camps, famine and collectivization drives during the Soviet leader's reign, according to an article by the respected Soviet historian Roy Medvedev. The story appears in today's issue of the national weekly *Argumenty i Fakty*. He estimates that another 20 million were arrested or driven from their homes. Medvedev's own father died in a labor camp.

The historian's calculations are in line with long-standing Western estimates, but the publication of his article marks the most complete information the Russians have received about Stalin's terrors. Many Soviets revere Stalin as the leader who prevented the Soviet state from crumbling after Lenin's death. But the measures he used, as Medvedev makes clear, were pathologically harsh. Among his victims were 6 to 7 million who died during the famine generated in 1932-33 as an outgrowth of the drive for industrialization; one million executed during 1937-38; and 10 to 12 million "repressed" during World War II (→ April 5).

Botha, ill, leaves party leadership

Feb 2. President P.W. Botha resigned today as leader of the National Party, but will remain as President of the regime that rules South Africa. Botha, who fell victim to a mild stroke on Jan. 18, will be succeeded by Frederik W. de Klerk as head of the party that has dominated South Africa's all-white parliament for 40 years. It was the National Party that first established apartheid as a legal system, and de Klerk seems ready to carry that torch in his new position. Blacks, who represent 75 percent of the country's population, are denied a political voice through legal repression and violence (→ March 11).

P.W. Botha, recovering from stroke.

Japanese plan to move underground

In Tokyo, if anyone asks where the next frontier is, the answer is, "You're standing on it." Japan's cities have eaten up so much space that far-sighted (or deep-sighted?) planners envision underground complexes complete with offices, libraries, public baths and space for up to 500,000 people. Japan's economy can handle such schemes even when the costs shoot through the roof. Consider the $80 billion price tag on Urban Geo Grid, a maze of tunnels and atriums covering 500 square miles of earth — 164 feet below the ground. Sunlight will be filtered in, naturally.

Paraguay's Stroessner is ousted in coup

A pro-Stroessner poster, as shredded as his regime, is washed from the wall.

Feb 3. After 35 years of dictatorial rule, Paraguay's President Alfredo Stroessner has been removed from office and placed under house arrest by his second-in-command, Gen. Andres Rodriguez. The coup followed several hours of heavy fighting in the streets of Asuncion between rebel troops and forces loyal to General Stroessner. Estimates of casualties run as high as 100 killed and wounded.

News of the 76-year-old president's ouster has been greeted with enthusiasm by people in the streets of the capital, but prospects for a return of democracy are slender. Rodriguez, who has already had himself sworn in as the new president, was closely associated with the Stroessner regime for many years and is believed to have engineered the coup only because he was losing out in a factional fight within the ruling Colorado Party. He is also reported to have close ties with the trade in narcotics.

Under Stroessner, Paraguay granted refuge to a number of notorious outlaws, including Josef Mengele, the Nazi doctor who conducted medical experiments on prisoners at the Auschwitz concentration camp, and Gen. Anastasio Somoza Debayle, the former Nicaraguan dictator who was assassinated in Asuncion in 1981. Croatian terrorists, European embezzlers and assorted drug traffickers have also found asylum there (→ 5).

The Black Clock, *from a Cezanne show at the National Gallery of Art.*

Boy in the band was really a woman

Feb 1. Thirty years ago, when baby-faced saxophonist Billy Tipton proposed marriage to entertainer Kitty Oakes, he told her a very sad secret: a car accident had rendered him impotent. Could she still love him, he asked. Of course she could, and during their 20-year marriage they happily adopted three boys. But Tipton's true and much sadder secret has been revealed by a Spokane, Wash., funeral director: he had been a she. Tipton, who led the Tipton Trio in the 1950s, died four days ago at age 74, having led a lifelong charade to pursue a jazz career in a world where male musicians wrote the score.

Masquerade: The Billy Tipton Trio, popular in the mid-1950s, featured Ron Kilde (left), drummer Dick O'Neil (right) and Tipton.

Mr. Noid is a little more than annoyed

Fed up with TV's commercial fare? Kenneth Noid knows the feeling. For years, Domino's Pizza has run ads featuring a nasty gnome called the Noid, which represents an imperfect pizza experience. The human Noid, having a history of psychiatric problems, sought revenge on his good name this week when he entered a Domino's Pizza outlet in Chamblee, Ga. Wielding a .357 Magnum, he took two workers hostage, demanded a getaway car, $100,000 and a novel about prisons he had read recently. Poor Noid. The hostages escaped, and he surrendered to authorities.

FEBRUARY
1989

Su	Mo	Tu	We	Th	Fr	Sa
			1	2	3	4
5	6	7	8	9	10	11
12	13	14	15	16	17	18
19	20	21	22	23	24	25
26	27	28				

5. Pakistan: Soviet Foreign Minister Eduard Shevardnadze arrives in a last-minute effort to avoid open civil war in Afghanistan (→ 15).

5. Asuncion: Deposed dictator Alfredo Stroessner flies into exile in Brazil.

5. Teheran: Iran's President dismisses possibility of improved relations with the U.S. until frozen assets are released.

5. Budapest: Media report 25 percent of Hungarian population is poor, 40 years after government declared poverty had been eradicated.

7. Rio de Janiero, Brazil: Eighteen prisoners die after police force 51 inmates into a four-by-ten-foot cell as punishment for attempted jailbreak.

7. Washington, D.C.: Navajo leader Peter MacDonald accused of fraud in $8 million land deal.

8. Portugal: American airliner crashes into mountain in Azores, killing all 144 aboard.

8. Washington, D.C.: National Cancer Advisory Board calls for ban on all tobacco ads.

9. Vancouver: Film director Peter Bogdanovich marries 20-year-old sister of former lover Dorothy Stratton, Playboy centerfold murdered by estranged husband.

9. New Jersey: In surprise to nation, professional wrestling deregulation hearings uncover that the sport is a fake.

9. Washington, D.C.: CIA Director William Webster tells Congress that the Third World is making gains in developing ballistic missiles.

9. Los Angeles: Storm drops up to six inches of snow on city and suburbs.

10. Kenya: President Daniel arap Moi, concerned over loss of nation's wildlife, has ordered poachers shot on sight.

DEATH

10. Wayne L. Hays, ex-Ohio congressman best known for scandalous relationship with staff member (*May 13, 1911).

Bush to give S&L bill to taxpayers

Feb 6. If President Bush gets his proposed $90 billion savings and loan bailout, depositors won't have to pay to stem a threatened bank run and plug a $100 billion leak. Taxpayers will.

The plan, proposed today, includes $50 billion in bonds, and $50 million a year to find and punish bankers involved in "fraud and criminality." Interest on the bonds would cost taxpayers $1.9 billion in 1990 alone. Savings and loans and other banks will share in the interest and also pay more for insurance. President Bush pledged "to see that the guarantee to depositors is forever honored" (→ March 31).

Yes, Congress will have no raise today

Feb 7. One of the bitterest floor fights in recent memory ended today when Congress, bowing to public outrage and hardball lobbying by consumer kingpin Ralph Nader, voted to kill a proposal that would have upped House and Senate wages from $89,500 to $135,000. Lawmakers were hot under the collar even as they sent the bill to crushing defeat. They said it consigns them to padding their income with pricey lecture fees, long an ethical sore point. The vote also stung federal executives and judges, who were included in the wage bill yet are barred from seeking outside cash.

Big Torn Campbell's Soup Can (Vegetable Beef): *at a MOMA Warhol retrospective, New York.*

Black woman becomes Episcopal bishop

Barbara Harris at her ordination: a sign of growing tolerance in the church?

Feb 11. The Rev. Barbara Clementine Harris, a 55-year-old black priest, today became the first woman bishop in the Episcopal Church. Fifty-five priests and thousands of guests collected in Boston's John B. Hynes Memorial Auditorium to watch the shattering of 2,000 years of church tradition.

Despite the throng of supporters, the expanding role of Episcopalian women threatens to split the church in half. Harris' consecration was opposed at the ceremony by John Jamieson of the Prayer Book Society, as "a sacrilegious imposture." The Rev. James Hopkinson Cupit Jr. said the ceremony was "contrary to . . . apostolic order."

Amid the objections, Harris was elevated to the bishopric by Edmond L. Browning, a former public relations executive who helped conduct an unauthorized ordination of 11 women in Philadelphia's Church of the Advocate in 1974. Harris became a priest herself in 1980.

The Most Rev. Robert Runcie, Archbishop of Canterbury and head of the Anglican Church worldwide, said from London that he doubted "every Anglican will yet feel able to acknowledge her as a bishop of the church" (→ Aug 3).

Man fights to care for comatose wife

Feb 7. A decision to appoint Martin Klein legal guardian of his pregnant, comatose wife Nancy was handed down today by a Mineola, N.Y., State Supreme Court justice. Only hours later, however, Mr. Klein was dealt a blow by an appellate court judge, who stayed the ruling pending appeal by abortion opponents.

Klein, of Upper Brookville, N.Y., sought to become his wife's legal guardian so he could authorize an abortion of the 17-week-old fetus in attempt to save his 32-year-old wife's life. Mrs. Klein has been in a coma at North Shore University Hospital in Manhasset since she suffered extensive brain damage in a car accident on Dec. 13 (→ 12).

Did Admiral Peary make it after all?

Feb 5. After 80 years of controversy, a re-examination of old documents suggests that the American explorer, Adm. Robert E. Peary, probably did reach the North Pole in 1909. Skeptical geographers, scientists and historians have long argued that Peary faked his records to indicate he discovered the Pole, when in fact he was at least 121 miles from his goal. The prestigious Navigation Foundation now says the allegedly doctored document in fact had nothing to do with Peary's navigational calculations. Peary's claim, which has been called by one debunker "one of the greatest scientific frauds of this century," will be discussed further in June by the Society for the History of Discovery.

Soviet publication attacks the party

The Soviet magazine *Neva* has given Mikhail Gorbachev something no other Soviet leader has ever had: criticism from the official press. This month's *Neva* carries an article that accuses Gorbachev of contradicting himself in remarks on democracy, and blames party workers for blocking his reforms. The author, identified as a 35-year-old geologist from Siberia, writes: "Naturally, even raising the question of sharing power with the people causes apoplexy in many party workers who have been taught for dozens of years that it is not the party that serves the people, but the people who serve the party."

U.S. women still earn less than men

Feb 8. Some 20 years after the birth of the contemporary women's liberation movement, women earn only 65 percent of men's wages, according to a study released today by the Rand Corporation. This disparity, coupled with the growing number of women who are heads of households, has made poverty an increasingly female problem: in 1980, 62 percent of poor adults were women.

The gap does, however, seem to be narrowing. Between 1980 and 1986 women wage earners gained 5 percent on their male counterparts. Researchers predict that women will earn at least 74 percent of men's wages by the year 2000.

West Germany outlaws neo-Nazi groups

Grim-faced West Germans demonstrate against the rising tide of Nazism.

Feb 9. Facing a resurgence of neo-Nazi activity, the West German government has banned the 170-member National Assembly. In a series of raids on party members' offices and homes, officials seized large quantities of ammunition, knives and swastikas. The new-right Republicans, who placed well in last week's Berlin elections, were not considered "extremist" enough to fall under the ban. But Interior Minister Friedrich Zimmerman said the strike "should be seen as an unmistakable warning signal. West Germany will not be a playing field for right-wing extremism." National Assembly leader Michael Kuhnen, however, has already created yet another party (→ April 20).

Film sparks to life smoldering memories

Willem Dafoe, Gene Hackman and a chilling symbol of the South's fiery past.

A storm of controversy rages over the film *Mississippi Burning,* the center being the state itself. Articles for and against, TV talk shows, attacks and defenses each make the summer of 1964 come to life in all its heroism and horror.

Undeniably, the Hollywood version of the June 1964 killing of three civil rights workers — two white and one black — is powerful, and brings back what some may wish to be forgotten. Mississippians tend to be ambivalent about having the closets of their past cleaned out in public. Dick Molpus, secretary of state in Jackson, points out that his state today is "a very different place." "We can't undo what took place," he mourns, "but we must

focus on the future and see to it that it never happens again."

The movie has also been greeted with some discomfort in black communities. The civil rights movement is silent in *Mississippi Burning.* The film's black characters are passive, cowed into submission by intimidating Southern whites. Its heroes instead are FBI agents.

When confronted with the argument that his slant does an injustice to history, director Alan Parker says calmly, "This is an investigative thriller, not the definitive film on the subject. There should be other films, giving other views. The black point of view, for instance. The only way to attack a work of art is with another work of art."

Worker-owned companies on the rise

Avis car-rental workers no longer say, "We Try Harder." They now proclaim, "Owners Try Harder" because they own the place. They are beneficiaries of the Employee Stock Ownership Plan (ESOP), the 30-year-old brainchild of lawyer Louis Kelso that is flourishing as a block to hostile takeovers and an alternative to raising wages. Some 10,000 U.S. firms with 10 million employees offer ESOPs, including 1,500 where workers own a majority of stock. Morale is soaring, and worker-owners at one steel mill have raised productivity 300 percent.

Speaking for the ozone: At a carnival in Mainz, West Germany, an effigy of Mother Earth tries to wrest aerosol cans from a human hand.

Su	Mo	Tu	We	Th	Fr	Sa
			1	2	3	4
5	6	7	8	9	10	11
12	13	14	15	16	17	18
19	20	21	22	23	24	25
26	27	28				

12. Moscow: First officially approved Jewish cultural center in Soviet Union is opened.

12. Islamabad, Pakistan: Thousands march on American cultural center to protest Salman Rushdie's *The Satanic Verses* (→ 15).

12. New York: Abortion performed on comatose patient Nancy Klein after court refuses to overturn ruling placing her in husband's guardianship.

13. Washington, D.C.: Oliver North's lawyers claim that then-President Reagan and other high-ranking officials were directly involved in raising money for contras at time it was forbidden by Congress (→ March 3).

14. Los Angeles: Desert power plant is now supplying power to 20,000 homes by burning cow manure, saving 300,000 barrels of oil annually.

14. Oklahoma: Oklahoma quarterback Charlie Thompson arrested on charges of selling cocaine one week after telling elementary school kids to "just say no."

15. South Africa: Officials identify body of black teenager believed abducted by Winnie Mandela's bodyguards, implicating her in the death (→ 16).

15. United States: Rolling Stone readers poll finds the band U2 most popular rock artists.

16. London: British authorities announce demolition experts have concluded that the bomb which destroyed Pan Am flight 103 over Scotland was concealed in a cassette player.

16. Los Angeles: Dodger pitcher Orel Hershiser becomes highest-paid ball player after signing $7.9 million contract.

18. United States: Sony and Canon have introduced camera that takes still pictures on floppy disks.

DEATH

17. Vernon "Lefty" Gomez, baseball Hall of Famer; pitched for N.Y. Yankees, 1931-1942 (*Nov 26, 1909).

Irreverent novel sparks death threats against Salman Rushdie

Feb 15. Iran's leader, Ayatollah Ruhollah Khomeini, has declared Salman Rushdie's novel *The Satanic Verses* to be blasphemous and has sentenced the author to death. The Ayatollah yesterday asked all Muslims to "execute" his orders and offered a reward of $1 million — $3 million if the executioner is an Iranian. Anyone killed in carrying out his order would, he claims, be considered a martyr.

Rushdie's "criminal" act apparently lies in his portrayal of a businessman/prophet named Mahound, who, like Martin Scorsese's Jesus in *The Last Temptation of Christ*, wrestles continually with worldly temptation. Though the objections have not been spelled out, many Muslims appear to have interpreted Mahound as a satirical depiction of the prophet Mohammed.

Rushdie, who lives in London, could not be reached. He is presumed to be in hiding under armed guard. The British Press Association has quoted the author as saying that he takes the death threats "very seriously indeed," and that he is very saddened by the recent turn of events.

Demonstrations against the book in Pakistan and India have left several dead and hundreds wounded. The turmoil has stirred up a diplo-

Not looking too worried, the author poses with his controversial book.

matic hornet's nest at a time when Iran appeared to be moderating its extreme revolutionary posture. Both Britain and France have recently normalized diplomatic relations with Tehran, but these changes appear to be threatened.

Observers of Middle Eastern politics have suggested that Khomeini's move against Rushdie is in reality a political ploy to unite Muslims by offering them a common foe. What

better enemy, they suggest, than one who appears to be attacking the very core of Islam.

Iran's image as a revolutionary model has slipped since last summer's cease-fire with Iraq and its apparent reversal of some fundamentalist policies. It now seems as if Khomeini may be shifting Iran back into a posture of fundamental revolution, the original goal of the Ayatollah's movement (→ 24).

Feb 16. *Seventy years after a molasses tank burst in Boston, Gering, Neb., gets a reprise, as 1.2 million gallons of the goop injures three and levels a factory.*

135-year-old record is broken at sea

Feb 12. Eighty days, 20 hours for a New York-San Francisco run isn't exactly an early-bird special. But it was good enough to break a record that stood untouched for 135 years. When the yacht Thursday's Child sailed into San Francisco Bay today just after noon, it clipped by eight days the round-Cape Horn mark set in 1854 by Flying Cloud. But the old clipper ship can still hold its head high, being one of only 13 vessels ever to sail more than 400 miles in one day. The best day for Thursday's Child was 310 miles; the poorest, 64. As the 60-foot yacht slipped under the Golden Gate Bridge, it was accompanied by a welcoming flotilla of pleasure craft. Commenting on the grueling, wet, cold voyage, skipper Warren Luhrs said, "Once is enough."

Union Carbide must pay people of India

Feb 14. Four years after a toxic cloud of methyl isocyanate killed 3,500 people and injured 200,000 in Bhopal, a city in central India, the Union Carbide Corporation has been ordered to pay $470 million in damages. The settlement, which was announced today by the Indian Supreme Court, did not say who was to blame for the incident. Carbide officials claim the disaster resulted from sabotage by a disgruntled worker.

The Indian government, which had asked for $3.3 billion on behalf of the victims, has agreed to accept the lower figure. As part of the final settlement, the Supreme Court dismissed all other civil suits against Carbide, as well as the murder charge brought against company chairman Warren Anderson.

Central Americans sign peace accord

Feb 14. Nicaragua will hold open elections in exchange for the closing of rebel camps in Honduras, under an agreement announced today by the presidents of five Central American countries. The accord is the product of a two-day summit meeting attended by the leaders of Costa Rica, El Salvador, Guatemala, Honduras and Nicaragua.

The Sandinista government of Nicaragua has promised to allow opposition parties four months to organize and six months to campaign for the presidential, legislative and municipal elections, scheduled for Feb. 25, 1990. Nicaragua will also free contras and National Guardsmen now in jail. A plan to relocate to third countries thousands of contras and their families, now in border camps in Honduras, will be drawn up within 90 days. Most of the rebels have been in the Honduran camps since last year, when the United States stopped providing military aid.

The nations that signed the pact have committed themselves to halt all aid to rebel groups and to negotiate cease-fires with guerrillas. Costa Rican President Oscar Arias Sanchez, who won the 1987 Nobel Peace Prize for his work in negotiating a regional peace accord, said today's agreement "shows that we have the will, and agree we need, to silence the arms of war through democracy" (→ March 3).

Last of Soviet troops leave Afghanistan

Feb 15. "There is not a single Soviet soldier or officer left behind me. Our nine-year stay ends with this." With those words the last Soviet soldier left Afghanistan, bringing to a close an embarrassing chapter in Soviet foreign policy. Like the Vietnam War, to which it was often compared, the Afghan war cost the Soviets dearly in men, money and prestige.

The Soviet departure seriously weakened the position of the Afghan government, which is fighting a war against Muslim insurgents. President Najibullah's forces have been well armed by the Kremlin. But the insurgents command a sophisticated array of American-supplied arms and maintain a vast advantage in popular support.

The Soviets began withdrawing their 100,000-plus forces from Afghanistan last spring in compliance with an accord negotiated with the United Nations. The agreement was really nothing more than a face-saving measure for the Soviets, who wished to withdraw from a war that became unpopular almost as soon as the first troops arrived on Dec. 27, 1979. Reports this week of Soviet atrocities suggest that the celebratory mood which greeted returning troops will not last long.

The United States pledged to continue its support to the Afghan rebels until there is "Afghan self-determination," according to the State Department (→ March 8).

The last Soviet troops leave behind what has been called Russia's Vietnam.

Murder case hurts Winnie Mandela

Feb 16. The leadership of the United Democratic Front, South Africa's dominant legally recognized anti-apartheid group, has denounced Winnie Mandela for her alleged involvement in the murder of a 14-year-old boy. Mrs. Mandela's bodyguards, the United Football Club, stand accused of a "reign of terror" in Soweto. South African police are investigating the disappearance of two other Soweto youths believed to have been abducted as police informers by the soccer club. The Front has publicly distanced itself from Mrs. Mandela, but recognizes her lifelong struggle against apartheid.

Report shows Arctic ozone in jeopardy

Feb 17. Look. Up in the sky. It's a bird. It's a plane. No, it's chlorofluorocarbons, chemicals that have already cut the ozone over the South Pole in half, weakening the earth's shield against harmful radiation. A team of government scientists said today that traces of the chemicals (used in solvents and refrigerators) are now swirling above the North Pole. This, said one expert, should send a "strong signal to the nation's policy makers," who have been slow to limit production of industrial pollutants (→ March 2).

Young as ever, Barbie celebrates her 30th

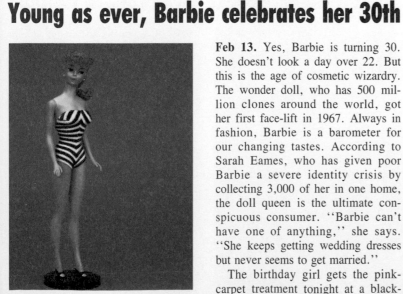

The "Eve" of Barbies — 1959.

Feb 13. Yes, Barbie is turning 30. She doesn't look a day over 22. But this is the age of cosmetic wizardry. The wonder doll, who has 500 million clones around the world, got her first face-lift in 1967. Always in fashion, Barbie is a barometer for our changing tastes. According to Sarah Eames, who has given poor Barbie a severe identity crisis by collecting 3,000 of her in one home, the doll queen is the ultimate conspicuous consumer. "Barbie can't have one of anything," she says. "She keeps getting wedding dresses but never seems to get married."

The birthday girl gets the pink-carpet treatment tonight at a black-tie party at Lincoln Center.

Hudson lover wins

Feb 15. Rock Hudson's "pillow talk" never got around to AIDS, and today it cost his estate $14.5 million, the sum awarded by a Los Angeles jury to the film idol's ex-lover, Marc Christian. Hudson, who died in October 1985, tested positive for the fatal illness in June 1984, but he kept the news from Christian and continued to have sex with him for several months before the pair broke up. In July 1985 Christian learned he'd been put at risk. He escaped infection, but lodged a suit, and came up a winner as the jury termed Hudson's off-screen performance "outrageous." Said Christian, "This shows people he had a duty to disclose."

Jane Fonda and Tom Hayden are splitting after 16 years. Under California divorce law, Hayden stands to gain in money what he may well lose in publicity.

FEBRUARY
1989

Su	Mo	Tu	We	Th	Fr	Sa
			1	2	3	4
5	6	7	8	9	10	11
12	13	14	15	16	17	18
19	20	21	22	23	24	25
26	27	28				

20. Dallas: Book repository from which Lee Harvey Oswald shot President Kennedy opens as a museum.

21. Prague: Playwright Vaclav Havel is jailed for inciting protest last month (→ 22).

21. Los Angeles: Olympian Florence Griffith Joyner is presented Jesse Owens International Trophy Award (→ 25).

23. Columbus, Ohio: Rep. Donald Lukens charged with having sex with teenage girl.

23. New York City: The Rev. Timothy Healy, president of Georgetown University, is named head of New York Public Library.

25. New York City: Track star Florence Griffith Joyner tearfully announces her retirement, to devote more time to writing and acting.

26. Nevada: Nevada Gaming Control Board fines casino owner Ralph Engelstad $1.5 million for displaying Nazi memorabilia in casino and celebrating Hitler's birthday.

27. East Berlin: Communist Party theorist Otto Reinhold categorically rejects Soviet reform movement (→ Aug 14).

27. Persian Gulf: Britain withdraws last of its mine-sweepers from gulf, leaving U.S. to do job.

27. Atlanta: Immigration officials arrest 79 on Eastern Airlines plane, saying flight is used regularly to shuttle illegal aliens from Los Angeles to New York City.

28. Berkeley, Calif.: Two bookstores firebombed in response to owners' support of Salman Rushdie (→ March 1).

28. Winston-Salem, N.C.: R.J. Reynolds announces it will stop market-testing "smokeless" cigarettes, as they taste bad and are difficult to light.

DEATHS

22. Aldo J. Jacuzzi, former chairman of family's whirlpool pump firm (*1922).

26. Roy "Little Jazz" Eldridge, jazz trumpeter (*Jan. 30, 1911).

"Satanic Verses" provokes Islamic furor

Rushdie may or may not burn in hell, but his image isn't faring well on earth.

Feb 24. Muslim rioting provoked by the publication of Salman Rushdie's novel *The Satanic Verses* has resulted in the death of 12 people and the wounding of 40 others in Bombay, Rushdie's birthplace. Accounts by the Press Trust of India and Reuters say that police set up barricades to block a protest march against the British diplomatic mission. Trouble began when a huge crowd of demonstrators broke down the barriers. One march leader, Sharafat Khan, said he pleaded with police to let the marchers pass when, without warning, the crowd surged forward and the police tried to fend off demonstrators with clubs. Rocks were thrown and

"then there was gunfire," said Khan. The march had been banned because of the possibility of violence, but this did not deter the protesters.

Rushdie's novel has been banned in India and in Pakistan, where further clashes in front of the American Information Center left six people dead and 83 wounded. Leading Islamic clerics have called for Rushdie's death and complete repression of the novel, which they deem highly blasphemous.

In New York two days ago, American writers held readings to support Rushdie and protest what they consider to be a violation of free speech (→ 28).

Israeli bombs kill 3 Palestinian youths

Feb 28. Twenty-two schoolchildren were injured and three others killed today when Israeli jets tore across the sky southeast of Beirut, dropping bombs on what were thought to be radical Palestinian bases. The air-to-surface missile that hit the schoolyard was intended for a base of the Democratic Front for the Liberation of Palestine, located in Chemlan, a nearby mountain resort. Israel maintains that only terrorist positions were hit. Despite cease-fire efforts led by Yasir Arafat, chairman of the PLO, hard-line Palestinian groups continue to attack Israeli-supported Christian militia groups (→ April 3).

Czechs clamp down, convict 7 dissidents

Feb 22. A Czech court has found seven people guilty of hooliganism for laying a wreath of flowers to commemorate the death of Jan Palach, a student who set fire to himself in protest over the 1968 Soviet invasion of Czechoslovakia. The sentences range from fines to a year in prison. The verdict comes one day after the dissident playwright, Vaclav Havel, was sentenced to prison — and one month after Czechoslovakia signed the Helsinki accords on human rights (→ Oct 28).

In the grip of economic depression, Venezuela erupts in rioting

After new bus fare hikes, many Caracans would rather riot than ride a bus.

Feb 28. Riots have erupted in nine Venezuelan cities during protests over economic policies. Dozens of demonstrators are dead and hundreds have been injured in clashes with the National Guard. To control the unrest, the beleaguered government of President Carlos Andres Perez has imposed a curfew and curbed civil liberties.

The riots were set off by a recent removal of price controls aimed at reducing the nation's $33 billion foreign debt. Prices skyrocketed, including fares for public transportation, which kindled the latest round of violence. The riots threaten a democratic state that flourished in the 1970s, when oil sales made Venezuela a stable, prosperous nation.

Solidarity to share power in Poland

Feb 19. The banned union Solidarity may be allowed to control 40 percent of the seats in Poland's Parliament if it will support the government's economic policies. This startling proposal comes two weeks after economic crises prompted the government to open talks with the renegade unionists. The two sides say they have reached a "fundamental accord" in which they would divide up districts before the election and then refrain from running a candidate in the other's district. If the accord goes into effect, Poland will join Hungary and Yugoslavia in trying a multi-party government (→ March 2).

Feds bust $1 billion heroin drug cartel

Feb 21. The FBI says heroin prices will be going up now that it has seized 800 pounds. The billion-dollar Queens seizure is the biggest in U.S. history and would have supplied New York City's 250,000 addicts for six months. Asians muscling in on the market hid their high-quality heroin, said to come from Thailand, in rental vans. The raid also netted $3 million cash and the owner of the liquor store where Chinatown's Democratic Club has its basement quarters.

Feb 24. *Nine people were swept away today as a hole was ripped in the side of a United 747. The plane landed safely in Honolulu.*

Bush, in China, optimistic over improving Sino-Soviet relations

Feb 26. President George Bush today characterized the upcoming meeting between Chinese leader Deng Xiaoping and Soviet leader Mikhail Gorbachev as "an important . . . step in providing stability to the region and the world." Bush, who is visiting China as part of a five-day Asian tour, stressed that improved Sino-Soviet relations would not have adverse effects on the United States' China policy, declaring himself "convinced that U.S.-China relations are strong."

Gorbachev will be the first Soviet leader to go to China since Nikita Khrushchev in 1959. His visit will normalize relations between the two nations, which were broken 30 years ago over ideological differences. Both countries now have active reform movements, though the Soviets have emphasized political openness in contrast to the Chinese stress on economic changes.

Although Bush was full of praise, at one point describing China as a "tree in the winter wind [that had] learned to bend and adapt to new ideas," the United States remains critical of certain Chinese policies. Bush addressed concerns over trade barriers. He also discussed Chinese sales of Silkworm missiles to Iran and other countries with Prime Minister Li Peng, who reassured the President but avoided any commitment to restrict sales. The issue of human rights was conspicuously absent from the agenda (→ 26).

Ex-KKK chief wins

Feb 22. An avowed white supremacist and former grand wizard of the Ku Klux Klan, David Duke, has been elected to the Louisiana state legislature with a stunning 78 percent of the vote. Now a convert to the Republican Party, Duke is a liability to the GOP. President Bush and Ronald Reagan urged Louisiana voters to reject Duke's candidacy. But their efforts seem to have backfired; said one voter, "We resent outsiders coming in trying to influence us." Nonetheless, Lee Atwater, Republican National Committee chief, labeled Duke "a pretender, a charlatan, and a political opportunist." Undeterred, Duke says, "I feel . . . comfortable in the Republican Party."

George Bush and Deng Xiaoping raise glasses together in the Great Hall.

Chinese bar dissident from Bush party

Feb 26. The Chinese government's tolerance of the growing democracy movement has its limits, as demonstrated today when Chinese police prevented dissident Fang Lizhi from attending a dinner to which he had been invited by President George Bush.

The Chinese have made it clear to Bush that they consider the pro-democracy movement a threat to economic reforms undertaken in the last few years. Zhao Ziyang, the Communist Party general secretary, told Bush that "the fact that some elements in American society support people who are dissatisfied with the Chinese government will not contribute to China's political stability and reform, nor will it help China's friendship with the United States." The harsh tone of Zhao's comments was surprising, because he is considered a moderate. Bush himself has not brought up the subject of human rights, though many expected him to in light of strong American support for the Chinese pro-democracy movement.

Fang, an astrophysicist, is a well-known dissident in China. He was thrown out of the Communist Party in 1987 because of his vocal support for democratic reforms. Bush was reportedly unaware that Fang had been prevented from attending the barbecue at the Great Wall Sheraton (→ May 15).

The man who didn't come to dinner. Fang Lizhi was stopped by security police.

MARCH
1989

Su	Mo	Tu	We	Th	Fr	Sa
			1	2	3	4
5	6	7	8	9	10	11
12	13	14	15	16	17	18
19	20	21	22	23	24	25
26	27	28	29	30	31	

1. Toronto: Charlie Francis, Olympian Ben Johnson's coach, testifies that Johnson began using steroids in 1981, and had used them in the two months before he set world record last year (→ June 13).

1. Washington, D.C.: First round of payments to victims suffering from effects of Agent Orange are mailed.

1. Baltimore, Md.: Research from Johns Hopkins shows homicide is leading cause of injury-related deaths of children under one year old.

1. New York: Isaac Yeffet, former security expert for El Al airlines, reports that "no airport in the United States is safe" from terrorist attack.

1. Tokyo: Japan announces it will reduce imports of Iranian oil by one-third in wake of Salman Rushdie affair (→ 2).

1. Washington, D.C.: State Department announces that worldwide drug production is up markedly from last year.

2. Warsaw: Government and Solidarity Union agree to issue joint appeal for international aid to relieve Poland's crushing debt crisis (→ March 9).

2. London: To relieve tensions with Iran, Britain calls Salman Rushdie's *The Satanic Verses* offensive (→ 6).

2. Los Angeles: Citywide ban on assault weapons takes effect (→ 13).

3. Washington, D.C.: Secretary of State James Baker urges interim aid for contras (→ 17).

3. Honolulu: Oil tanker Exxon Houston runs aground, spilling 2,800 barrels of oil into sea, threatening Oahu's beaches.

4. Los Angeles: Mystery of murdered "strawberries" — women who sell sex for drugs — appears solved; suspect is Ricky Ross, 40, Los Angeles narcotics investigator.

4. London: Two passenger trains collide, killing nine and injuring 70.

4. Maine: Republican Governor John McKernan weds Republican Congresswoman Olympia Snow.

Machinists wage strike for worker rights

March 4. Idled behind the picket lines of some 8,500 striking machinists, Eastern Airlines has been forced to ground 90 percent of its 250 planes and cancel all but 50 of its 1,040 daily flights.

The International Association of Machinists and Aerospace Workers, one of the most militant and cohesive unions in the country, seems eager for a fight. Irate over the $1.5 billion in concessions given up by Eastern employees over the last decade, workers authorized the strike by a 97 percent majority. And they have the support of Eastern's 3,500 pilots and 5,900 flight attendants.

The inadvertent cause of all this solidarity appears to be one Frank Lorenzo, chairman of Texas Air, which owns Eastern. In 1983 Lorenzo crushed the union at Continental Airlines by using bankruptcy to break contracts and slash wages. At Eastern, Lorenzo has been selling off assets in a slow dismemberment, and claims to be losing more than $1 million a day. He says he is seeking to revitalize the airline in a deregulated environment. But his name adorns picket signs across the country, one of which labels him "the AIDS of working people."

As for public opinion, there was no shortage of ire among the 100,000 stranded passengers today, though most of it remains unfocused. Said one sobbing vacationer upon aborting her trip to the Bahamas, "I'll sue someone for this" (→ 5).

Tooling up for what could be a long haul, machinists form a picket line.

Urban shadow falls over small-town U.S.

Rural areas, now hemorrhaging residents at a rate of one million a year, increasingly find themselves locked in a life-and-death struggle against the relentless tide of urban America. Rural flight, of course, has plagued the small town since mechanization began to liberate farming of its need for farmers. Says John Keller, a professor at Kansas State, "This has been the longest deathbed scene in history."

But the 1980s have subjected the heartland to a new set of forces, most of which lie beyond its control. Light manufacturing, the rural answer to the decline of the family farm, has been siphoned away by low-wage foreign suppliers, allowing small towns a job-growth rate only 40 percent that of the cities.

And deregulation has accelerated the process. Jimmy Carter and Ronald Reagan eagerly defended small-town values on the campaign trail, but the policy room was a different matter. Without government subsidies, many firms can ill afford to cater to regions where people are few and far between. Defense contracts follow the well-represented coastal populations. And, deprived of adequate infrastructure, small towns remain cut off from the high-tech route advocated by most economists. In the words of one Kansas official, "in the long term . . . rural America will pay a terrible price."

West Europe will cut harm to ozone

March 2. Chlorofluorocarbons, the chemical agents used as coolants in refrigerators and air-conditioners, and as propellants in aerosol cans, will be eliminated throughout the European Community by the end of the century, it was announced in Brussels today. The move goes far beyond the 1987 Montreal accord, which called for a 50 percent reduction by the year 2000. It was hailed by William K. Reilly, head of the Environmental Protection Agency, who is seeking a worldwide phaseout. The United States and the European Community each produce about one-third of the world's chlorofluorocarbons (→ June 19).

Likud wins in vote

March 1. By winning major victories in municipal elections, the Likud Party has become the dominant political body in a beleaguered Israel. The triumph comes despite the fact that 80 percent of Arabs with Israeli citizenship voted, compared with only 48 percent of Jews. Likud opposes self-determination for the 1.5 million Palestinians living in Israel's occupied territories.

Today's defeat adds to the woes of the Labor Party, which lost November's national elections. Likud leader Yitzhak Shamir says the world must now recognize his party as Israel's guiding force (→ April 5).

Bonn breaks Soviet computer spy ring

March 2. Glasnost or not, spies march to their own beat. West German police have uncovered a computer spy ring that fed the KGB with American military passwords and software. Though the information was not classified, it was termed "highly sensitive," and the fact that computer hackers could pull it off has alarmed U.S. military leaders. The ring has operated for several years, gaining access to more than 30 computers associated with American defense. The five arrested include ringleader Marcus Hess, a 25-year-old West German computer programmer.

McFarlane is fined for Iran-contra role

March 3. Federal District Judge Aubrey Robinson today fined ex-national security adviser Robert McFarlane $20,000 and placed him on two years' probation for witholding Iran-contra information from Congress. He was also ordered to perform 200 hours of community service. McFarlane, who attempted suicide three months after the scandal broke, is the first Reagan administration official to be sentenced in the Iran-contra affair. One of the most visible of the administration's "loose cannons," McFarlane told the judge that while he "regretted" his actions, he was still "proud to have served my country" (→ 13).

Familiar pose for ex-Reagan aides.

Corporate sponsors pull ads from show

March 1. "Appalling!" cried Terry Rakolta, 41, about the situation comedy *Married . . . With Children.* Sexual innuendo, abasement of women, references to homosexuality, and a scene where a woman removes her bra in public made the Michigan mother write angry letters to 45 advertisers on the show. Giants such as McDonald's, Procter & Gamble, Tambrands and Kimberley-Clark withdrew commercials, and Mrs. Rakolta continues her crusade to "identify, target and boycott" advertisers sponsoring shows she finds depicting the American family negatively.

Time and Warner announce merger plans

Time and Warner, multi-billion-dollar cornerstones in communications.

March 4. Time, Inc. and Warner Communications, Inc. announced plans today to merge and form the largest media and entertainment conglomerate in the world. The new company, to be called Time Warner, Inc., will have a total stock market value of $15.2 billion and a total value of $18 billion.

Time is a major magazine and book publisher and owner of the country's largest cable television programming service. Warner is a large producer of motion pictures, records and cable TV.

The merger of these two New York-based giants, both founded in the 1920s, will insure the new firm a place in the 1990s as one of a handful of global media giants able to produce and distribute information in any medium. Time and Warner executives explain the merger as a bulwark against foreign competition. "Only strong American companies will survive after the formation of a unified European market in 1992," said Steven J. Ross, chairman of Warner. The merger will also make the new company a tough target for a hostile takeover.

The deal, subject to shareholder and government approval, is called a "merger of equals" because Time chairman J. Richard Munro and Warner chairman Steven J. Ross will share power as co-chairmen and co-chief executives. Time's president, N.J. Nicholas Jr., will take control eventually (→ July 24).

Almost extinct from overhunting in the 19th century, buffalo have staged a minor comeback. But Montana law permits shooting bison that leave Yellowstone Park. Buffalo roaming near homes are shot for sport.

D.C. Council orders curfew on young

March 1. In an effort to offset the rash of drug-related murders in Washington, D.C., Mayor Marion Barry and the City Council have voted to impose a curfew for anyone under 18 years. Parents of those teens violating the curfew would face fines after one warning.

So far this year, 90 people have been murdered. At the present pace, the crime spree will break last year's record of 372 killings, which gave the city the title "Murder Capital." Some say the law will not slow the violence. Legal experts say it is unconstitutional and will not withstand a challenge in court; police question its enforceability (→ 20).

D.C. Mayor Barry sweats it out.

Gourmets flip over hamburger's 100th

Let's hear it for the hamburger's 100th birthday — maybe. The burger's origins are clouded by competing claims. But the Oxford English Dictionary says it arrived in the United States from Hamburg, Germany, in 1889. The 19th-century Hamburgers (the people) acquired a taste for scraped raw beef through their trade with the Baltic regions. By 1921, hamburgers were offered (cooked) to millions at White Castle; in the 1930s they became known as "Wimpy burgers" after Popeye's beef-addicted friend; and in 1955 the first of billions was sold by McDonald's.

MARCH
1989

Su	Mo	Tu	We	Th	Fr	Sa
			1	2	3	4
5	6	7	8	9	10	11
12	13	14	15	16	17	18
19	20	21	22	23	24	25
26	27	28	29	30	31	

5. South Korea: Four sisters commit suicide with rat poison so their parents can give all personal and financial attention to their brother.

5. United States: Machinists announce they will temporarily refrain from calling upon railway workers to strike in support of their cause (→ 9).

5. California: Some 100 participants in "Aryan Woodstock" — organized by new-Nazi groups — are jeered by 500 protesters.

6. Rome: The Vatican newspaper condemns *The Satanic Verses* as blasphemous, but also condemns death threats against Salman Rushdie.

6. New Delhi: Some 125 people now dead from drinking illicit alcohol in Gujarat State, which is officially dry.

7. Washington, D.C.: Christopher Dodd becomes second Senate Democrat to voice support for John Tower, after Howell Heflin; Tower is three votes short of tie (→ 9).

8. Afghanistan: Rebels open major assault on Afghanistan's second largest city, Jalalabad; two army outposts east of city fall (→ April 8).

9. Wisconsin: Right-wing John Birch Society announces it will move to Appleton, Wis., birthplace of Communist-hunter Joseph McCarthy.

9. Newport, R.I.: Kitty Dukakais announces she is an alcoholic two days before release from rehab center.

11. Moscow: American psychiatric experts conclude upon completing extensive on-site study of Soviet psychiatric hospitals that system is still prone to abuses.

11. Johannesburg, South Africa: President P.W. Botha announces he will not follow the wishes of fellow National Party members and step aside as President (→ April 6).

11. Los Angeles: Roman Catholic Archbishop Roger Mahony, in order to cover 8,700-square-mile archdiocese, has accepted $400,000 helicopter from wealthy friends.

Senate topples Tower for Pentagon post

March 9. The sharp debate over the nomination of John Tower for secretary of defense came to an end today as the Senate rejected the nominee by a 53-47 vote. It was the first time in 30 years that a president was refused his choice of a Cabinet member.

Under a public microscope for several weeks now, Tower has been accused of excessive drinking, philandering and unsavory business ties. Following the decision, he read a statement calling for an end to the "bitterness, rancor and anger" that marked the debate. The former Republican senator and arms negotiator went on to state that, despite recent events, "I depart from this place at peace with myself, knowing that I have given a full measure of devotion to my country."

The Tower issue has sparked a furor over Democratic intentions and the selection process. Republicans are accusing their Democratic

Tower thinking about his sinking.

colleagues of using an unreasonable ethical standard to discredit Tower and the new President. Democratic senators' refutation of the charges have yet to put out the fires (→ 17).

Bush urges death for drug-related killings

March 9. Declaring that "hunting season is over," President Bush today urged a mandatory death penalty for people who kill law-enforcement officials in the course of drug-related crimes. Current law permits such sanctions for that crime or for any murder by someone who has been involved in at least two continuing criminal operations involving drugs. But the death penalty is not

required by law.

In the martial rhetoric of the current "war" on drugs, the President said Drug Enforcement Administration officers are "the special forces, the Green Berets, if you will, of narcotics enforcement." While this is not the first administration to try to eradicate drugs in the United States, it hopes it will be the last to have to make the attempt.

Battle of the Crows, *by Friedemann Hahn, from "Refigured Painting: The German Image 1960-88" now at the Toledo Museum of Art.*

Asians try to limit flow of boat people

March 9. The vast outpouring of refugees from Indochina could face more stringent regulations as they try to resettle in other countries, according to draft proposals from a conference in Kuala Lumpur, Malaysia. Representatives from some 30 nations this week discussed the vast increase of boat people over the last two years. Most of the refugees are fleeing economic strife in Vietnam, and nearby countries such as Thailand, Malaysia, Indonesia and Hong Kong have complained of the economic strain caused by the flood of needy immigrants.

The proposals, which will be considered again at a Geneva confer-

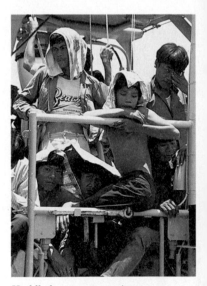

Huddled masses yearning . . .

ence in June, encourage Indochinese nations to better regulate their citizens. Countries like Thailand are urged to reaffirm the principle of first asylum for refugees, while Western nations are asked to accept more refugees and set up screening for new arrivals to determine whether they qualify as refugees.

According to a 1951 Geneva convention, refugees are individuals who can prove a well-founded fear of persecution. Economic disadvantage alone does not open the door to refugee status.

Thailand wants those who do not qualify taken to a holding spot somewhere outside the country. Or, as one official put it, "We should put them in a place sufficiently uncomfortable that they decide they do want to go home" (→ May 6).

Beijing places Tibet under martial law

Anger overflows into violence as Tibetans assault a Chinese man in Lhasa.

March 8. China imposed martial law yesterday in Lhasa, the capital of Tibet, following three days of violent protest against Chinese rule. Thousands of Chinese soldiers were deployed this morning after the government announced a ban on all meetings, petitions and strikes. Violators, said Chinese officials, would be severely punished.

Chinese officials report 12 people killed and more than 100 wounded in the latest round of clashes between police and protesters. Unofficial accounts place the number significantly higher. The turmoil apparently started on Monday, when 13 Buddhist monks and nuns shouting, "Independence for Tibet!" were joined by some 600 protesters. For the past few days, angry Tibetans have been marching, looting stores and stoning government buildings.

Experts say that the Tibetans' recent struggle, which started 18 months ago, is the most serious challenge to Chinese rule since the 1959 uprising, during which some 87,000 Tibetans were killed.

Soviets are blamed for Katyn massacre

March 7. Forty-five years after the bodies of 4,443 Polish officers were found in a mass grave in the Soviet forest of Katyn, the Polish government has decided to set the record straight. The government today blamed the Soviets for the atrocity, finally rejecting the Soviet explanation that Nazis committed the crime. Coming at a time when the government is negotiating with Solidarity, the act goes a long way toward diffusing one of the central issues of Polish nationalism, the charge that Stalin intentionally destroyed a generation of Polish leaders. The dead men were part of a unit of 15,000 officers who were captured by the Soviets in 1939 when they occupied eastern Poland. The remaining 10,600 men simply vanished.

Solidarity, regime to form free Senate

March 9. The Communist Party may soon find out how popular it really is in Poland. According to a plan that has been tentatively agreed to by the Polish government and Solidarity, Poland's Senate is to be restored and free and open elections held to fill its seats. The Senate, or second chamber, was disbanded in 1946 in referendums rigged by the Communists to cement their control of Poland.

In exchange, Solidarity has agreed to accept a new office of president, whose sweeping powers will include the right to disband Parliament. "A process has begun under which democracy is to be rebuilt in an evolutionary manner, not upsetting the political balance or stability," said Solidarity spokesman Bronislaw Geremek (→ April 5).

Lorenzo's Eastern files for bankruptcy

March 9. Embroiled in a bitter six-day-old strike and hemorrhaging cash at $1 million a day, Eastern Airlines has filed for bankruptcy in federal court. Frank Lorenzo, head of Texas Air and storm center of the strike, had some harsh words for the 8,500 striking machinists and the 3,500 pilots who have refused to cross picket lines. Many lower-paid ground support workers, he said, would not be rehired after the strike, while others would return to lower wages and tougher work rules. Lorenzo hopes to use reduced credit obligations to wait out the strike. Eastern president Phil Bakes predicted the picket line will cease to thrive on "the self-deluded struggle of good versus evil."

Lorenzo, foe of the machinists.

Tom Landry leaves

"America's Team" is at mini-camp, but that familiar figure with the snap-brim fedora is not patrolling the sidelines. Tom Landry, who led the Dallas Cowboys as coach for 29 seasons, is out, the first victim of a change in the football team's ownership. Landry, 64, had wanted to return for at least another year to make up for a 3-13 record in 1988. But the new owner wanted his own man. As Dallas' only coach, Landry set an NFL record with 20 winning seasons in a row. After taking the Cowboys to five Super Bowls, Landry says he won't coach anywhere else.

Hangman wanted

"Wanted: Person good at tying knots. Must have an understanding of physics (as in body weight-to-rope-length ratio) and a firm belief in capital punishment. Please apply in person at Walla Walla State Prison, Washington. Disguises are recommended." Walla Walla has not gone to the absurd length of placing a want ad, but it is indeed actively recruiting a hangman for two executions slated for next month. The American applicants, say state officials, have not displayed the proper qualifications. So, despite the obvious commuting problems, they are looking abroad.

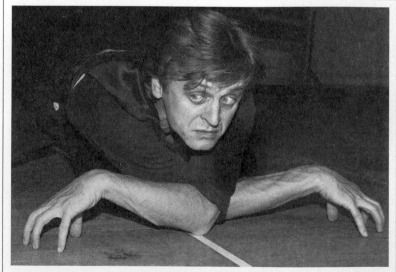

Preparing for his stage debut as an actor, Mikhail Baryshnikov transforms into the dung beetle Gregor Samsa, rehearsing for Kafka's Metamorphosis.

MARCH

1989

Su	Mo	Tu	We	Th	Fr	Sa
			1	2	3	4
5	6	7	8	9	10	11
12	13	14	15	16	17	18
19	20	21	22	23	24	25
26	27	28	29	30	31	

12. San Salvador: Salvadoran army admits killing 10 unarmed civilians last year (→ 20).

12. United States: Georgetown wins sixth Big East Conference basketball title by beating Syracuse 88-79.

13. Sacramento, Calif.: State Assembly votes to ban assault firearms, first state in union to do so (→ 14).

13. Tucson, Ariz.: Air Force helicopter crashes in night flight, killing all 15 aboard.

14. Washington, D.C.: American court convicts Lebanese highjacker Fawaz Yunis of commandeering a Jordanian jet in 1985.

14. North Carolina: Team of researchers announces it has found strain of AIDS virus resistant to drug AZT, only known drug effective against disease (→ May 8).

15. United States: Heavy metal band Guns N' Roses dropped as main act at upcoming AIDS benefit because of anti-gay lyrics in song *One in a Million*.

16. Frankfurt, West Germany: After going AWOL, then returning, U.S. soldier Michael Peri is charged with selling secrets to East Germany.

16. Washington, D.C.: Surgeon General C. Everett Koop tells congressional panel there is not enough evidence to conclude that abortion has lasting adverse effect on mother (→ 25).

17. Washington, D.C.: Conservative Republican Richard Cheney wins unanimous Senate confirmation as secretary of defense.

17. Managua: Sandinista government releases 1,894 former National Guardsmen from prison in accordance with five-nation peace accord (→ 24).

17. Pavia, Italy: Nine hundred-year-old, 255-foot medieval tower collapses, killing two and injuring 15; there were no signs of tower's weak state prior to disaster.

18. Giza, Egypt: Researchers discover 4,400-year-old mummy at Pyramid of Cheops.

Bush said to know of North's actions

March 13. Former national security adviser Robert McFarlane told a federal court today that he had informed President Reagan and Vice President Bush in 1985 that Lt. Col. Oliver North had provided both advice and financial assistance to the contra rebels in Nicaragua, even though Congress had clearly prohibited such action. When asked about Reagan's reaction to the disclosure, McFarlane said the President simply replied, "O.K." McFarlane did not elaborate on his conversations with either Reagan or Bush.

Both men have repeatedly maintained that their knowledge of North's activities in the Iran-contra affair was limited. It appears that either someone is being deceitful, or that a cavernous communication gap existed at the highest levels of government (→ 28).

Chilean markets hurt by tainted grapes

Chilean fruit waiting in warehouses.

March 15. American stores are removing Chilean fruit from their shelves after two cyanide-tainted grapes were discovered in Philadelphia. The amount of poison found was too small to make anyone sick, but the Food and Drug Administration is not taking any chances. The federal agency has decided to impound all fruit imported from Chile and is urging consumers not to eat any. Earlier this month, the American and Japanese embassies in Santiago received anonymous telephone calls warning that fruit exports would be poisoned.

The cyanide scare has already resulted in massive layoffs in Chile, and officials there say it is a major threat to the $850 million fruit export industry. They are blaming both communists and the United States. The military government says the poisoning of the grapes is an act of "terrorism backed by the Communist Party." A member of the ruling junta called the FDA's action "roguish." "Americans think we are all banana republics," charged Adm. Jose Merino. "Chile is not a banana republic."

"Mommy Track" advocated in workplace

You've come a long way, baby — and maybe you've come far enough. That is the conclusion of an article by commentator Felice Schwartz in the latest issue of Harvard Business Review. "Management Women and the New Facts of Life" examines the family-business conflict faced by workingwomen with young children, and suggests that it might be resolved if corporations placed such employees on a less competitive path.

Feminist critics have nicknamed that route the "Mommy Track" and denounced it as an unrealistic and demeaning solution to working mothers' scheduling problems. They advocate flextime, parental leave and corporate-sponsored daycare to make the business world conform to the reality of the working mother, rather than the other way around. Get ready, they say: 66 percent of the new work force in the 1990s will be female.

Bush backs gun ban

March 14. President Bush has ordered a ban on the import of semi-automatic assault rifles. The move, unexpected from a president who is a lifetime member of the National Rifle Association, follows the recent murders of five California schoolkids by a man firing an assault rifle. Some say the ban is a prudent step in fighting crime. Others say Bush should take tougher measures, starting with a ban on semi-automatics (→ July 12).

Japan plane deal

March 15. A $1.2 billion plan by General Dynamics and Mitsubishi of Japan to build the FSX tactical fighter plane, an advanced version of the American F-16, received the support of President Bush today. A formal decision is yet to be reached, but the President is seeking to arbitrate conflicts between the Commerce and Defense departments over the project. Defense supports the plan, which it says will strengthen security ties with a Pacific ally. Commerce is concerned about sharing technology with a nation that is surpassing the United States in many high-tech areas (→ April 28).

The brilliant orange flash of a solar flare that erupted this week.

Kremlin backs Gorbachev farm reform

Lithuanian farmers: soon to be free-holding capitalists?

March 16. Soviet leaders convened today at an emergency Central Committee meeting and approved sweeping changes in farm policy. Under the "new agrarian plan," which was proposed by Mikhail Gorbachev, farmers will be allowed to lease land from the state for life and pass it on to their children. In the past, leases had 15-year limits. Farmers will also be given greater freedom in deciding where to work. The goal of the new reforms, ex-

plained Gorbachev, is to allow farmers "to display independence, enterprise and initiative."

The need for Soviet agrarian reform is critical. The state-owned collectives that are the mainstay of Soviet agriculture require billions of rubles in subsidies, and even then the Soviets are forced to import grain and meat. Because of the system's inefficiencies, as much as one-third of the food rots before it gets to market.

New Cabinet will confront chaos in Sudan

March 12. Succumbing to an army ultimatum, Sudanese Prime Minister Sadiq el Mahdi will form a new Cabinet whose mandate is to end the ongoing civil war. It will reflect the new government — el Mahdi's recent effort to placate the army — which represents major labor unions and 30 political parties. The war, of ancient origin, erupted anew in 1983. It has been fueled by el Mahdi's imposition of Islamic law upon a rebellious south whose people are either Christian or animist. The six-year conflict has claimed about a million lives, and the U.N. estimates that last year alone some 250,000 southern Sudanese died from famine and war-related starvation (→ June 30).

Famine and war plague the people.

Americans jumping on abstinence wagon

Moderation is the key word for the '80s. A bevy of health-promoting activities and much less alcohol is the style. Wine use fell 14 percent between 1980 and 1987, consumption of distilled spirits dropped 23 percent and membership in Alcoholics Anonymous doubled. Even beer drinking dropped 7 percent. "A real change of life style," is the

comment of Dr. Howard Shaffer, director of Harvard's Center for Addiction Studies. "Hard liquor is out," said one restaurant owner.

Many believe the trend has a lot to do with an increased focus on work. Ford Motor Company's director of public affairs agrees. "People work harder," he observes. "The pace is quicker."

American colleges prey of Japanese

The Japanese have added American colleges to their U.S. shopping list, which already ranges from Manhattan skyscrapers to Honolulu mansions. At least one of the sought-after institutions has said no to the mighty yen. Refusing a $24 million offer from the Kyoto Institute of Technology for their entire campus in Enid, Okla., officials at Phillips University declared, "Colleges are not bought and sold. We're not Quaker Oats." But other schools, such as financially pressed Warner Pacific College in Portland, Ore., see Japanese money as an opportunity too enticing to pass up. Selling 49 percent of its physical plant to a Japanese firm, the college says it needs the $6 million. "There is no question," says an assistant to the president there, "higher education will be more international in the future."

Flag-desecrating artwork in Chicago sparks nationwide protest

March 12. The streets of Chicago are today awash in a sea of patriots, marching to protest an exhibit at the Chicago Art Institute. Designed by student "Dred" Scott Tyler, the piece is entitled *What is the Proper Way to Display the U.S. Flag?* Against a background of photography showing flag-draped coffins from the Vietnam War, the work contains a sign-in ledger for comments by viewers about the art. The catch is that, in order to write in the book, would-be critics have to walk on an actual flag that the artist, a self-proclaimed Maoist, has arranged on the floor. The work has enraged a broad spectrum of people, from war veterans who consider sacred the flag for which they fought, to average citizens who feel that the symbol of the nation deserves better treatment.

The controversy has brought into national focus several important issues, including censorship of the

arts by people hostile to a specific piece, and the issue of the flag itself. As does a case of flag burning to be heard by the Supreme Court, the dispute over Tyler's work seems to

ask whether or not a legitimate symbol of patriotism can also serve as a legitimate symbol of protest. Which is more important: the flag or what it represents?

Protesters outside Chicago's Art Institute try to lift patriotism above art.

MARCH
1989

Su	Mo	Tu	We	Th	Fr	Sa
			1	2	3	4
5	6	7	8	9	10	11
12	13	14	15	16	17	18
19	20	21	22	23	24	25
26	27	28	29	30	31	

19. Ponte Vedra Beach, Fla.: Tom Kite captures the Players Championship, becoming second golfer this year to win consecutive PGA titles.

20. Washington, D.C.: U.S. District Court Judge Charles R. Rickey blocks curfew in capital.

20. Jerusalem: Group of Hasidic men attack women praying at Wailing Wall, which the men consider blasphemous.

20. Belfast, Northern Ireland: Two senior policemen are killed returning from a meeting in the Irish Republic; IRA claims responsibility (→ July 13).

20. Los Angeles: Record 13 people killed and nine wounded over weekend in shootings across county.

21. Washington, D.C.: In first underwater test launch, Trident 2 missile explodes seconds after takeoff, delaying deployment scheduled for next year.

21. Washington, D.C.: Supreme Court upholds right of federal government to test employees for drug abuse.

21. Sydney, Australia: Prime Minister Bob Hawke admits he was unfaithful to wife of 33 years, and vows not to do it again.

21. Washington, D.C.: Oregon Sen. Mark Hatfield admits to witnessing a shooting on a city street and not telling authorities because it wouldn't have made any difference.

22. Washington, D.C.: In unanimous decision, Supreme Court voids New York City's Board of Estimate because it gives boroughs power disproportionate to population.

22. Palm Desert, Calif.: National Football League commissioner Pete Rozelle announces intention to retire when replacement is found.

24. New York City: Convicted child killer Joel Steinberg sentenced to 8.3 to 25 years for death of illegally adopted daughter, Lisa.

25. Washington, D.C.: Career lawyers in Justice Department protest department's active anti-abortion efforts (→ April 9).

Rightist Arena Party wins in El Salvador

Cristiani celebrates a victory for conservatives in his war-torn country.

March 20. Alfredo Cristiani of the right-wing Nationalist Republican Alliance (Arena) has won the presidential election in El Salvador by a wide margin. He will succeed President Jose Napoleon Duarte, whose five-year term ends June 1. Fidel Chavez Mena of the Christian Democrats finished second in the field of seven candidates, but Cristiani's majority has eliminated the need for a runoff election.

Leftist guerrillas, who have been waging a war against the U.S.-backed government for nine years, called on voters to boycott the election. The Christian Democrats attribute their loss to the low turnout, which official estimates place at 40 percent of registered voters. Arena contends that the guerrilla activity discouraged supporters of all parties. Cristiani's victory completes the transformation of Arena from a paramilitary organization to El Salvador's dominant political party, with a majority in the National Assembly and control of most municipal and provincial governments.

Arena's victory was not welcomed by policy makers in Washington. The United States, which has given more than $3.2 billion in aid to El Salvador since 1981, supported the centrist policies of Duarte and his Christian Democrats. Arena's links to human rights violations may endanger the bipartisan congressional support necessary to continued financial aid (→ April 19).

Pete Rose hit with charges of betting

March 22. Pete Rose refuses to swing hard at those making charges that he has bet on baseball games. "No comment," has been Rose's reply to published reports that the baseball commissioner's office is investigating "serious allegations."

Rose capped a long playing career by breaking Ty Cobb's record for base hits. Now the manager of the Cincinnati Reds, he bristles at suggestions the betting charges might jeopardize his election to the Hall of Fame. If it is found that Rose bet on other baseball teams, he could be suspended for a year; if he bet on the Reds, he faces a lifetime suspension (→ June 25).

Charlie Hustle's feathers are ruffled.

Scientists claim to have created cold fusion; met with skepticism

Fusion or illusion; science can tell.

March 23. An American and a British researcher created a sensation in the world of science today and catapulted from the laboratory to the front pages by announcing they had created nuclear fusion in a test tube. Ordinarily, it would require temperatures of hundreds of millions of degrees to force two nuclei to fuse. Dr. B. Stanley Pons of the University of Utah and Dr. Martin Fleischman of England's University of Southampton said their experiment took place in room-temperature water. Most other scientists were quick to throw cold water on an experiment they deem highly suspect.

If the results of the two electrochemists can be confirmed, their work would have staggering implications. Energy could be produced very cheaply for entire cities without creating dangerous radioactive wastes. A meltdown, the greatest danger created by nuclear fission reactors, would be impossible.

Pons and Fleischman say their test tube, filled with heavy water and lithium, heated up unexpectedly when an electric current passed through. They insist that nuclear fusion, the squeezing together of two lighter nuclei into a heavier one, is the only possible explanation. Many other scientists disagree. They say there must be a different answer that Pons and Fleischman simply have not found (→ July 12).

Exxon Valdez runs aground, spilling oil

Seals try to avoid the poisonous slick.

March 25. Environmental officials in Alaska are criticizing the Exxon Corporation for moving too slowly to clean up the 240,000 barrels of crude oil that have spewed from one of its tankers into Prince William Sound. The Exxon Valdez, filled with more than a million barrels of crude oil from the Trans Alaska Pipeline, ran aground and ruptured early yesterday. Tonight, the slick from the spill is eight miles long and more than three miles wide. Critics of oil drilling on Alaska's North Slope say it is the environmental disaster they have always warned would happen. Exxon has already accepted responsibility for the damage, but it could take years to clean up the area (→ 30).

U.S. gives contras humanitarian aid

March 24. The Bush administration and Congress signed an agreement today that gives the Nicaraguan opposition $4.5 million a month for food, clothing and medical supplies. The accord, orchestrated by Secretary of State James Baker, signals a change in the foreign policy thrust of the last eight years, which aimed to overthrow the Nicaraguan government by arming the contras. It is also the first bipartisan foreign policy decision of the new administration. Nicaraguan President Daniel Ortega says the aid package violates a Latin American accord designed to disassemble the contras (→ June 18).

"Thin Blue Line" prisoner released

March 23. Randall Dale Adams spent the past 12 1/2 years of his life behind bars. Today, when the Dallas district attorney's office announced it would not retry the recently freed convict, it virtually admitted that those years were the product of an incredible injustice. Adams, sentenced to death in 1977 for shooting a Dallas police officer, escaped execution in 1980 on a technicality. A documentary film entitled *The Thin Blue Line* examined his case and documented another man's confession. Thanks to the film's director, Errol Morris, Adams is now at home in Columbus, Ohio.

L.A. approves massive clean-air program

March 22. "I refuse to breathe air I cannot see," goes a standard joke in Los Angeles, where smog indeed gets in your eyes. Now, a regional planning board, under attack in the courts, has passed a plan calling for more than 120 air pollution controls by the year 2007. Among the activities proposed: cleaning up emissions from cars, buses, boats and industry; trading aerosol deodorants for sticks; banning barbecues that use starting fluids; replacing dirty paints and solvents; telling people to work at home with fax machines and phones; and more.

House of ill repute takes on Wall Street

March 21. There's a new development in the world's oldest profession. Mustang Ranch, the biggest brothel in the United States, is preparing to sell stock to the public at $20 a share; investment bankers plan to close the offering before April at $23.3 million. Located nine miles east of Reno, Nev., the house of ill but legal repute has 102 rooms and 30 women available to satisfy male fantasies for $80 a half hour. Who will profit most from the stock offer? Mustang Ranch owner Joe Conforte, who owes the IRS $12 million in back taxes and penalties.

House report claims class gap widening

March 22. The rich are getting richer and the poor are getting poorer, according to a study conducted for the House Ways and Means Committee. Personal income for the poorest American families dropped by 6.1 percent in 1987 compared with figures from 1979. In the same period, the report shows an 11.1 percent increase for the nation's wealthiest families.

Rep. Thomas Downey, chairman of the Subcommittee on Human Resources, said the widening gap is likely to lead to an increase in crime and social unrest: "You're not going to have enough locks on the doors or police in the streets to protect you from a generation of people who are not part of the mainstream of American economic life."

The study also found that although federal assistance may not be able to reduce the number of poor people, it can reduce the degree of destitution.

March 25. *The Louvre reopened today with architect I.M. Pei's new pyramid adorning its courtyard. But is it intrusion or addition? Critical opinions are mixed as to whether it will become the classic it was meant to be.*

Su	Mo	Tu	We	Th	Fr	Sa
			1	2	3	4
5	6	7	8	9	10	11
12	13	14	15	16	17	18
19	20	21	22	23	24	25
26	27	28	29	30	31	

27. Washington, D.C.: Iraq agrees to pay a total of $27.3 million to families of those killed on USS Stark, accidentally attacked in the Persian Gulf in 1987.

27. Albany, N.Y.: Manufacturers of latex condoms agree to put expiration dates on every package.

27. United States: Anti-missile satellite fails in first test in space, as sensor malfunctions.

28. Washington, D.C.: Former Atty. Gen. Ed Meese reveals at North trial that many Reagan aides feared President might be impeached for Iran-contra affair (→ April 6).

28. Washington, D.C.: Air Force grounds all B-1 bombers after wing punctures fuel tank in one plane.

29. New York City: Broker Michael Milken is indicted on 98 counts of financial wrongdoing.

30. Atlanta: Researchers at Center for Disease Control report that death rate for cigarette smokers is increasing while rate for population as a whole decreases.

30. Athens, Greece: Prime Minister Andreas Papandreou files for divorce from American-born wife (→ June 19).

31. Newfoundland, Canada: France and Canada sign pact ending 3-year dispute on fishing rights off Canada's coast.

31. United States: Wrestlemania V, championship starring Hulk Hogan and Macho Man Savage, is largest pay-per-view program in cable TV's history.

31. South Korea: Police, 14,000 strong, storm workers at Hyundai plant in Ulsan, trying to end three-month strike.

31. Los Angeles: Federal government takes over two West Coast savings and loan firms, biggest federal bank rescue to date (→ July 21).

DEATH

27. Malcolm Cowley, critic, writer, chronicler of the "Lost Generation" (*Aug. 24, 1898).

Soviets elect legislature in free vote

March 26. Soviet citizens went to the polls today and managed to find ways to reject the status quo whenever possible, even where candidates ran unopposed. In the freest elections since 1917, a sizable minority of independent candidates was elected to the new national congress.

The day's biggest winner was Boris Yeltsin, who swept to a landslide victory against a candidate backed by the Communist Party. Yeltsin, who resigned from the Politburo in 1987 after criticizing the slow pace of reforms, ran a popular campaign against party privilege.

One of the most embarrassing losses went to Yuri F. Solovyev, regional Communist Party leader in Leningrad. So many voters crossed his name off the ballot that even though he ran unopposed, he was unable to win a majority, forcing a new election. The same thing happened to the party leader and the mayor in Kiev, and to several Ukrainian officials.

Soviet leader Mikhail Gorbachev cautioned the Soviets not to get overexcited. "We must not commit stupidities, attempt great leaps forward, or overreach ourselves because we could put the people's future at risk." In truth, the Communist Party did not take that much of a risk, since it never stood to lose control of the legislature.

The vote was for half the 2,250 seats in the new national Congress

Maverick politician Boris Yeltsin.

of Deputies. The other seats were reserved for people appointed by the party. The 2,250 must now choose from themselves 1,500 who will actually make up the legislature.

But the election results still presented the Communist leadership with a stunning rebuke. One woman, when asked how she voted, simply replied, "Against what we have now." Voters seemed to prefer radical candidates. In Yaroslavl, an army general was defeated by a lieutenant colonel who favored doing away with the draft. In the Baltics, separatist candidates did well.

The last competitive elections in the Soviet Union took place in 1917. Lenin's Bolshevik party was defeated by the Socialist Revolutionaries, and shortly after he established a one-party state. Perhaps with that in mind, court clerk Boris Mamedov said what many must be feeling: "I hope this is all for real" (→ April 25).

Soviet voters hail their candidate in a Western-style political rally.

Pulitzers and Oscars given; 1960s and Hoffman are winners

March 30. Both Academy Awards, and Pulitzer Prizes were bestowed this week.

The 61st Oscar ceremony was a grand, glittery night, televised for 1.5 billion viewers in 91 countries, including the Soviet Union for the first time ever. Top Oscar winners — Dustin Hoffman, Jodie Foster and the movie *Rain Man* — received quite a bit more media atten-

tion than the 73rd Pulitzer Awards for journalism, letters and music, where echoes of the '60s resonated favorably among members of the judging committee.

Neil Sheehan was rewarded for the 16 years he spent delving into the Vietnam War to write *A Bright and Shining Lie: John Paul Vann and America*. Taylor Branch chronicled the civil rights struggle in

Parting of the Waters: America in the King Years, 1954-63. He shared the history prize with James M. McPherson, who wrote *Battle Cry of Freedom: The Civil War Era*. Wendy Wasserstein won for *The Heidi Chronicles*, a play about a child of the '60s alienated from the consciousness of the '80s. And Anne Tyler won for *Breathing Lessons*, her 11th novel.

127 charged with money laundering

March 29. "The Mine" has been sealed for good, federal drug fighters declared today, referring to "La Mina," a Los Angeles-based scheme that annually sneaked more than a cool billion in drug profits from the United States to Colombia. The operation is by far the biggest of its kind, said Atty. Gen. Dick Thornburgh, who announced the indictments of 127 people. All took part in a tricky, three-part scam: First they mixed millions of drug dollars in with profits skimmed from gold imports; next they deposited the disguised sums in American banks; then the money was quietly moved to branches in South America. Were the stateside banks — Continental Illinois and others — in on the game? The feds don't know yet.

Red star to Canada

March 29. Hockey right-winger Sergei Priakin, the first Soviet athlete permitted to play for a professional North American team, today signed a contract with the National Hockey League's Calgary Flames.

Cliff Fletcher, Flames' president and general manager, said "Sergei is a pioneer" paving the way for more spectacular Soviets such as the Red Army's Vyacheslav Fetisov, who has been drafted by the New Jersey Devils.

Eternal teen-ager Dick Clark retires

When Dick Clark spun his first disks on television's *American Bandstand* in 1956, he appeared, though 26, no older than the gaggles of local Philadelphia teenagers gyrating and bopping to the latest hits each week. His boyish good looks have remained remarkably intact through 33 years hosting the show, but pop music's Dorian Gray is calling it quits at age 59. Clark, who built a financial empire producing TV game shows, hands the *American Bandstand* reins to David Hirsch, who is 26. If he proves as successful as Clark, Hirsch will retire in the year 2022.

Exxon spill pollutes miles of Alaskan coast; wildlife endangered

March 30. Oil from the biggest tanker spill in United States history has spread over 500 square miles of Alaskan waters and coated hundreds of miles of coastline. The oil is more than a foot deep on some beaches. Dead birds, their feathers coated with oil, wash onto the shore. Sea otters, blackened by the spill, rub their eyes helplessly as they try to swim home in what used to be one of the most pristine and majestic areas of the country.

President Bush today called the spill a "major tragedy," as Exxon admitted it had given up trying to contain the oil from its tanker Exxon Valdez. "This spill has pretty much blown into Prince William Sound," an Exxon official said. "We will never get back those 240,000 barrels, but we will continue to try and clean it up, even if it takes months." Environmentalists say it will take much longer.

Scientists studying the enormous oil slick said today that it may poi-

Rocky, oil-soaked beaches show the effects of sluggish clean-up efforts.

America's addiction to oil . . .

son the area for years. Toxic chemicals like benzene and xylene are trapped in the calm, cold water beneath the slick, and experts say the poisons will almost certainly enter the food chain and kill fish eggs before they hatch.

The spill has already hurt Alaska's valuable fishing industry. This is the season that salmon migrate toward the ocean and herring move toward the shore. Fishermen in Valdez and Cordova say their catches are off, and they have begun to file claims against Exxon.

Exxon says it will reimburse the fishermen within reason, but the company is being widely criticized for doing too little, too late to clean up the spill. Company officials acknowledged yesterday that Exxon did not start deploying booms around the grounded tanker until 10 hours after the accident. Experts say a critically important barge into which oil could have been pumped was out of commission at the time of the accident. Exxon is blaming federal and state officials for the cleanup delays.

Lt. Gov. Stephen McAlpine bristled when told of the company's charges. "Trying to shift the burden of the blame in this situation," he said, "is something that just cannot and should not be done" (→ 30).

Tests show tanker captain was intoxicated

March 30. Federal officials investigating the massive oil spill in Alaska say the captain of the Exxon Valdez had unacceptably high levels of alcohol in his blood just after the accident. The captain, Joseph Hazelwood, has been dismissed by Exxon. The National Transportation Safety Board reports that the alcohol content of Hazelwood's blood was 0.061 percent, well above the maximum permissible level of 0.04 percent. Earlier this week, it was revealed that Hazelwood was not at the helm when the 987-foot tanker ran aground. In violation of both federal regulations and Exxon company policy, Hazelwood had left an unlicensed third mate in command.

Authorities in New York say this is not the first time Hazelwood has run into trouble for drinking. He has been convicted of drunken driving twice in five years. His license to drive a car has been suspended or revoked three times; his license to drive a tanker, however, remained untouched (→ April 3).

Hazelwood in a New Jersey court.

Su	Mo	Tu	We	Th	Fr	Sa
						1
2	3	4	5	6	7	8
9	10	11	12	13	14	15
16	17	18	19	20	21	22
23	24	25	26	27	28	29
30						

1. Toulouse, France: Concorde supersonic jet celebrates 20th birthday.

2. New York City: In major editorial, New York Times declares Cold War to be over.

2. Covington, Tenn.: Bridge collapses over river, sending seven motorists to watery death.

2. Smithton, Pa.: Workers at John Brewing company have been stripped of twice-daily beer breaks; management says they reduce productivity.

3. Valdez, Alaska: Herring fishing banned for season due to oil spill (→ 10).

4. Chicago: Richard Daley Jr., son of late political boss, wins mayoral race (→ 24).

5. Stockholm: Carl Gustav Christer Pettersson is charged with 1986 assassination of Swedish Prime Minister Olof Palme (→ July 27).

5. Moscow: Soviets allow publication, for first time, of Khrushchev's 1956 denunciation of Stalin (→ Aug 10).

6. Cape Town, South Africa: P.W. Botha announces in Parliament he will resign after upcoming election (→ May 26).

6. New York City: Archeologists unearth remains of 1735 almshouse, possibly New York's first homeless shelter.

6. United States: Researchers have found that ex-smokers put on weight because nicotine increases metabolic rate.

6. Washington, D.C.: Document at trial of Oliver North reveals that Panama's Manuel Noriega offered to kill Sandinista leaders for the U.S. (→ 7).

6. Lebanon, N.H.: FAA introduces new landing system for planes that operates on microwaves; destined for all U.S. airports by year 2000.

7. Washington, D.C.: At his trial, North admits to lying to group of congressmen at White House in 1986 (→ May 4).

8. Kabul, Afghanistan: Government admits it accidentally fired a Soviet Scud-B missile into Pakistan (→ 16).

Polish accord promises free elections

Democratic inroads in the Eastern bloc: Solidarity and the government hold their historic round-table discussions on the political future of Poland.

April 5. Poland is on its way to becoming the first Communist state to evolve into a democracy. Accords signed today between the union Solidarity and the Polish government set free elections in June for the upper house of Parliament. Union leader and Nobel Peace laureate Lech Walesa praised the peaceful round-table negotiations that led to the accords and said he hoped that such talks can "become the beginning of the road for democracy and a free Poland."

If carried out, the accords will bring sweeping changes to Poland. The government will end its eight-year ban on Solidarity. Free elections will be held in Poland for the first time since World War II for the 100 seats of the newly restored upper house of Parliament. The upper house was disbanded after World War II as the Communists cemented their control of Poland.

Thirty-five percent of the seats of the lower house of Parliament will be distributed to Solidarity.

The Communist Party will hold 38 percent, giving it a minority position there for the first time since 1944. The remaining seats will be held by parties that usually vote with the Communists.

The main concession on the union's part was in allowing the creation of a new office of president. The officeholder will be elected by the two houses for a six-year term. The new president, who is expected to be Gen. Wojciech Jaruzelski, will have the power to dissolve Parliament and to veto laws.

The accords are the culmination of negotiations that began last August when the country was on the verge of economic collapse following two waves of strikes. Said Walesa, "I have to emphasize that for the first time we have talked to each other using the force of arguments, not the arguments of force."

Public reaction to the accords was muted, with people taking a wait-and-see approach. This response was largely a reflection of the political seesaw Poland has been riding for the last decade.

In the United States, the White House welcomed the accords as a "great day for the Polish people and for freedom," and declared that the move should improve ties between the two countries (→ 17).

Vietnam to quit Cambodia unconditionally

Has Cambodia become Vietnam's Vietnam? Withdrawal continues.

April 5. Ten years after its armed forces crossed into Cambodia and drove out the Chinese-backed Pol Pot regime, the Vietnamese government has announced that it will withdraw the last of its troops by Sept. 30. Estimates of the number of Vietnamese troops remaining in the war-torn country range from 50,000 to 70,000.

No conditions are attached to the pledge, although Hanoi had earlier insisted on a cutoff of all military aid to the factions opposing the present Cambodian government, headed by Premier Hun Sen. The opposition coalition, led by former ruler Prince Norodom Sihanouk, includes the Khmer Rouge, which held power from April 1975 to December 1978 and was responsible for the deaths of at least one million Cambodians (→ Aug 27).

March 3. *Rumeal Robinson's free throws with three seconds to go lift Michigan over Seton Hall 80-79 for the NCAA title.*

In U.S., Israeli P.M. presents vote plan

April 5. Secretary of State James Baker says that his first meeting with Prime Minister Yitzhak Shamir of Israel, regarding ways to settle the Israeli-Arab conflict, was "very encouraging." Shamir proposed supervised elections in the occupied territories after the intifada, or uprising, has ended. Israel would then negotiate with the elected representatives. The PLO has rejected this plan but might be willing to accept elections supervised by the United States or the United Nations. Shamir will present detailed plans to President Bush later this week (→ 14).

Soviet troops sent to Georgia republic

April 8. Thousands of people demonstrated and held strikes in the Georgian capital of Tbilisi today as pressure mounted on Soviet leader Mikhail Gorbachev to grant more autonomy to the republic of Georgia. Some of the demonstrators demand complete independence. Gorbachev and Foreign Minister Eduard Shevardnadze, himself a Georgian, are trying to use quiet diplomacy to end the rebellion, but the government has also stationed tanks and soldiers in the streets of Tbilisi. Crowds carrying signs denouncing "Russian imperialism" have surrounded the tanks (→ 9).

Gorbachev takes "new thinking" abroad

April 7. Soviet leader Mikhail Gorbachev tested glasnost in Cuba and London this week and found that the 1980s have put an ironic twist in East-West relations. His "new thinking" got a better audience among Britain's hard-core capitalists than among the revolutionary ideologues of Havana.

Meeting with the fatigue-clad Fidel Castro, Gorbachev appeared the consummate pragmatist. He declared the Soviet Union to be "categorically opposed to . . . all forms of foreign interference in the affairs of sovereign states." And though he mentioned U.S. aid to rebels in Afghanistan and Nicaragua, he extended his disavowal to "doctrines that seek to justify the export of revolution." Castro, in turn, did a balancing act, making clear his opposition to Soviet-style economic reforms, yet insisting Cuba and the Soviet Union agree on all matters.

Moving on to London, Gorbachev elicited praise from Prime Minister Margaret Thatcher, who called their talks "very deep, very wide ranging and very friendly." One poll found that in eight years, the percentage of Britons who feel the U.S.S.R. "wishes to extend its power over other countries" has been cut in half. Queen Elizabeth even accepted an invitation to visit Russia, where her Romanov cousins were executed 70 years ago.

Rockets and artillery ravage Lebanon in new round of fighting

April 3. Muslim and Christian forces in Lebanon continued their vicious infighting today, raising the human toll in their relentless conflict yet another notch. Radio stations representing both sides reported 12 Lebanese killed and 15 wounded in today's fighting, which brings the casualty count to 120 dead and 450 wounded since hostilities resumed on March 14.

Most of the carnage is a result of the rocket and artillery fire that continues to rain down on the Bekaa Valley and Beirut. Foreign embassies in Baabda, near Beirut, have been hit by the fire, but no diplomats have been hurt. An Arab committee in Damascus, Syria, has been trying unsuccessfully to arrange a cease-fire.

The ante in Lebanon was upped by Gen. Michel Aoun, commander of the Christian forces, who vows he will not stop fighting until the Syrians agree to leave his country. Some 40,000 Syrian soldiers now control 65 percent of Lebanon. The rest of the country is divided into several political and religious factions, and southern Lebanon is still controlled by Israel with a proxy force of Christian militia.

Since General Aoun's force of 15,000 Christian militia began to attack Syrian positions surrounding Beirut, the Syrians have poured Katyusha rocket fire and heavy artillery into the Christian sectors of a city, once beautiful, that has been almost destroyed (→ 16).

Even the heavens hold no answers for the human tragedies on Earth.

Soviet sub sinks; may bear nukes

April 7. A Russian submarine has reportedly sunk in the Norwegian Sea. According to Norwegian and American sources, the huge Mike-class submarine apparently caught fire while submerged. American officials believe the 6,400-ton Soviet craft was equipped with nuclear-tipped cruise missiles in addition to conventional torpedoes. U.S. Navy officials are playing down the danger of radiation leaks. Since the sub has a double hull, they claim, the chances of nuclear seepage are minimal. White House spokesman Marlin Fitzwater told reporters, "We understand there has been a loss of lives, but we can't confirm how many" (→ 9).

Get your sushi here

Baseball is the Great American Pastime. So vendors at major American ballparks are serving great American foods like . . . tacos and sushi? Responding to the needs of bored and health-conscious fans, food services at Anaheim Stadium, Wrigley Field and other ballparks are offering a wider variety of munchables. Hot dogs, beer and popcorn remain popular (they make up nearly 90 percent of Wrigley's concession sales). But last season, when fans sampled sushi at San Diego Padre games, they roared for more raw fish.

Su	Mo	Tu	We	Th	Fr	Sa
						1
2	3	4	5	6	7	8
9	10	11	12	13	14	15
16	17	18	19	20	21	22
23	24	25	26	27	28	29
30						

9. Moscow: Soviet officials put death toll from sinking of nuclear submarine off Norway at 42.

9. Augusta, Ga.: Englishman Nick Faldo wins Masters golf tournament.

10. Washington, D.C.: Drug czar William Bennett opens drug offensive, indirectly accusing Washington Mayor Marion Barry for unchecked drug violence in capital.

10. United States: Gasoline prices have risen by 12 percent since Easter as result of Alaskan oil spill (→ May 5).

11. Tokyo: Prime Minister Takeshita admits to Parliament that he accepted payments from major corporations, but insists they were political contributions, not bribes (→ 25).

12. Washington, D.C.: House Ethics Committee votes to charge Speaker Jim Wright with breaking House rules (→ 17).

12. Matamoros, Mexico: After finding mass grave of 12 people, authorities search for drug gang engaged in ritualistic murder.

12. U.S.S.R.: Because of sugar shortage, first ration cards since World War II are issued.

13. Ontario: Human rights tribunal rules that homosexual couples can constitute a family.

13. Colombo, Sri Lanka: Bomb planted by Tamil separatists kills 38 in marketplace.

15. Illinois: Ron Miller, hog buyer from Little York, is one of four winners of $69.9 million state lottery.

DEATHS

14. George Burrows, a founder of the American Civil Liberties Union (*1900).

14. Herbert Mills of Mills Brothers singing group; recorded total of 2,246 records since 1930s (*1912).

15. Frances ''Fanny'' Steloff, founder of Gotham Book Mart (*Dec. 31, 1887).

15. Hu Yuobang, former leader of Chinese Communist Party (*November 1915).

Thousands march in Washington in support of Roe v. Wade

April 9. In one of the largest demonstrations in Washington, D.C.'s history, hundreds of thousands of people today filled the streets in support of abortion rights. Mothers and daughters, senior citizens and dozens of celebrities filed past the White House with banners and buttons that read, ''Keep your laws off my body,'' or ''Who decides? You or them?'' From inside the President's domicile, the only comment was, ''We have no comment.''

The march, estimated to have attracted between 300,000 and 600,000 protesters, also drew several hundred counter-demonstrators. At one point, pro-choice advocates, some dressed in the white, purple and gold of the suffragettes, faced off against a group of bonneted baby-impersonators. ''Shame! Shame! Shame!'' shouted the abortion rights marchers. ''Life! Life! Life!'' screamed their opponents.

Organizers of the march hope

Coathangers everywhere symbolized the dangers of illicit abortions.

their show of force will send a message to the Supreme Court, which next month considers a Missouri law restricting the use of public funds for counseling or performing abortion. Many pro-choice advocates fear the court lacks the needed margin to uphold the Roe v. Wade decision, which affirmed abortion rights in 1973 (→ July 3).

Fiery 1960s radical's life is quenched

A man out of time. The '60s radical lived through '80s conservatism.

April 12. Abbie Hoffman, the '60s radical whose biting sarcasm and instinct for the absurd lent a theatrical edge to the protest movement, is dead at 52. Hoffman was a member of the Chicago Seven, a group accused of disrupting the 1968 Democratic Convention, and co-founder, with Jerry Rubin, of the protest group the Yippies. Whether naming a pig for president or trying to levitate the Pentagon, he aimed to mix politics and humor. But Hoffman grappled all his life with manic depression, and according to friends, found life in the '80s increasingly irrelevant. The cause of his death is undetermined (→ 18).

Sugar Ray is dead

April 12. The prizefighter described as ''pound for pound, the best'' is dead at 67. Sugar Ray Robinson, who won the middleweight title five times and also held the welterweight title, died in Culver City, Calif., of Alzheimer's disease and diabetes. In a 25-year career, Sugar Ray won 175 bouts and lost 19. Five of those defeats came in the last six months of his career, when he fought solely to avoid poverty, having run through an estimated $4 million. In the words of the champ himself, ''Money is for spending.''

Mexican drug raid

April 10. Just as Congress was debating the extent of Mexican cooperation with the United States war on drugs, Mexico provided a dramatic answer by arresting Miguel Angel Felix Gallardo, its leading cocaine king. Eighty policemen were also arrested, but only two were detained. Felix Gallardo's operation slipped about two tons of cocaine a month into the United States. The arrest is seen as a personal triumph for President Carlos Salinas and reflects a recent get-tough crackdown on corruption.

The flesh may be dead, but the soul lives on as the spirit of political dissent.

Rioting in Soviet Georgia claims 16 lives

April 9. Nationalist demonstrators clashed before dawn today with Soviet troops in the streets of Tbilisi, the capital of Soviet Georgia. The government says 16 civilians were killed and more than 100 were injured. Military authorities imposed a curfew and banned further rallies. According to Tass, the Soviet press agency, the square of the capital is now under army control. "My God, it is so tragic, so awful," one demonstrator told a reporter. "Young girls and boys are dead. The situation is very dangerous."

Soviet troops and tanks were sent to Tbilisi last week following new demands for Georgian independence and strikes in factories and the television station. A leader of the rebellion said the show of force today will not end the movement. "We are intellectuals and workers," she said, "and we will no longer allow ourselves to be silenced. This is a real struggle, not a show."

Soviet leader Mikhail Gorbachev has condemned nationalist movements, but his reforms have breathed new life into them. More than 80 people died over the past year in clashes between Muslim Azerbaijanis and Armenian Christians in Nagorno-Karabakh. In Georgia, the situation is more complicated. The latest round of trouble began when Muslims in the small republic of Abkhazia, which is under Georgian control, demanded independence from Georgia (→ 25).

Armored cars and troops enforce calm in the streets of Tbilisi.

First Star Wars test is a stellar success

April 10. Pentagon officials announced today that the first major Star Wars anti-missile weapons system has been successfully tested. The top-secret, $250 million "Alpha" laser, fueled by a mixture of hydrogen and fluorine, is designed to produce a concentrated light beam of 2.2 million watts. When fully operational, it should be capable of destroying a large number of incoming enemy missiles almost simultaneously. The ground test was conducted at a TRW plant near San Juan Capistrano, Calif., the Pentagon says. The new laser weapon is scheduled for deployment in space in 1994, though Star Wars funding must first pass critical tests in Congress.

Did Bell invent the phone, or Meucci?

April 9. Who doesn't identify the telephone with Alexander Graham Bell, who patented the device and founded the Bell Telephone Company in 1876? The answer is John N. LaCorte, president of the Italian Historical Society of America and lobbyist for Italian-American inventor Antonio Meucci.

In 1871 Meucci filed a notice of intent to take out a patent for an instrument that transmitted speech by electricity, but he lacked money to pursue the project. In New York today, at a ceremony honoring Meucci, LaCorte said Bell commercialized the telephone, but Meucci first invented it.

In 1940, New York's Meucci Square was named after Meucci.

British soccer crowd turns ugly; 93 die

Some fans managed to escape the chaos of the crushing crowds below.

April 15. British soccer fans have once again been forced to watch their fervor for the sport turn brutally to tragedy. Ninety-three people were killed and more than 180 injured today at a match in Sheffield, where Nottingham Forest and Liverpool met for a tournament contest. The disaster began when a mob surged into the overcrowded standing area of Hillsborough stadium, crushing hundreds of others against cement barriers and steel bars. It is not known how so many fans got into the stands at once. Witnesses said ticket takers were overwhelmed by the incoming stream. Others said rowdies overran the restraining gates.

Officials asserted that the disaster — the worst in British soccer history — was not the result of fighting, as has often been the case, but of misbegotten "safety arrangements." Ironically, the fences and barriers that trapped the fans were originally erected in an effort to control unruly crowds.

Israelis deny Arabs right to worship freely

April 14. Despite a long-standing Israeli policy of allowing Arabs freedom of worship in Jerusalem, police today sealed off the Al Aksa Mosque, which was turned into a battleground by riots in the Old City last week. By closing one of Islam's holiest sites, the Israelis hope to block protests over the killing by Israeli Border Police of five Arabs in the West Bank village of Nahalin. The pre-dawn police action has been highly criticized in the Israeli press (→ May 22).

Palestinians protest the deaths of five Arabs at the hands of Israeli commandos.

Su	Mo	Tu	We	Th	Fr	Sa
						1
2	3	4	5	6	7	8
9	10	11	12	13	14	15
16	17	18	19	20	21	22
23	24	25	26	27	28	29
30						

16. Beirut: Spain's envoy to Lebanon, Pedro Manuel de Aristegui, is killed in the latest round of fighting (→ May 7).

16. Islamabad: Pakistani officials report that Afghan rebels' latest actions have been led by Pakistanis with direct involvement of U.S. Embassy officials (→ 23).

17. Hamtramck, Mich.: President Bush announces extensive aid program to Poland, linked to Warsaw's recent democratic reforms (→ July 12).

17. Warsaw: Solidarity, outlawed in 1981, receives legal status from a Polish court (→ June 5).

18. Switzerland: At request of U.S., Swiss arrest tycoon Adnan Khashoggi for fraud in conjunction with Ferdinand and Imelda Marcos (→ July 19).

18. Pennsylvania: State coroner rules Abbie Hoffman's death a suicide.

18. Luxembourg: Nation's 150th anniversary celebration is attended by the 45-member army band, about 7 percent of the country's military.

18. Indianapolis: Pipe bomb in a toothpaste container explodes at a K-Mart, seriously injuring a 5-year-old girl.

19. United States: Large asteroid passes within 500,000 miles of the Earth, a close call in cosmic terms.

20. Washington, D.C.: White House announces Dr. Allan Bromley has been appointed Bush's chief science adviser.

20. Washington, D.C.: Census Bureau reports a record 17 million people are employed by the government, partly due to rising prison population.

21. United States: Researchers report that viral hepatitis in nation's blood supply causes 150,000 new cases per year.

21. Moscow: The KGB announces the discovery of two bombs in a subway station.

22. Manila: Communist rebels claim responsibility for murder of U.S. Col. James N. Rowe, saying they will kill again (→ Sept 27).

Battleship blast kills 47

With a force that can hurl a 2,700-pound shell 20 miles, the guns blow inward.

April 19. The largest naval guns in the world — branded obsolete by many — today killed 47 of the sailors who manned them aboard the battleship Iowa. In training near Puerto Rico, 27 of the victims were inside the close, 17-inch-thick hardened-steel walls of one of the Iowa's three main turrets when an explosion and fire tore through the interior and beyond, claiming their lives and those of 20 more on deck.

Each turret contains three of the mammoth guns, each one so powerful it can hurl a 2,700-pound shell more than 20 miles. The massive projectiles are stored below, separated from silk bags of highly flammable powder, until shells and explosives come together inside the steel turrets where there is no escape from accidental explosion. Today's blast was the first in an American warship's gun turret since 1972, when 20 were killed and 36 injured on a heavy cruiser off Vietnam. The last main-gun explosion on a battleship took 43 lives when a turret blew up aboard the Mississippi during the World War II shelling of Makin Island.

With missiles now the principal battleship weapon, only a few 16-inch guns remain, at the insistence of those who say they are required for heavy shore bombardment during amphibious landings. They are no longer manufactured, however, and spare parts are a major problem (→ July 22).

April 20. *On the centennial of Hitler's birth, polls show 44 percent of West Germans think German blood should be kept pure.*

"Wilding" results in rape, beating

April 20. It has happened before, but today there is a new name for it: "wilding." Defined by the suspects, it means to canvass an area, raping, robbing or brutalizing all comers. Six young teen-age boys stand accused of the beating and raping of a 28-year-old woman yesterday in Central Park. She now lies comatose in the hospital. The suspects are black and Hispanic, hailing from Harlem, the victim a white investment banker from Wellesley and Yale. The brutal and indiscriminate nature of the crime has brought national attention to the problems of race, class and violence in New York City.

HDTV broadcasting system is shown

April 20. Scientists at the David Sarnoff Research Center in Princeton, N.J., have announced the successful demonstration of the world's first broadcast system for high-definition television (HDTV) that is compatible with current TV sets. HDTV, which offers sharp, highly-detailed images, is considered to be the television technology of the 21st century. With an obvious eye toward Japanese competitors, one Sarnoff scientist said the test "clearly puts us in a leadership position" (→ June 3).

Drug-dealing women cause prison boom

The number of women in New York City jails today is four times what it was in 1981 and rising at more than twice the rate of male prisoners, due to a sharp increase in female drug users and dealers. And the disturbing trend is echoed around the country. Apparently, as the number of single mothers rises, so does the number of women who sell crack to help support their children. To deal with the women's needs, Rikers Island opened a nursery in 1985 for newborn babies. A former shelter for homeless men on Wards Island is being converted into an auxiliary 300-bed women's jail. And a formerly all-male state prison will now house only women.

A rising tide of women in prisons.

Chinese students mark reformer's death

Students mourn Hu Yaobang.

April 22. A crowd estimated at 100,000 gathered yesterday in Beijing's Tiananmen Square. Composed primarily of students and workers, the crowd assembled to mourn publicly the death last week of Hu Yaobang, a reformist government official. Demanding democracy and chanting, "We will die for freedom," the demonstrators appear to be ready for a confrontation with the government. The Communist Party has banned such mass demonstrations, and a force of 2,000 heavily armed policemen has reportedly taken up positions around the square. One student, Yan Xinghua said, "Even if we risk a crackdown, this is something we must do" (→ May 20).

Rock and Roll boom grips Red China

More than 30 years after Elvis Presley first rattled the foundations of Western Civilization, the People's Republic of China is starting to rock. Once branded decadent and counter-revolutionary by Chairman Mao Zedong, rock music is now just one more Western influence in a nation embracing everything from jeans to Coca-Cola. But a People's Motley Crue appears far off: Chinese rock is long on syrupy strings and disco beats and short on Western rock's most crucial ingredient — defiance.

Connecticut in lead

The wealthiest Americans aren't about to pull up stakes, according to the Commerce Department. For the third year in a row, Connecticut ranks first among all 50 states in per capita personal income. Its $22,761 is well above the national average of $16,444. What makes Connecticut so special? For one thing, jobs; last year unemployment was only 3 percent. For another, there's no state income tax; just ask Donald Trump, Phil Donahue, Paul Newman and other denizens of Connecticut's southwestern Gold Coast. Outlanders, though, should think twice about moving to the "promised land." The average home in Connecticut costs $169,700.

Costs push young to live with parents

The latest results of the Census Bureau reveal that 18 million adults between the ages of 18 and 34 live with their parents, a 30 percent increase since 1974. Contributing factors are the high cost of housing and low starting salaries.

To some this means deepened family ties, to others only a cramped social life. Many parents are plagued by "boomerang kids," who leave home but keep returning. The trend may indicate an unwillingness to grow up, and an elongated concept of youth in society.

Loonies for Canada

April 30. Canada's last $1 greenbacks rolled off the presses of the Canadian Bank Note Co. Ltd. today. In a year, their average lifespan, the bills will be replaced by 11-sided, gold-colored $1 coins stamped with a loon and known as loonies.

The loonie, expected to last 20 years, is popular with transit companies, vendors and the Canadian National Institute for the Blind. But Canadians nostalgic for the $1 bill have already bought 55,000 uncut sheets as souvenirs, paying $50 each for a set of notes worth only $40 at face value.

Within a year, 450 to 600 million loonies will be in circulation.

Bomb atop car kills Salvadoran official

April 19. Salvadoran Atty. Gen. Roberto Garcia Alvadora was killed today by a blast from a bomb planted on the roof of his car. Government officials are blaming leftist guerrillas for the murder, the second fatal bombing of a rightist Nationalist Republican Alliance official in a week; Vice President-elect Francisco Merino was killed on Friday. Opposition forces are incensed over their declining political fortunes, claiming fraud in the election of the right-wing Alfredo Cristiani administration last month. Garcia is the highest-ranking leader killed in the nine-year war against the U.S.-backed government (→ June 9).

House committee blasts Jim Wright

April 17. The House Ethics Committee today accused House Speaker Jim Wright of a "scheme to evade" House income rules. In a harsh indictment, the committee leveled 69 charges of wrongdoing against Wright. It found that bulk sales of Wright's book, *Reflections of a Public Man,* were a deliberate effort to avoid House limits on outside income. It also charged that outside fees paid to the Speaker's wife, Betty, were in fact illegal gifts. Although Wright will have an opportunity to defend his actions, the committee's scathing report may have irreversible political repercussions (→ May 31).

Thomas Hart Benton's Persephone *(1939) in a Nelson-Atkins Museum of Art show, Kansas City. Considered by some the greatest American artwork to that time, it hung in a bar for some months as Benton had wanted.*

23. New York City: The 100-year-old Players Club, all-male theatrical group, inducts 30 women on its centennial, including actress Helen Hayes and columnist Liz Smith.

23. Kabul, Afghanistan: Officials report 277 people killed in latest rebel attacks (→ Oct 23).

23. New York City: Actor portraying George Washington re-enacts first President's arrival in New York for bicentennial of his inauguration.

25. Tbilisi, U.S.S.R.: Communist Party officials admit some 20 deaths in recent rioting were result of poison gas used by riot control (→ May 18).

25. Arcadia, Fla.: James Robinson released after 21 years in jail for murder of seven children; courts think he didn't get fair trial.

26. Washington, D.C.: Researchers find that two drugs designed for heart attack patients in fact kill in the long run.

26. New York City: Frank W. Cyr, 88, is honored for making yellow school bus standard in New York as a safety measure 50 years ago.

27. United States: Center for Women Policy Studies claims in report that Scholastic Aptitude Tests are biased in favor of boys (→ June 30).

28. Washington, D.C.: U.S. and Japan agree to proceed with joint project to produce new version of F-16 fighter.

28. New York City: Mobil announces it will pull out of South Africa because of stiff congressional laws.

29. Hartford, Conn.: Colt Industries, which first made the Colt revolver in 1836, is selling firearms division.

30. Hundwil, Switzerland: Armed with ceremonial swords, 5,000 men vote to give women of half-canton (state) of Appenzell Outer-Rhodes right to vote.

DEATH

28. Roy L. Williams, former Teamsters president (*March 22, 1915).

Japanese Prime Minister quits in scandal

Takeshita will leave office under a cloud of financial shenanigans, as the sun sets on his administration.

April 25. The bribery and corruption scandal that has rocked the Japanese government and, according to one poll, brought its popularity rating to a record low of 4 percent, has finally forced the resignation of Prime Minister Noboru Takeshita. Like his predecessor in that office, Yasuhiro Nakasone, Takeshita has been accused of accepting large sums of money from the Recruit Company, an information services conglomerate that has attempted to buy political favors from the government.

So many leading members of the ruling Liberal Democratic Party have been tainted by the Recruit scandal that Takeshita is said to have turned to former Foreign Minister Masayoshi Ito to succeed him as Prime Minister. Ito, who served briefly in that office in 1980, is now 75 years old and suffering from diabetes.

As the scandal has unfolded, three Cabinet ministers have been forced to resign, and Nakasone has stubbornly refused to testify under oath in Parliament about his role in the affair (→ May 31).

TV show sparks debate on black athletes

April 25. A documentary airing tonight on NBC reopens a volatile debate on race and athletics by offering both biological and cultural explanations for black excellence in sport. Since Jesse Owens' refutation of Hitler's racial theories at the 1936 Olympics in Berlin, scientists and psuedo-scientists have often claimed that blacks are innately disposed to certain kinds of physical activity. That argument, considered racist by many, cost Jimmy the Greek and Al Campanis their jobs.

Kareem Abdul-Jabbar spoke for the other side when he identified himself as one of the many black athletes who "put all their waking energies into learning the moves." "That's the way it's going to be," he said, "until black people can flow without prejudice into any occupation they can master."

Performance, by Jo Ann Callis, in a Smithsonian photo show.

Lucille Ball dead; we all loved Lucy

Red hair no American can forget.

April 26. One of the brightest lights in American entertainment history has been extinguished. Lucille Ball, the comedienne who delighted audiences for four decades has died of an aortal rupture at the age of 77. Best known for the title role in the sitcom *I Love Lucy,* her life was the ultimate Hollywood success story. Rising from the stables of RKO Pictures, she eventually bought the studio with the fortune she earned as the nation's leading funny lady. Her innovative sitcom, the first to be filmed before a live audience and to use motion picture-style editing, continues in syndication as one of the most popular ever. She has left a legacy of laughter.

Kareem's last regular season "sky hook"

April 23. He may be basketball's greatest ever. And today, Kareem Abdul-Jabbar was paid a fond farewell before his Los Angeles Lakers played their last regular season game with the big guy at center. Fans, teammates and city officials lavished gifts on the man who groomed the "Sky Hook" into an awesome weapon. Inglewood, Calif., Mayor Ed Vincent announced in the pre-game ceremony that a street near the Forum, where the Lakers play, would be renamed Kareem Court. Jabbar holds a host of records, including most points (38,387), games (1,560) and rebounds (5,920). He will reappear for a swan song with the Lakers when the playoffs begin (→ June 13).

Jabbar bids adieu to his loyal fans.

Short-range missiles cause fuss in NATO

Kohl: pressured home and abroad.

April 29. Washington officials to-day charged that Helmut Kohl's West German government is put-ting domestic politics ahead of NATO unity by pressuring the alli-ance into quick talks with the Sovi-et Union to eliminate short-range nuclear weapons in Europe. The United States wants to modernize the Lance missiles, not eliminate them. Refusing to retreat, the Bush administration insists Kohl is play-ing to anti-nuclear sentiment at home. Said one official, "If there are tensions in the alliance, they will be responsible." Though based in West Germany, the missiles are operated by U.S. troops and consti-tute a front-line defense against any Warsaw Pact attack (→ May 12).

110 members of Soviet leadership purged

April 25. The Communist Party ac-cepted the resignations today of 110 of its inactive members, purging the Central Committee of a group of political holdovers who are deri-sively known as the "dead souls." At the same time, 24 junior leaders were promoted to fill open spots on the Central Committee.

The purge appeared to come in response to last month's elections, in which voters favored a more rap-id pace of reform. The removal of the 110, 74 of whom had full voting rights, should eliminate a signifi-cant drag on Gorbachev's leader-ship. Among those who resigned were former President Andrei A. Gromyko and former Prime Min-ister Nikolai Tikhonov (→ May 31).

Gorbachev: undeniably the top man.

Yet another Mayor Daley in Chicago

April 24. Flanked by his wife and three children, Richard M. Daley was sworn in today as Chicago's 45th mayor. Daley, who is the son of former Mayor Richard Daley Sr., was elected to fill out the re-maining two years of the late Har-old Washington's term.

Invoking the spirit of his late fa-ther before a crowd of 2,500, Daley promised a "new season" in Chica-go. Mayor Daley faces the daunting task of reducing the racial tensions which now divide the Windy City.

Was TV host trashed by skinheads?

April 25. The biggest mouth on tele-vision may have opened too wide. Morton Downey Jr., the host of a talk show in which he devotes him-self heartily to haranguing both guests and audience, claims that he was attacked by skinheads in a San Francisco airport. Downey alleges that the bald-headed bullies corn-ered him in a bathroom, where they cut his hair and painted swastikas on his face and clothes.

Inconsistencies abound, how-ever. One 15-year-old in the area says he saw no skinheads. Police say the marks on Downey's face when the incident was reported dif-fered from those in later photos. Further, they say, he refused to file a police report, which, if proved false, would constitute a misde-meanor. He also refused a physical exam. So the question remains as to whether the clown prince of trash television was himself trashed by marauding youths, or if a premier publicity hound is dogging the me-dia for exposure. Right now, the nation can only echo the words of a spokesman for the *Morton Down-ey Jr. Show*: "I don't know. I don't know anything."

Violence flares on Senegalese border

April 30. A seemingly minor border incident on the Senegalese-Mauri-tanian border has sparked wide-spread ethnic violence in which hun-dreds have been killed. The unrest began when animals belonging to Mauritanian tribesmen damaged nearby Senegalese crops. Wide-spread killing and looting broke out in both countries following the news that two Senegalese farmers had died in the incident. Curfews and troops have been used to halt the violence in both countries.

1989 terrible year for 1789 Margaux

April 26. There's no use crying over spilled wine, even if it is priced at $519,750. William Sokolin, a New York wine merchant, realized this tonight after he broke a bottle of 1787 Chateau Margaux which, ru-mor has it, once belonged to Thom-as Jefferson. Sokolin had gone to Manhattan's fashionable Four Sea-sons restaurant to join some fellow wine lovers for a sampling of the 1986 Bordeaux vintage. Hoping to whip up some publicity for his Mar-gaux, which he thought he could sell at a profit, he carted it along. Rushing to show it to an admirer, he cracked the bottle on a table — and left, he said, "in shock."

April 23. *A carpet of flowers — symbol of mourning for the 20 nationalists killed by Soviet troops two weeks ago — covers a street in Tbilisi, Soviet Georgia. Today, 47 people were arrested while protesting the deaths. They were flying the flag of pre-revolutionary Russia and shouting, "Fascists."*

Suntan oil machine has you covered

Keeping a youthful look and do-ing things the easy way are two American trademarks of the '80s. Skin protectors such as sunscreens and lotions are big business, so Charles King of Memphis decided to capitalize on the nation's predi-lection for ease. Who likes to han-dle greasy, gritty bottles, he rea-soned. So King has invented Sun Center, a vending machine that dis-penses tanning lotion. Deposit 50 cents and let a hand-held nozzle spray you lightly for 40 seconds.

King began putting out machines last August and expects to distrib-ute 500 more this year along beach-es and at swimming pools.

1. Lakeville, Ind.: A pastor, his wife and two children are found shot dead in their home; doors are all locked; no motive known.

1. Peking: Finance Minister Shirley Kuo is first Taiwanese official to visit mainland since Communist revolution.

1. Bangkok, Thailand: Marilyn Quayle, wife of vice president, reveals on Pacific tour her "official cause" will be disaster relief.

2. Paris: PLO leader Yasir Arafat meets with President Francois Mitterand on Middle East situation; French Jews protest.

2. Washington, D.C.: President Bush tells Panamanian government U.S. will not recognize outcome of elections if there is evidence of fraud (→ 9).

3. Moscow: Unions are granted right to strike after wildcat walkouts (→ July 13).

3. Washington, D.C.: William Rehnquist is first Chief Justice to testify before Congress, for increased salaries for federal judges.

4. Washington, D.C.: Surgeon General C. Everett Koop announces he will resign in July.

4. Washington, D.C.: President Bush denies visiting Honduras while vice president to offer U.S. aid in exchange for Honduran aid to Nicaraguan contras (→ 4).

5. Washington, D.C.: Commerce Department reports jobless rate rose 0.3 percent in April, sparking recession fears.

5. Anchorage, Alaska: Vice President Quayle visits oil spill region to show federal support for cleanup effort (→ July 24).

6. Louisville: Sunday Silence rides to upset victory in Kentucky Derby.

6. Kuala Lumpur, Malaysia: It is reported that 130 people died over last month as pirates attacked boatloads of refugees from Vietnam.

6. Switzerland: Muammar al-Qaddafi, Libyan dictator, establishes $10 million Qaddafi Prize for Human Rights.

Colonel North convicted

Outside the courthouse: hero, or the pawn of a deceitful administration?

May 4. Oliver North, the man who ran the secret war against Nicaragua and won the hearts of many Americans during the Iran-contra hearings, was convicted today on three of 12 counts against him. The jury found that North destroyed and falsified documents, failed to pay for a $13,800 security system and aided the obstruction of Congress. But the ex-Marine was acquitted of the most serious charges, one of which was lying to Congress.

Vowing to appeal the verdict, North spoke in the swaggering, sentimental tone that Americans have grown to love or hate. "As a Marine," he said, "I was taught to fight, and fight hard, for as long as it takes to prevail."

The eight-week trial disclosed much about the secret arms sales to Iran and the diversion of funds to the contras. But, constrained by government refusal to disclose key documents, it shed only circumstantial light on the roles played by former President Reagan and then-Vice President Bush.

North's conviction strips him of his Marine pension and bars him from public office. It also carries a possible 10-year jail term and fines of up to $750,000 (→ July 5).

Meyerowitz's Provincetown Porch, *from a National Gallery photo show.*

Report calls U.S. education stagnant

May 3. Public education in the United States is "a disaster that we must turn around," said Education Secretary Lauro F. Cavazos at a presentation of the annual federal student performance report today in Washington. He angered state educators by claiming that despite a 26 percent increase in federal spending per student, indicators such as graduation rates and college entrance exam scores have not improved in the last three years. Critics insist the findings are biased against women and minorities and do not allow for the sharp increase in poverty-level students. The report, they charge, is an opening salvo in the administration's battle to cap federal spending on education.

Gay back in Army

May 3. A San Francisco court held today, 7-4, that the Army could not bar a former soldier from re-enlisting because it had allowed him to serve for 14 years despite his homosexuality. Perry J. Watkins will be the first gay to be admitted to the armed services with the backing of a full appellate panel. The ruling, however, sidestepped constitutional issues and did not directly challenge the military's long-standing policy of excluding gays from its ranks.

Mom is responsible

May 3. Some mothers are just too understanding. At least that's what Los Angeles police think. Under California's new anti-gang act, they've booked Gloria Williams, 37, for failing to "exercise reasonable care, supervision, protection and control" of her 17-year-old son, who is being held on rape charges. Mrs. Williams' arrest came after police toured the family apartment and termed it a "gang museum." The exhibit featured assorted gang insignia, along with two family photo albums showing the Williams kids aiming weapons and the lady of the house clad in a gang shirt. "All I can say," Mrs. Williams declared, "is that they are wrong. My son is not in a gang."

KGB pledges to refrain from state terror

KBG men guarded British leader Margaret Thatcher on her visit to Russia.

May 6. A kinder, gentler KGB? That, at least, is what the chief of the Soviet secret police and intelligence agency promised the public today in a front-page article in the official Soviet newspaper *Izvestia*. "The activity of our offices won't be so secret as it has been until now," declared Vladimir A. Kryuchkov, pledging "an expansion of democracy" in the KGB's operations.

The new look is a radical departure for an organization that once prided itself on the ruthlessness with which it eliminated counter-revolutionaries. "Frankly speaking, we have to learn to work under new conditions," Kryuchkov said, alluding to the political reforms known as glasnost that have been intro-

duced by Soviet leader Mikhail S. Gorbachev.

How open is the KGB likely to become? Kryuchkov promised to inform the public about "all major and important operations" carried out by the agency's half a million employees. He did not spell out details of this remarkable promise, but Soviet opinion polls indicate that the KGB has already done a credible job of softening its public image. In a poll published this week, the KGB's approval rating was higher than that of the Central Committee of the Communist Party or the Academy of Sciences.

Hungary tearing down barrier to Austria

May 2. The "Iron Curtain" that separates the East from the West is not just a figure of speech. Miles of barbed-wire fences seal off the borders of the East European countries. But in Hungary, the curtain is coming down. Hungarian soldiers have begun removing the barbed-wire fence that runs the length of Hungary's border with Austria. Said the head of Hungary's border guards, "It makes Hungarians feel much better that we no longer have such an old-fashioned border with the West." He added that the entire 150 miles of fence should be pulled up by the end of the year.

But will floods of East European immigrants now pour into Austria? That was the question Austrian officials were asking even as they applauded the change (→ Aug 14).

Churchill called it an Iron Curtain; here it is just 150 miles of barbed wire. The curtain is swept aside by Hungarian soldiers in Hegyeshalom.

Selling big names

Nostalgia is in — and expensive for the devotees of baseball's golden age. One-time greats like Ted Williams, Joe DiMaggio, Ernie Banks and Willie Mays are charging from $12 to $30 for their autographs at baseball-card shows. They sign rapidly while their mostly young fans are rushed impersonally through long lines. It wasn't that long ago that players signed their names for free, especially for kids. Many of today's players also set a price before they'll sign anything.

Pyramids are ailing

Next time you visit the pyramids of Egypt, do the 4,500-year-old edifices a favor: don't park your car near them, don't climb up their sides, and breathe on them as little as possible. Egyptologists are warning the public that the factors of modern life — air pollution, sewage water and vibration from car traffic — are destroying the Sphinx and other historic treasures. Even breathing in a tomb is risky, raising the humidity and encouraging the growth of destructive fungi.

Shuttle launches space probe Magellan on mission to Venus

New York Mayor Ed Koch, up for re-election in November, tries to pacify a Manhattan version of the GOP mascot with a bagel.

May 5. Don't hold your breath, but 15 months from now, in August 1990, the spaceship Magellan will reach Venus. The unmanned craft, launched into orbit yesterday from the space shuttle Atlantis, is already some 170,000 miles away. It got off to a flying start, according to Elliott Cutting, head of mission planning. "The way it looks now, the insertion was very accurate and we will need only very small course corrections." Not only small, but few. Just three adjustments should be called for on a trek that will cover 800 million miles at a clip of 6,000 mph. The goal of the well-aimed craft? Scientists hope the mission will send back radar images of the planet's surface.

Its namesake braved the waters of this world; this Magellan will hazard space.

Su	Mo	Tu	We	Th	Fr	Sa
	1	2	3	4	5	6
7	8	9	10	11	12	13
14	15	16	17	18	19	20
21	22	23	24	25	26	27
28	29	30	31			

7. Beirut: Heavy shelling takes the lives of 20 people and injures 100 (→ 16).

8. London: Tests begin on humans for a third American AIDS vaccine (→ June 26).

9. Washington, D.C.: President Bush calls on world community to drive General Noriega from power in Panama; U.S. is considering military action (→ 11).

9. Hong Kong: Six sailors on USS White Plains die in unexplained fire off coast.

11. Washington, D.C.: John Mack, top aide to House Speaker Jim Wright, resigns after it is revealed that he was jailed for beating a woman.

11. Bar Harbor, Maine: Massive fire at genetic research lab kills 500,000 mice, a setback for researchers.

11. United States: Controversial film *The Last Temptation of Christ* has been released on home video, but many stores refuse to carry it.

11. Florence, Italy: Researchers have discovered mental condition known as ''The Stendahl Syndrome,'' whereby its victims lose control of their mental faculties in the presence of great art.

12. Los Angeles: Runaway freight train hits several houses, killing three people.

13. Cambridge, Mass.: Harvard's gays and lesbians force university to reverse decision to allow ROTC on campus, because U.S. military discriminates against homosexuals.

13. Bonn, West Germany: Soviet Foreign Minister Shevardnadze warns NATO that modernization of short-range nuclear missiles could jeopardize disarmament plans (→ 15).

13. New York City: Federal court rules ''Murphy bed'' has become a generic term and thus Murphy Door Bed Co. can no longer lay full claim to name.

DEATH

13. Christine Jorgensen, one of the first sex-change patients (*1926).

Panama's bloody elections prompt American military response

May 11. Widespread violence during elections in Panama has left the nation in disarray, opponents of Gen. Manuel Noriega bloodied and the Bush administration outraged.

Opposition leaders have won an electoral victory over Noriega's hand-picked candidates, according to a team of independent observers that includes ex-President Jimmy Carter. But Noriega has rejected the election results and sent paramilitary squads into the streets of Panama City to silence all protests. Witnesses say the squads brutalized demonstrators with lead pipes and baseball bats. Opposition vice presidential candidate Guillermo Ford was photographed as he was bloodied by Noriega's soldiers. Presidential candidate Guillermo Endara was also attacked and at least one opposition supporter was killed. In the hospital, a wheelchair-bound Endara remained determined: ''Noriega stands for everything

The U.S. deploys more troops . . .

but Noriega has forces of his own.

bad,'' he said, ''and he has to leave.''

President Bush concurs. He condemned the violence, called the election a fraud and deployed 2,000 troops in the region, saying he will not rule out the use of force to oust Noriega. Bush also ordered military families living in Panama to leave the country or seek shelter on U.S. bases (→ 18).

Asians are changing the face of Vancouver

Immigrants from Hong Kong are pouring into the western Canadian city of Vancouver, driving real estate values up 50 percent in one year and arousing hostility from local residents. The mainly affluent Chinese are racing to establish themselves in North America before Hong Kong reverts to Communist China in 1997. Some 5,000 arrived in Vancouver last year, comprising 20 percent of all newcomers.

Hong Kong Chinese now own $2.1 billion in Vancouver real estate and are involved in 60 percent of condominium construction. Longtime residents, angered that land is often sold in Hong Kong before it is offered in Vancouver, are demanding government restrictions.

Drug czar backs boot camps for addicts

Harsh measures from Bill Bennett.

May 8. Drug czar William Bennett, convinced that 4 a.m. wake-up calls and rigorous exercise will rehabilitate the prisoners of the drug war, came out today in support of a series of boot camps for drug convicts. The camps are voluntary, and require convicts to endure a basic training-style regimen of work, exercise and discipline. Georgia and Oklahoma were the first states to inititate boot camp programs in 1983, and now eight states utilize the camps. The recidivism rate for camp inmates is 38 percent, just a bit better than the rate of 41 percent for inmates in status quo prisons. But, if nothing else, America will have a healthier collection of drug dealers and addicts.

Egypt back in OPEC

May 13. After 10 years of ostracism, Egypt is being allowed to return to the Arab fold and rejoin OPEC. A decade ago the moderate nation was ejected by the nine-member group for having signed a peace treaty with Israel. Iraq initiated the move to bring Egypt back to OPEC because Egypt had supported that country in its eight-year war with Iran. Libya has been the only country to express reservations about the conciliation.

H-bomb near Japan

May 8. A long-lost hydrogen bomb has revived bitter Japanese memories of atomic destruction. As reported today by the environmental group Greenpeace, the bomb was en route from Vietnam in 1965 when it slipped from a U.S. aircraft carrier into 16,000 feet of water off the Ryukyu Islands — right on Japan's doorstep. Though losing power with age, the bomb has been politically potent in Japan, where it is fueling anti-nuclear and anti-American sentiment. Greenpeace says the bomb is only one of 50 warheads that have been scattered in the ocean by accident since 1956.

Bush, Gorbachev vie for Western Europe

May 12. Competition between the United States and the Soviet Union continues, but the emphasis, at least on the American side, has shifted from arms to public relations. George Bush today gave his first presidential address on East-West relations only a day after Soviet leader Mikhail Gorbachev surprised visiting Secretary of State James Baker with a new arms plan.

Bush's speech was clearly an effort to win support from a Western Europe that is infatuated with the Soviet leader. The long-awaited address did not stray far from Reagan administration policy. Bush called for a revival of President Dwight D. Eisenhower's "open skies" proposal, under which NATO and War-

saw Pact countries would allow unarmed surveillance aircraft to fly over each other's territory. The open skies plan was never put into practice because of deteriorating relations in the 1950s. And many observers note that widespread use of surveillance satellites makes the plan primarily symbolic in the '80s.

Bush did not respond to Gorbachev's promise yesterday that the Soviets will cut 500 weapons from their nuclear arsenal in Europe. Baker, however, appeared resentful that his first visit to the Soviet Union was being upstaged by yet another Gorbachev peace initiative. The secretary of state rejected Gorbachev's call for talks on short-range missiles in Europe (→ 13).

Smiles on the faces of Gorbachev and Baker belie the tension over West Europe.

Religious revival hits Russia and China

Patriarchs of the Russian church are gaining renewed respect in the U.S.S.R.

Lenin and Mao notwithstanding, the opiate of the people is nourishing millions in the two great empires of state-decreed atheism.

Church bells are tolling again in the Soviet Union, where Orthodox Christianity took root 1,000 years ago. Onion-domed churches, many of which were converted into storehouses, stables or factories by the Bolsheviks, are welcoming more and more of the faithful.

Orthodox leaders praise not just the Lord, but Soviet leader Mikhail Gorbachev, who gave his blessing to religion after meeting with church luminaries last year. Since then, 1,600 groups have won state approval and 937 churches have reopened. Says the Rev. Georgi Studenov, people want "to find themselves . . . to find God, but also to

find explanations to many things."

In China, Christianity is also growing rapidly, though it remains a novelty of sorts. "This is Western culture," said one new churchgoer as he left the chapel. "I want to learn more about it." So do millions more, including subterranean Roman Catholics who secretly defy the anti-papal stance of China's official Catholic Church. God is far from replacing Mao as the arbiter of morality in China, but Protestants say they number four million, nearly six times their total before the revolution of 1949. And the halls of worship continue to fill, perhaps offering a welcome respite from political ills. As one recently baptized 20-year-old said, "Young people love to come to church. It is very quiet and spiritual here."

A Jewish Klansman

The Ku Klux Klan has preached hatred for a lot of different people, but what about a grand dragon who hates himself? Jordan Gollub, who was born of Jewish parents, has been grand dragon of both the Virginia and the Mississippi chapters of the anti-Semitic and anti-black organization. Virgil Griffin, national leader of the KKK, dismissed Gollub from both posts, citing his "Jewish background." The 30-year-old Semitic anti-Semite, however, refuses to go quietly. Still in search of a racist forum that will tolerate his own roots, Gollub has vowed to form his own klan.

The Bakkers, again

Guess who's staging a comeback? Here they are, Jim and Tammy, mikes in hand, dewy smiles aimed at the cameras in a last-ditch attempt to save their televangelical show. The setting has changed — to a seedy mall in Orlando, Fla. "It's the crossroads of the world," said Jim Bakker as he greeted reporters at his makeshift studio, a run-down department store not far from a gin mill called Nasty Ed's. Outside, a protester held a sign that read, "Just Say No. Keep Our City Clean." He may get his wish. It seems the Bakkers never applied for an occupational license (→ Aug 31).

Chinese nuns can't fly but they're finding that their religion does.

MAY
1989

Su	Mo	Tu	We	Th	Fr	Sa
	1	2	3	4	5	6
7	8	9	10	11	12	13
14	15	16	17	18	19	20
21	22	23	24	25	26	27
28	29	30	31			

14. Norfolk, Va.: Fire breaks out on the aircraft carrier America; two sailors are killed.

14. Atlantic City, N.J.: First Tour de Trump bicycle race ends in controversy as Eric Vanderaerden goes off course, losing lead to winner Dag Otto Lauritzen of Norway.

15. Beijing: Soviet leader Gorbachev arrives for first summit meeting between China and U.S.S.R. in 30 years, normalizing relations (→ 20).

15. Washington, D.C.: New York Times/CBS poll finds 26 percent of Americans consider Soviet Union a direct threat to the U.S., down from 64 percent seven years ago (→ 28).

15. Washington, D.C.: President Bush announces $1.2 billion anti-crime plan.

16. Rome: Vatican releases a report condemning pornography and violence in film, specifically mentioning Kung Fu movies.

17. Addis Ababa: Coup fails to topple Ethiopian Marxists.

18. Washington, D.C.: Defense Department charges Panama violated Canal Treaty by attacking and harassing Americans (→ July 19).

18. Chicago: Rudy Linares will not be charged after removing brain-damaged son from life support.

18. Lithuania: Legislature adopts declaration seeking independence from Soviet Union (→ July 27).

18. Washington, D.C.: FAA orders the repair of older jets; affects 2,200 airplanes.

18. Arizona: Ten-year-old boy survives bicycle accident that left his head attached only by muscle and skin.

19. London: Former Beatle Paul McCartney prepares for first world tour in 13 years.

20. Berkeley, Calif.: Violent protest in People's Park marks 20th anniversary of similar protest.

20. Nepal: Walter McConnell, 57, is oldest man to reach Mount Everest's 27,000-foot level.

Gorbachev greeted in China by massive pro-democracy marches

Gorbachev and Deng: A smile and a handshake melt the 30-year glacier.

Liberty's effigy in Beijing.

May 20. Nearly two million students and other citizens clamored for democracy in the streets of China today, defying the government's attempts to impose martial law. The growing reform movement is a great embarrassment to the Chinese leadership, which lost face considerably earlier this week during the summit meeting in Beijing between Deng Xiaoping and Mikhail Gorbachev. The two Communist leaders agreed to end three decades of hostility, but Gorbachev's itinerary and motorcade route were both changed repeatedly to avoid the thousands of student hunger strikers in Tiananmen Square.

The pro-democracy movement spread quickly this week to Shanghai, where half a million people demonstrated, and Xian, where 300,000 protesters poured into the streets. More than a million people rallied for democracy in Beijing and defied Prime Minister Li Peng by preventing Chinese troops from entering the capital. Men and women lay down before advancing tanks; students even offered the soldiers breakfast and Coca-Cola. "We absolutely won't repress the people," one officer said. "We are the people's soldiers." Hopeful protesters in Shanghai carried posters urging Li Peng not to "use the people's army against the people."

Reports from inside the Communist Party indicate that the leadership generally supports Li Peng's plan to crack down on the students. Earlier this week, General Secretary Zhao Ziyang was stripped of most of his powers after he supported the students' demands (→ 22).

Army develops robot to measure humans

It could truly be the super-soldier.

The U.S. Army has enlisted its newest recruit — a soldier who is not afraid to embark on the most dangerous of missions. Manny, the new trooper, has one major advantage over his fellow G.I.s — he's a robot. But he walks, talks, breathes and even sweats like his human counterparts. At the Army's Dugway Proving Ground in Utah, he will test the effects that certain battlefield encounters may have on a soldier. In October, "Robogrunt" will walk into clouds of nerve gas to test how body movements may affect the leakage of gas through protective clothing. Based mainly on Disney technology and built by Battelle's Pacific Northwest Laboratories, Manny cost $2.35 million.

Anti-Semitism cut from Shakespeare

May 18. The Shakespeare festival at Stratford, Ontario, has cut two allegedly anti-Semitic items from its future productions of the Bard's *The Merchant of Venice*. The traditionally controversial scenes deal with the forced conversion to Christianity of Shylock, the play's Jewish moneylender, and a joke about how pork costs would skyrocket if all Jews converted. Festival officials discussed the play with the Canadian Jewish Congress before making their decision, but deny they acted under pressure.

Two years ago, an Ontario school board banned *The Merchant of Venice* from its curriculum.

"Family Ties" are tearfully severed

May 15. After seven years of popularity, *Family Ties,* reputedly Ronald Reagan's favorite television show, has taped its 176th and final episode. Actors Michael J. Fox (who has movie projects lined up until 1992), Meredith Baxter Birney, Tina Yothers (who was 9 years old when the show started), Justine Bateman, Michael Gross and the rest of cast and crew bid one another tearful farewells. The comedy series about a couple of grown-up flower children and their very proper kids has tried to deal with serious subjects, such as teen suicide, Alzheimer's disease, divorce and the healing powers of family.

The show is still widely popular. "It's good to quit while you're ahead," says creator Gary Goldberg. "But it feels strange."

Alar-less apples

May 15. Stunned by a $50 million drop in sales, the apple industry will voluntarily stop using the chemical Alar, a carcinogen. Alar ripens and preserves apples. But the Environmental Protection Agency decided earlier this year that the risks outweigh the benefits, and said it would ban the substance. Alar is said to cause cancer in 45 out of every one million adults exposed.

CBS TV's *60 Minutes* is responsible for nailing down Alar's coffin. A piece on the EPA announcement provoked a consumer reaction that led many retailers to pull Alar-treated apples from their shelves.

Playboy is stripped

Missing: $1 million worth of videos featuring sexy, scantily clothed women. If found, please return to a Los Angeles warehouse, care of Playboy founder Hugh Hefner. . . . Sometime in April someone carted off 421 hours worth of ogling, but Playboy has only recently admitted the disappearance and offered a $50,000 reward for the videos' return. Of course, even if the tapes are found, the profits may be lost; thieves could easily dupe the tapes, re-edit them and sell them overseas before claiming their 50 grand.

Saturday Night's Gilda Radner dies

May 20. "It's always something," her half-witted alter-ego journalist Roseanne Roseannadana was apt to say. Now, sadly, there will no longer be "something" to look forward to. Comedian Gilda Radner died today after a two-year struggle with ovarian cancer. She was 42.

Radner was part of the first *Saturday Night Live* crew, a slim, gangly, sweet-tempered clown whom fellow *SNL* member Dan Aykroyd called his "little sister." Born in Detroit, Radner performed with Toronto's Second City and New York's National Lampoon, specializing in mildly irreverent characterizations. She left *SNL* in 1980 to make a few films with her husband, Gene Wilder. He was with her when she died this morning at a Los Angeles hospital.

Lebanon's grand mufti dies in bombing

Putting out yet another fire in the rubble-strewn streets of Beirut.

May 16. If a man's worth could be calculated by the weight of TNT used to kill him, the religious leader of Lebanon's Sunni Muslims rated with that nation's most valued.

Terrorists packed more than 300 pounds of explosives into the booby-trapped car they detonated today as the grand mufti of Lebanon drove through crowded Muslim-controlled West Beirut. Sheik Hassan Khaled was killed instantly, along with 21 others.

Sheik Khaled's political moderation seems only to have added to his daily risk in a city dominated by extremists. As mufti, he had presided over the Sunni religious courts for 23 years, serving also as chairman of the Islamic Coalition, which includes past government officials of the highest rank.

Today's assassination and massacre was only the latest round in the terror that continues to shake Beirut. Syrian-backed Muslims are still regularly exchanging fire with forces of the Christian-dominated government led by army commander Michel Aoun (→ Aug 11).

Terrorist sentenced for TWA hijacking

May 17. Mohammed Ali Hamadei stood in the dock expressionless, his head slightly bowed, as he heard a West German court sentence him to life imprisonment for the hijacking of a TWA jet. Hamadei's trial lasted 10 months under a blanket of West German security and American scrutiny. The United States, seeking justice for the death of an American in the 1985 ordeal, had pushed unsuccessfully for the Lebanese terrorist's extradition. A White House spokesman praised the judge for demonstrating "the effectiveness of the rule of law against terrorism." Judge Heiner Muckenberger, in turn, extolled the independence of the German judiciary, which he said was particularly important "after the dark experience of the Nazi regime."

Peronists back in power in Argentina

With a victor's smile, Menem votes.

May 15. Jubilant at the prospect of returning to policies of government handouts, high pay and full employment, ardent crowds took to the streets of Buenos Aires today to cheer the election victory of Peronist Carlos Saul Menem. But the chances that Menem, the 59-year-old son of Syrian immigrants, will deliver on his campaign promises are dim. Conditions were different in the '40s when Juan Peron came to power on an anti-American platform and began nationalizing industry. Today, Argentina has paid no interest in over a year on its foreign debt, which exceeds $60 billion. A massive flight of capital continues, and the economy languishes in the grip of double digit inflation (→ 30).

Roll for your rights

Here is a weighty question for equal opportunity employers: should you discriminate against obese employees? The 2,000-member National Association to Advance Fat Acceptance says "No!" Headquartered in Sacramento, Calif., the group has rallied around the case of Sharon Russell, a young pediatric nurse from St. Petersburg, Fla., who sued her former nursing college because it forced her to resign when she failed to shed enough of her 328 pounds. According to Russell, "Fat is an OK word."

MAY
1989

Su	Mo	Tu	We	Th	Fr	Sa
	1	2	3	4	5	6
7	8	9	10	11	12	13
14	15	16	17	18	19	20
21	22	23	24	25	26	27
28	29	30	31			

21. Kings Island, Ohio: Nancy Lopez wins LPGA championship for the third time, her 40th career win.

22. Beijing: Students and workers block entrance to center of city, preventing army units from breaking up demonstrations (→ 23).

22. Washington, D.C.: Secretary of State James Baker calls upon both Israelis and Palestinians to exercise restraint and seek compromise (→ July 7).

22. New Delhi: India reports testing new mid-range missile capable of carrying a nuclear warhead.

23. Beijing: Seven former top military leaders sign a statement against using military to put down youth uprising (→ 23).

23. Beijing: Three men arrested for splashing paint on Mao Zedong's portrait in Tiananmen Square (→ 30).

24. Paris: Nazi collaborator Paul Touvier is arrested in Catholic priory.

28. Indianapolis: Emerson Fittipaldi wins Indy 500.

28. Washington, D.C.: President Bush sends a troop-cutting plan to NATO leaders, hoping to heal rifts in the alliance (→ 31).

30. Buenos Aires: Bombs and riots rock Argentina as rising prices spark unrest (→ July 8).

30. Beijing: Eleven demonstrators are arrested as officials condemn the erection of a Statue of Liberty in Tiananmen Square (→ June 5).

30. Hollywood: *Indiana Jones and the Last Crusade* is first movie to sell $10 million in tickets on opening day.

31. Tokyo: Foreign Minister Sousuke Uno designated as next Japanese Prime Minister (→ July 2).

DEATHS

30. Claude Pepper, Florida congressman who championed cause of the elderly (*Sept. 8, 1900).

30. Zinka Milanov, a leading Metropolitan Opera soprano for 30 years (*May 17, 1906).

NATO summit success for President Bush

As East and West turn toward each other, one graffitist's query on the Berlin Wall has again become a pressing question at the highest levels of state.

May 31. President Bush's stunning success at the Brussels NATO summit has surprised his supporters as well as his critics. After four months of simply responding to Soviet proposals, Bush has seized the arms-control initiative. During the two-day meeting, the President presented an agenda that goes beyond any Soviet plan, and forged a compromise among the allies on short-range nuclear forces (SNF), a topic that had threatened to tear the alliance apart. According to the British daily the *Guardian,* he "rode to the rescue like the proverbial U.S. cavalry, at the last possible minute."

Bush's "double hit" may put an end to complaints about his lackadaisical foreign policy. His proposal calls for reductions in combat aircraft and deep cuts in troop levels in Europe: 20 percent of U.S. troops and as much as 50 percent of Warsaw Pact forces. The plan also offers a faster timetable, aiming for troop withdrawals by 1992, five years ahead of the Soviet schedule.

Bush's plan has been hailed by liberals and conservatives alike. But the arms cuts will save only $1 billion, scarcely a dent in the U.S. budget deficit. And the timetable is being taken with a grain of salt. "I think it's a little optimistic," said British Prime Minister Margaret Thatcher. "It's quite optimistic. It's very optimistic."

Sanguine mood intact, Bush went on to Mainz, West Germany, today and called on the Soviets to tear down the Berlin Wall (→ June 15).

Mel Gibson and Danny Glover once again, in Lethal Weapon II.

Rep. Coelho resigns in ethics scandal

May 26. The ethics scandal that has dogged Capitol Hill Democrats for weeks has claimed its first victim. Rep. Tony Coelho of California, the House majority whip, announced today that he will resign from Congress. Coelho, who is under attack for the undisclosed 1986 purchase of $100,000 in junk bonds, faces possible House and Justice Department investigations.

In an emotional appearance, Coelho expressed confidence that he could, if willing, clear himself of all charges and win election as House majority leader. But, he concluded, he could not put his party, his family or himself through so exhausting an inquiry.

Lowe's low video

A new genre for film star Lowe?

May 24. A touch of scandal has hit actor Rob Lowe, 25, over an alleged videotaped liaison with a 16-year-old girl during the Democratic National Convention last July in Atlanta, Ga. The girl's mother filed suit for damages today, claiming that Lowe used his fame to seduce her daughter into appearing in a pornographic video. Under Georgia law, having sex with a 16-year-old is statutory rape, but prosecuting attorneys will probably have to prove the actor was aware of her age. Neither the girl nor her father, who has custody of her, has taken any legal action. Lowe, who in earlier interviews has claimed to be "mostly shy around girls," is not commenting.

New Soviet legislature opens — loudly

Physicist and rights activist Sakharov adds politician to his resume.

May 31. Russian television has been running a remarkable show for the last six days. In its live broadcasts of the opening session of the Soviet Union's new Congress, it has displayed such never-before-seen acts as Soviet leader Mikhail S. Gorbachev being cross-examined; the legislature being forced by public opinion to reverse its decision not to seat maverick Communist Boris N. Yeltsin; and a blistering speech against the KGB by former Olympic star Yuri P. Vlasov. Theoretically, the Congress of People's Deputies is, with the smaller Supreme Soviet, the ruling body of the Soviet Union. Based on the opening sessions, the newly elected legislators will be tenacious in protecting their powers (→ Aug 10).

House Speaker Wright resigns in disgrace

May 31. In an impassioned speech before a packed House chamber today, Jim Wright announced his resignation as Speaker and offered to leave the House of Representatives. Wright's address came in the aftermath of a year-long investigation into the financial dealings of both him and his wife, Betty.

In a speech laced with sadness, humor and fist-banging, the 34-year House veteran from Texas said neither the questionable sales of his autobiography nor certain "consulting" fees paid to his wife were of an improper nature. Wright instead blamed the House Ethics Committee and a "season of bad will" for his predicament. The Speaker went on to recap the work of the 100th Congress and declared that it was

Wright unravels before the House.

his love of Congress that compelled him to leave. "I don't want to be a party to tearing up this institution," he said. "I love it" (→ June 6).

Death sentence for 14 in South Africa

May 26. A South African judge has sentenced 14 blacks to hang for the murder of a black constable. Eleven others who allegedly participated in the mob action will be sentenced next week. The incident occurred three and a half years ago when a policeman was stoned to death by demonstrators in Upington after he had fired into a converging crowd. The fact that 25 people may die for one murder has created an uproar among South African blacks. Condemned defendant Evelina de Bruin, 60, charged, "This court is the guilty party in this case" (→ July 8).

130 days' solitude in a Carlsbad cave

May 23. What do you say after 130 days in a cave with no human contact? "Wow, man!" Or so said Stefania Follini as she emerged from a cave in Carlsbad, N.M. The 27-year-old Italian interior decorator was participating in an experiment to learn how people are affected by the long solitude of interplanetary travel. Disoriented, Follini would stay awake for 20 to 25 hours at a time and sleep for 10; her menstrual cycle stopped. Further tests will analyze the other effects of her stay 30 feet below the ground.

Campus minority rights spark white anger

College campuses, long considered bastions of liberalism and tolerance, have been erupting with racial tensions. Fueled in part by resentment toward affirmative action policies in college admissions and scholarships, some white students at dozens of colleges — including the University of Michigan, Brown and Smith — have aired racial jokes on radio stations, written racist fliers and letters and even set up white student unions. "We feel that giving scholarships, jobs or anything else because of race is wrong and they should be given on merit alone," said one student. Administrators attribute the problem in part to the generation's distance from the civil rights movement.

The strain of protest begins to show in the face of a young Chinese nurse, overwhelmed for a moment by the task of caring for Beijing's student hunger strikers. The fast for freedom is now in its second week.

Montreal is burned by Flames for cup

May 25. The Stanley Cup is going to Calgary for the first time since the Flames joined the National Hockey League 17 years ago. Calgary beat Montreal in the sixth game of the cup finals tonight, 4-2, to take the title by the same margin. Tradition took another blow too; the defeat marks the first time the Canadiens have lost a cup-clinching game on their home ice. Montreal has won the cup a record 23 times. Lanny McDonald, a player since 1973 but never on a championship team, scored the go-ahead goal for the Flames.

U.S., Soviet vets meet, commiserate

May 23. The veterans and survivors of two futile wars embraced today at Dulles Airport in Virginia. The Americans at the airport were Vietnam veterans, and they were there to greet Russians who had fought and lost in another unpopular conflict, the war in Afghanistan. "They are us 15 to 20 years ago," one American said. "They're looking to us for some kind of leadership and understanding," said another. The first stop for the two groups is the Vietnam Veterans' Memorial in Washington.

Su	Mo	Tu	We	Th	Fr	Sa
				1	2	3
4	5	6	7	8	9	10
11	12	13	14	15	16	17
18	19	20	21	22	23	24
25	26	27	28	29	30	

1. New Jersey: John E. List, wanted since 1971 for five murders, is found through TV's *America's Most Wanted*.

1. New York City: J. Paul Getty Museum acquires the Pontormo portrait in auction for $35 million.

1. New York: After failing to gain control of Texaco, corporate raider Carl Icahn sells 17.3 percent of stock.

1. Cambridge, Mass.: Harvard researchers now believe pigs can be developed as source of transplant organs.

2. Italy: Scientists report discovering way to transport genes by using sperm as vehicle.

2. London: Dustin Hoffman opens as Shylock in Shakespeare's *Merchant of Venice*.

3. Lagos, Nigeria: Rioting spreads in reaction to government's austerity measures.

3. Tokyo: Japan begins broadcasting high-definition television, while U.S. struggles to compete.

4. Tehran: President Sayyed Ali Khamenei is appointed Iran's supreme religious leader following the death of Ayatollah Khomeini (→ 6).

4. Colombo, Sri Lanka: A monsoon kills 171 people and strands 100,000.

4. Moscow: Gas pipeline explodes, killing at least 500.

5. Washington, D.C.: Supreme Court, 5-4, makes it easier for employers to justify why they did not hire a woman or minority (→ 12).

5. Washington, D.C.: Government places ban on all ivory imports (→ July 18).

6. Washington, D.C.: Rep. Thomas Foley (D-Wash.) is elected Speaker of the House.

9. San Salvador: Jose Antonio Rodriguez Porth, newly appointed minister of the presidency, is assassinated by leftist terrorists (→ 22).

10. Washington, D.C.: Marilyn Harrell, former HUD official, admits to illegally diverting millions (→ 11).

Solidarity sweeps to victory in Poland

Walesa's triumph: Solidarity's seed has blossomed into the flower of freedom.

June 5. In a stunning rebuke to the Communist Party, Polish voters yesterday gave Solidarity candidates an overwhelming victory in Poland's first competitive elections in four decades. "The elections were of a plebiscite character, and Solidarity has achieved a decisive majority," conceded Communist Party spokesman Jan Bisztyga.

Solidarity candidates swept the popular vote for the newly restructured two-house Parliament. The union proved so popular that Solidarity leader Lech Walesa feared the results would provoke the government into declaring martial law. Walesa cautioned his followers to be careful. "I think that too big a percentage of our people getting through would be disturbing and might force a fight on us," he said.

But Polish voters were not in a cautious mood. Of the 100 Senate seats up, at least 96 went to Solidarity candidates. Most of the 460 seats of the lower house, or Assembly, were allocated exclusively to the Communist Party in a pre-election agreement, and its candidates ran unopposed. Even so, many Polish people simply voted "No," denying quite a few Communists the required 50 percent of the vote. Prominent among the losers were eight of the 17 Politburo members.

Following its losses, the government urged Solidarity to join it in a governing coalition. Solidarity has rejected such offers in the past on the grounds that it would not truly be sharing power. "When the system of rule changes, when the heritage of the Stalinist system falls apart, room will be created for new political solutions," said a Solidarity spokesman. "This is not a matter for today or tomorrow" (→ 15).

Iran plunged into mourning over death of Ayatollah Khomeini

June 6. Crying, "we have lost our father," a crowd of almost three million frenzied Iranian mourners today buried the Ayatollah Ruhollah Khomeini in the "martyrs cemetery" near Tehran. Khomeini, the long-exiled cleric and leader of a fundamentalist Shiite clique, had returned to Iran from Paris in February of 1979 after Shah Mohammed Reza Pahlevi was toppled from his Peacock Throne. Khomeini and his Shiite followers have since ruled Iran with a revolutionary heart and an iron fist. Khomeini died on June 3 after a long illness that Western reporters and observers surmised to be cancer. He was born in either 1900 or 1902.

The Imam's funeral was a pastiche of bizarre scenes. Fire hoses doused mourners to cool them down; those who still collapsed from the heat and frenzy were shoved unceremoniously into ambulances. The anguished crowd, choking with dust and beating their heads in grief, at one point pulled the Ayatollah's body from its refrigerated coffin. Soldiers, firing their weapons into the air, finally got the body back, but not before the Imam's son Ahmed was knocked to the ground. On Monday, eight people were trampled to death by fellow mourners.

When Western journalists appeared with cameras and helicopters, the crowds began shouting, "Death to America." Americans will always remember the Ayatollah as the man who kept them glued to their TVs for 444 days while his revolutionary guards held the U.S. Embassy staff hostage (→ July 29).

Swarming the coffin in grief, mourners dislodge the body of the Ayatollah.

Tiananmen massacre stems democracy movement

Chinese communist troops kill students

June 5. Fires are still burning in Beijing today and the sounds of automatic weapons can be heard throughout the city as tens of thousands of Chinese soldiers tighten their control over pro-democracy demonstrators. Student leaders say more than 2,000 people were killed after the tanks started rolling into Tiananmen Square early yesterday morning. The government refuses to release a list of casualties, and doctors have been ordered to remain silent. Victims were reportedly cremated before their families were even notified of their deaths.

Protest leaders are calling for a general strike, but the hard-liners who are in control of the government vow to crush the "counterrevolutionary rebellion." For the past 24 hours, soldiers have shown little mercy as they fired wildly into crowds and drove tanks over occupied vehicles. The goodwill that existed earlier between soldiers and civilians has vanished. "We don't fear being beaten by you people," a platoon commander said. "We just fear that our guns will be taken and then we will have chaos." Outrage over the massacre spread quickly, and protests are reported in Shanghai and other cities (→ 5).

The power of passive resistance: a lone citizen stops a row of tanks.

Disarming the People's Army: students with a liberated machine gun.

Bush halts the sale of arms to China

June 5. President Bush condemned the crackdown in China today and suspended the sale of military equipment to Beijing. He rejected calls to impose economic sanctions or break diplomatic relations. "I don't want to see a total break in this relationship and I will not encourage a break," the President said. "When you see these kids struggling for democracy and freedom, this would be a bad time for the United States to withdraw."

Conservative lawmakers were disappointed that the President did not announce more extreme measures, but his actions were generally supported on Capitol Hill. Bush said his "careful" response "takes into account both our long-term interests and recognition of a complex internal situation in China."

The President's action affects $600 million worth of military hardware that has been ordered but not delivered. The Chinese have been counting on new U.S. electronic technology to modernize their F-8 fighter jets. Bush also suspended the visits of Chinese and American military delegations and indicated that thousands of Chinese students who are in the United States may extend their visits (→ 9).

Deng emerges; hardliners are prevailing

Deng vilified as a Nazi by students.

June 9. If there were any questions about who is in charge of China, they were answered tonight as Deng Xiaoping emerged from three weeks of seclusion and spoke on television. The aging Chinese leader praised the troops who crushed the pro-democracy rebellion and condemned the revolt's student leaders. "They are trying to overthrow the Communist Party," the 84-year-old Deng declared, "topple the socialist system and subvert the People's Republic of China so as to establish a capitalist republic." Prime Minister Li Peng, who invoked martial law, appeared with Deng. Zhao Ziyang, the Communist Party leader who urged moderation, was noticeably absent (→ 10).

Chinese regime strikes; 400 arrested

June 10. Chilling pictures of pro-democracy student leaders being arrested in Beijing were shown on Chinese television today. Their supporters fear a large-scale purge. Some 400 people have been taken into custody over the last few days. To the students, they are heroes. On TV, they are called "thugs and hooligans." The announcer reported, "Some of these people have attacked soldiers and burned or smashed military trucks. Others have stolen guns, bullets and ammunition." The arrests have forced many protest leaders into hiding. "It is not safe here in Beijing anymore," one of them said. It is not safe in other cities either; arrests are being made all over China (→ 15).

Tanks roll in the early dawn light.

Su	Mo	Tu	We	Th	Fr	Sa
				1	2	3
4	5	6	7	8	9	10
11	12	13	14	15	16	17
18	19	20	21	22	23	24
25	26	27	28	29	30	

11. Las Vegas: Jerry Falwell announces that the Moral Majority will dissolve, its work completed.

12. Washington, D.C.: President Bush unveils his clean air program (→ July 21).

12. Charleston, W.Va.: Hundreds of coal miners walk off the job, leaving southern West Virginia's coal industry at a standstill (→ July 10).

13. Philadelphia: Dr. Joseph Melnick is found guilty of murder for killing a fetus through abortion; he claims fetus was dead.

13. United States: Scientists have found a direct relationship between sunspots and the earth's weather patterns.

13. Washington, D.C.: House Democrats elect Richard Gephardt majority leader and William Gray majority whip.

14. Cape Canaveral, Fla.: Biggest unmanned rocket owned by the U.S., the Titan 4, is launched.

14. London: Former President Reagan is knighted by the Queen of England.

15. Washington, D.C.: Supreme Court upholds a Reconstruction law allowing minorities to sue for private acts of racial discrimination (→ July 9).

15. Warsaw: French President Francois Mitterrand announces France will give new loans to Poland (→ July 12).

15. Beijing: Three Chinese workers are sentenced to death for role in the pro-democracy protests (→ 17).

16. Pittsford, N.Y.: Four golfers fire four hole-in-one shots on same hole at U.S. Open (→ 18).

16. Pennsylvania: Researchers discover simple changes in light can change the human body clock.

17. Beijing: Sharply denouncing American interference, the Chinese government sentences eight more workers to death.→

DEATH

13. Fran Allison, star of *Kukla, Fran and Ollie* (*1909).

Olympian Ben Johnson admits steroid use

Johnson cries as he admits his guilt.

June 13. Canadian sprinter Ben Johnson, known as "The Fastest Man in the World," confessed yesterday that he has used banned anabolic steroids since 1981. At the 1988 Seoul Olympics, Johnson was stripped of his 100-meter world record and his gold medal after a urine test revealed traces of the steroid stanazabol. But until now, Johnson has staunchly denied using drugs.

The sprinter made the emotional admission before the Dubbin inquiry into drug use in amateur sport, which was set up after his Olympic fiasco. "I lied because I was ashamed for my family and other Canadian athletes and for kids who would look up to my position," he testified, as his mother and sisters watched intently from the packed courtroom gallery. The fallen Jamaican-born hero said he began taking steroids at the urging of coach Charlie Francis, but realized only in 1983 that the substances were banned.

Today, Johnson concluded his testimony with a wish to compete for Canada again. "I can run without drugs," he declared, "and I can beat anybody in the world."

Quayle supports allies in Central America

June 14. Vice President Dan Quayle has sewn a thread of respectability to his tarnished image after a visit to Latin America. While condemning Panama and Nicaragua and affirming support for El Salvador — in compliance with Bush administration policy — he avoided making any rhetorical bloopers. Aides to President Bush reportedly view his blunder-free trip as a success and a confidence booster for Quayle.

His performance in Latin America is a far cry from Quayle's recent speech to the United Negro College Fund, whose motto is "A mind is a terrible thing to waste." The vice president jumbled the slogan, saying, "What a waste to lose one's mind or not to have a mind at all."

Discussing the task of fighting leftist guerrillas with leaders in El Salvador, Quayle happily aims a Soviet-made grenade launcher at his own elbow.

Chinese authorities cover up massacre

Official story: flowers not bullets.

In China, the official word is that it never happened. Thousands of students did not die when soldiers broke up their protest in Tiananmen Square. Soldiers were attacked, not students.

History is being rewritten, and the big lie is the story line. Chinese authorities, hoping that lies repeated will become the truth, are saturating the media with the "official story." The lies strike fear into listeners. Afraid of the soldiers, people have started to turn on their neighbors and brothers. The brothers end up arrested on television and that's when it all starts to blur. If the protest never happened, who are the people in handcuffs? (→ 21).

Hitler's yacht down for count, almost

June 14. Like a bad memory, Hitler's yacht Ostwind has come back to haunt Holocaust survivor Abe Resnick. Resnick, who owns the yacht, arranged for its sinking off Miami Beach on June 4. It was a symbolic scuttling: 50 years earlier, 900 Jewish-German refugees had sailed on the "Voyage of the Damned." Refused entry at U.S. ports, they were returned to Europe and Nazism. This month, as the Ostwind sank, 100 concentration camp survivors cheered. Unfortunately, the yacht lies in just 20 feet of water in navigational lanes; law requires it be raised and moved.

Court deals yet another blow to minorities

June 12. The Supreme Court ruled today that affirmative action programs are open to legal challenges by white and male workers. The 5-4 ruling is seen as a victory by conservatives, while liberals have lambasted it as a setback to blacks and women.

The justices' vote permits white firefighters in Birmingham, Ala., to fight a court-approved settlement that encouraged the hiring and promotion of blacks and women. Writing for the majority, Chief Justice William Rehnquist referred to this policy as "reverse discrimination." In dissent, Justice John Paul Stevens said the decision would bring forth a "never-ending stream of litigation" and that it is "counter-productive" to ending job bias.

The ruling is one of many recent court decisions that have eroded protections against discrimination. Last week in Wards Cove v. Atonio, the high bench ruled that the burden of proof rests with plaintiffs, not employers, in cases that use statistics to show discrimination in hiring practices. As in the Birmingham case, Justices Anthony Kennedy and Antonin Scalia, both Reagan appointees, held the key votes in the 5-4 decision. Earlier this year, the court ruled unconstitutional a Richmond, Va., law that set aside a number of public works projects for minority contractors. In the words of Rep. Don Edwards (D-Calif.), "The Supreme Court is dealing blow after blow to 25 years of civil rights law" (→ 15).

West Germans hail Mikhail Gorbachev

His charisma follows wherever he goes; Soviet leader Gorbachev receives a welcome in West Germany that would turn any elected official green with envy.

Wide scandal dug up at Reagan's HUD

June 11. Another of the Reagan administration's skeletons is pushing its way out of the closet in congressional hearings. The vast Department of Housing and Urban Development, it appears, has equally vast closets. HUD Secretary Samuel Pierce let billions earmarked for low-income housing bulge the wallets of high-income Republicans, who in turn skimmed off sums for lobbyists like ex-Interior Secretary James Watt and one-time Nixon crony John Mitchell (→ 29).

Bush vetoes bill for minimum wage

June 13. President Bush "is not going to budge on the minimum wage," said a presidential aide, commenting on Bush's veto today of a bill to raise the minimum pay rate to $4.55 an hour. Although both the Senate and the House approved the legislation, it is unlikely that Democrats can muster enough votes to override the veto. While supporters of the bill maintain that the wage increase would help the poor, Bush believes the move would increase inflation (→ Nov 1).

Pistons beat Lakers to gain NBA title

June 13. Basketball's "bad boys" are the professional champions of the country, having lifted "Motown" over "Showtown" in four straight games. Revenge was sweet for the Detroit Pistons, who lost last year's final to this year's victims, the Los Angeles Lakers. Tonight's 105-97 victory gave Joe Dumars and the Pistons their first NBA title. The team's aggressive style of play has earned it the "bad boy" reputation, some commentators describing the Pistons' play as "mugging" and "thuggery." Hometown fans revel in the image, saying it fits Detroit's blue-collar style.

June 15. Mikhail Gorbachev's visit to West Germany can be described in one word: triumphant. A recent poll says 90 percent of West Germans trust the Soviet leader and approve of his momentous reforms. Though the main purpose of his visit was to attract money and technology for the faltering Soviet economy, applause was more than welcome. The cheers never stopped as Gorbachev traveled from city to city, meeting with bankers and industrialists in Cologne, Stuttgart and the Ruhr Valley. He seemed deeply impressed to receive such praise from a nation whose aggression of 50 years ago is still bitterly remembered in the Soviet Union.

But Gorbachev, the consummate politician, did not fail to use his popularity to establish stronger economic ties with Bonn. Though West Germany is already the Soviet Union's biggest trading partner, he described economic ties between the countries as "ridiculously low."

There were, however, no concessions on the Berlin Wall, the longstanding symbol of the Cold War. Gorbachev did leave some hope, saying that "the wall can disappear when those conditions that created it fall away." But the Soviets apparently fear that Europe's economic unification in 1992 will create a wall far more impenetrable than the concrete one in Berlin (→ July 6).

June 17. *Happy birthday, Eiffel Tower! The world renowned Parisian landmark is 100 today.*

June 12. Indiana Jones and the Last Crusade *last weekend broke a record held by* Return of the Jedi, *and became the fastest movie to pass $100 million in sales. Here, Harrison Ford donates items to the Smithsonian.*

Su	Mo	Tu	We	Th	Fr	Sa
				1	2	3
4	5	6	7	8	9	10
11	12	13	14	15	16	17
18	19	20	21	22	23	24
25	26	27	28	29	30	

18. Managua, Nicaragua: Americans are now required to get visas before entering country (→ Aug 4).

19. Freiburg, West Germany: Scientists have found unexpectedly high levels of ozone and acid rain damage in Africa's rain forests (→ July 1).

19. Washington, D.C.: Government officials announce creation of 30,000-acre refuge for Florida panther.

20. Chicago: Air traffic controllers at the nation's busiest airports are given a 20 percent raise.

20. Greenland Sea: After hitting an iceberg, 1,000 people are rescued from Soviet tour ship Maxim Gorky by the Swedish Navy.

20. Atlanta, Ga.: Former Rep. Pat Swindall is convicted of nine counts of perjury.

21. West Palm Beach, Fla.: Fifteen-year-old Tomontra Mangrum receives $81.28 after suing her no-show prom date.

21. Washington, D.C.: Kentucky Rep. William Natcher casts 16,000th consecutive vote in the House; he hasn't missed one since his election in 1954.

22. Gbadolite, Zaire: After 14 years of civil war, Angola's Soviet-supported Marxist government and nationalist rebels agree to a truce (→ Aug 23).

22. El Salvador: An American nun, Sister Mary MacKey, is shot in the head in ambush; killer unknown (→ Sept 5).

23. Washington, D.C.: Supreme Court rules that businesses offering phone sex cannot be restricted without violating freedom of speech.

23. San Francisco: Stanford University places tribal ritual above study, agreeing to return the remains of 550 Ohlone Indians for tribal burial.

24. Beijing: Communist Party ousts General Secretary Zhao Ziyang from all posts (→ 29).

DEATH

23. Michel Aflaq, founder of Iraq's Baathist Party and political theorist (*1910).

Court OKs flag-burning

The court has opted to protect the Constitution rather than its symbol.

June 21. The Supreme Court today opened a fiery storm of debate, ruling that the Constitution does not outlaw the burning of the American flag as a sign of protest.

The case stemmed from a protest at the 1984 Republican Convention in Dallas, where Gregory Johnson led protesters in burning the flag and chanting, "America, the red, white and blue, we spit on you." He was convicted of violating a Texas law barring flag burning. An appeals court overturned the ruling and the state asked the Supreme Court to overrule the reversal on grounds that the law protects the flag as a "symbol of nationhood."

The decision elicited passionate opinions from the high bench. Justice William J. Brennan wrote, "If there is a bedrock principle underlying the First Amendment, it is that the government may not prohibit the expression of an idea simply because society finds the idea offensive or disagreeable." Chief Justice William Rehnquist cited *The Star-Spangled Banner* and patriotic poetry from Emerson and Whittier in his dissent. Ironically, Justices Antonin Scalia and Anthony M. Kennedy joined the court's liberals, while Justice John Paul Stevens sided with the conservatives.

Free speech advocates laud the ruling as a victory for First Amendment rights. But many others concur with Patrick McGuigan of the Free Congress Center for Law and Democracy, who called the decision "an exercise in absurdity" (→ 27).

Andrew Wyeth's The Prussian, *in a Brooklyn Museum show.*

Historic tree has brush with assassin

The good people of Austin, Texas, would like to get to the root of a mystery: Who is trying to kill their favorite tree? Their historic 500-year-old Treaty Oak is suffering from the deliberate and secret application of Velpar, an herbicide that is used to destroy hardwood trees. Mayor Sally Shipman has hired botanical experts to cure the problem, but the prognosis is not good. Among the suspects are real estate developers looking for more cleared land, and people who are just plain nuts.

Papandreou ousted by Greek electorate

June 19. Although Prime Minister Andreas Papandreou is the loser in yesterday's Greek elections, no winner has yet emerged. Voters soundly rejected the Socialist Papandreou, 70, whose affair with Dimitra Liani, a 35-year-old former flight attendant, has not enhanced his political fortunes. But early returns show no parliamentary majority for Constantine Mitsotakis' conservatives. Since Mitsotakis has said he does not want to form a coalition government, Papandreou may be given another chance. Or, divorced last week, he may choose to retire his bruised public image and pursue a life with Ms. Liani free from the camera's prying eye (→ July 1).

Scandal-ridden Papandreou speaks to the press after casting a futile vote.

Pianist Van Cliburn returns to the stage

June 20. The hair may be graying, but the fingers that carried Van Cliburn to victory in the 1958 Tchaikovsky competition are as youthful as ever. Returning to the concert stage after an 11-year layoff, the master ended critical speculation about a possibly tarnished technique with sterling performances of two of his favorite concertos — the Liszt No. 1 and the Tchaikovsky No. 1. Backed by the Philadelphia Orchestra, the hero of 30 years ago, now 54, played with a power and grace undiminished by time.

Socialists, Greens gain in West Europe

June 18. The shape of a new and united Europe may have been clarified today by international elections for the Strasbourg-based European Parliament, which serves as a check on the European Council in Brussels. In a 12-nation vote, Socialists and environmentalist Greens wrested seats from the right and center.

Whether the results signify a general shift to the left is yet unclear. The voting may have been influenced more by local matters than by international vision. In West Germany, Helmut Kohl is under fire from anti-nuclear advocates, and Britain's Margaret Thatcher suffers from broad disillusionment with her conservative "revolution."

Later motherhood

June 21. Recent statistics confirm that motherhood is coming later and later for women of the '80s. In the 12 months ending June 1988, 33 percent of new arrivals in the United States were born to women in their 30s, compared with 19 percent in 1976. With more work experience under their belts, many of these women are likely to return to their careers long before their mothers might have. This trend is expected to put increased pressure on the country's already overburdened and underfunded day care system.

Strange no stranger to U.S. Open title

Strange interlude: kissing his cup.

Bush calls for new volunteer spirit

June 22. Addressing 1,000 business, community and education leaders gathered at the New York Hilton, President Bush today called for a new spirit of national volunteerism to help those in need of assistance, from the homeless to AIDS victims to the illiterate.

The President announced that he would ask Congress for $25 million to establish a foundation called the Points of Light Initiative. The group would assist private efforts to help the less fortunate in American society. President Bush will serve as honorary chairman, while outgoing New Jersey governor, Thomas Kean, will head a preliminary advisory committee.

Do the right thing

Is it riot-provoking propaganda or enlightening art? Everyone who has seen *Do the Right Thing*, Spike Lee's new movie, seems to have an opinion. The film gives a glimpse of racial tensions on a relentlessly hot summer day in Brooklyn's Bedford-Stuyvesant district, a black ghetto. The movie's conclusion, in which blacks destroy a white-owned pizzeria after a black man is slain by police, has led moviegoers to question whether Lee is advocating violence or just saying, "This is the way it is."

June 18. Curtis Strange shot his way to the United States Open golf championship today in Pittsford, N.Y., becoming the first man to win back-to-back titles since Ben Hogan did so in 1950 and '51. The key to Strange's victory was his steadiness. He shot one birdie, one bogey and 16 pars, giving him an even 70 for the day and 278 for the tournament, good enough for a one-stroke victory over three players. The others had opportunities, but faltered on the back nine. Strange, a 34-year-old Virginian, dedicated last year's Open victory to his father and friends. This time, he hugged his wife and thought in more intimate terms: "This one is for Sarah and me," he said.

China executes pro-democracy leaders

The condemned appeared on television as a warning to would-be protesters.

June 21. China ignored worldwide criticism today and executed three men in public for participating in a violent anti-government protest in Shanghai. Beijing radio also announced that 45 people have been sentenced to death or imprisoned in the city of Jinan. Both developments reveal that the hard-liners who are in control of China are resorting to Mao-era techniques to impose order. Secretary of State James Baker denounced the executions, but said the United States is not planning any new sanctions against China (→ 24).

Germany's Bismarck found on sea floor

June 22. The infamous Bismarck, Hitler's most powerful battleship, is still the subject of mystery nearly 50 years after its watery demise. Robert T. Ballard, who located the ship two weeks ago 600 miles off the coast of France, believes the Bismarck met its end at the hands of its Nazi owners. The warship, he says, was scuttled on May 27, 1941, when the British Royal Navy found it steaming around in circles with a broken rudder. The fatal deed was previously credited to three torpedoes from the cruiser Dorsetshire. Ballard says he has taken nothing from the ship and will reveal its location only to German officials.

Ballard holds a replica of the ship; the real thing lies in 15,000 feet of water.

JUNE
1989

Su	Mo	Tu	We	Th	Fr	Sa
				1	2	3
4	5	6	7	8	9	10
11	12	13	14	15	16	17
18	19	20	21	22	23	24
25	26	27	28	29	30	

25. Cincinnati, Ohio: A court rules that the baseball commissioner may not hold a hearing on betting charges against Pete Rose (→ Aug 24).

25. Oakville, Ontario: Steve Jones wins the Canadian Open golf tournament.

26. Washington, D.C.: The Supreme Court, in a 5-4 ruling, sanctions death sentences against the retarded and the young.

26. Israel: International group of scholars accuses the Israeli keepers of the Dead Sea Scrolls of blocking research.

26. Washington, D.C.: FDA gives unusually quick approval to two new AIDS drugs (→ Aug 3).

27. Washington, D.C.: Federal court overturns former Reagan adviser Lyn Nofziger's conviction on influence peddling charges.

27. Washington, D.C.: President Bush calls for constitutional amendment against flag-burning in response to recent Supreme Court ruling (→ July 5).

27. Atlanta, Ga.: New figures show that 60 percent of U.S. hospitals are short of nurses with no sign of crisis easing.

28. Newport, R.I.: Captain of a Greek oil tanker is arrested by U.S. officials for running his ship aground and dumping 420,000 gallons of oil.

28. Tokyo: Japan pledges to give U.S. greater access to mobile phone market.

29. Hong Kong: Wuer Kaixi, most wanted student protester, has fled here with other pro-democracy leaders on an underground railroad (→ July 22).

29. Dublin, Ireland: For the first time in history, the Irish Parliament is unable to form a government (→ July 12).

30. New Delhi: India admits that it sold a chemical used in poison gas to Iran.

30. Texas: School administrators report that principals may now forbid students from displaying peace symbol because it signifies defeat of Christ when turned upside down.

Cleanup begins at scandal-ridden HUD

June 29. Poor Jack Kemp. Misdeeds at the Department of Housing and Urban Development, now headed by Kemp, have thrown the ex-quarterback for a loss and left him pondering the hidden meaning of supply side economics.

During the drowsy tenure of Kemp's predecessor, "Silent Sam" Pierce, unqualified housing moguls were supplied with illegal subsidies, with commissions for lobbyists on the right side of the political fence. Frederick M. Bush, a top campaign fund-raiser who is now ambassador to Luxembourg, told a House panel yesterday that his tiny lobbying firm reeled in $600,000. A Maryland escrow agent skimmed off $5.5 million in agency money, allegedly in order to aid the poor. Investigators call her "Robin HUD."

So Secretary Kemp is scrambling while congressmen rush with lowered helmets. Yesterday, he said he had scrapped a mortgage insurance program, and promised to root out fraud tainting current projects. Critics wonder why Kemp waited so long. A 1986 audit disclosed that 16 out of 17 projects failed to create inexpensive housing, a task that is HUD's *raison d'etre*. Worse, a follow-up report shows that HUD may still be a soft touch. A new beneficiary — the largest project now bankrolled — offered "low-income" condominium units starting at a tad under $200,000 (→ July 12).

Caped Crusader leads movie blockbusters

Holy blockbusters! The Dark Knight promises to hunt down all moviegoers.

Ecstatic exhibitors are bat-dancing to all-time highs at the box office, making the movie summer seem sweeter than Baby Ruths. *Batman*, the movie, proved to be no Joker as it clobbered the competition, bringing in a record $42.7 million over its first three days.

Other mega-movies taking in big bucks this summer are *Ghostbusters II*, *Indiana Jones and the Last Crusade* and *Star Trek V*. Combined with *Batman*, this trio of lucrative sequels has already garnered $276 million in ticket sales. Last weekend, the top 10 films took in an uparalleled high of more than $93 million. And that only accounts for actual moviegoers. *Batman*, which is as much a franchise as it is a movie, is said to have taken in more money in concessions — bat hats, bat shirts, bat buttons, bat boxer shorts and more — than it ever will at the box office.

As movie producers count to I, II, III and even IV and V, $40 million to $50 million films are increasingly green-lighted by the studios. Three of the "Big Four" films right now are sequels and *Batman* is almost certain to beget a few more — which will sell more tickets, popcorn (sales are up 123 percent since mid-May) and merchandise. The Caped Crusader's arch nemesis (Jack Nicholson) is disposed of at the end of the original. But, as producer Jon Peters notes, "He could come back. He's the Joker."

Gender gap in tests finally narrowing

June 30. Results of a variety of tests show the gap between the sexes narrowing in math and disappearing in verbal skills. Just a decade ago, females scored better on verbal tests and males better on math tests. The change may be due in part, researchers say, to decreasing sex biases in education. Dr. Carol Jacklin of the University of Southern California, however, points out that standardized tests have changed as well. "If you ask questions about . . . gear ratios," she says, "boys give the correct answers. . . . If you ask about recipes and cutting patterns for clothing, girls do better."

June 29. In a confrontation more peaceful than most in the abortion battle, activists on both sides of the debate await the Supreme Court's decision.

Rock's legends launch whirlwind revivals

Not yet extinct, rock dinosaurs like The Who are touring. Geritol anyone?

When Led Zeppelin stepped on stage last year for Atlantic Records' birthday party, the rock 'n' rollers in the audience felt their age. Drummer John Bonham, who died several years ago, had a replacement named Jason — his son.

As the genre ages, early rock 'n' roll has acquired, ironically, a classical status; and the Bachs and Beethovens of rock have nearly been deified. As in boxing, when there are no exciting contenders, the legends return from retirement.

It's been a long time since they've rock 'n' rolled, but reputation is drawing larger crowds than originality. Without saying anything new, the bands of yesterday are filling the grandstands today. The Who, The Rolling Stones, The Allman Brothers, Yes and The Doobie Brothers are mostly intact and definitely back in concert. They are also definitely selling out in more ways than one. The stadiums and arenas are brimming with rock 'n' roll consumers. The Who performed *Tommy* in a sold-out Radio City Music Hall, and ticket prices went as high as $1,000 per seat. The Stones sold out their reunion concert instantly, and radio stations everywhere used ticket contests to keep listeners tuned in.

Just as in horror films, the theme of the decade is the sequel. Viewers flock to see Freddy play razor tag; at least The Who had something interesting to say — again.

Cubans condemn general for drug dealing

June 27. Gen. Arnaldo Ochoa Sanchez, a high-ranking officer in the Cuban Army, has been found guilty of drug trafficking and corruption and will probably die in front of a firing squad. Displaying Cuba's eagerness to be seen as a front-line soldier in the war on drugs, a military tribunal unanimously found the general guilty and recommended he be sentenced with the "full weight of the law."

Ochoa has led troops in Angola, Nicaragua and Ethiopia and used his assignments to engage in worldwide drug, ivory and diamond smuggling. He also laundered money and arranged flights across Cuba for the Colombian-based Medellin drug cartel (→ July 13).

General Sanchez on trial in Havana.

Army takes over Sudanese regime

June 30. The army is in charge of Sudan today following the pre-dawn overthrow of Prime Minister Sadiq al-Mahdi's regime. The new strongman is Brig. Omar Hassam Ahmed al-Bashir, who announced he would become Prime Minister, defense minister and head of the armed forces. He suspended the constitution, dissolved Parliament and imposed emergency rule. Sudan, Africa's largest nation, has been in the throes of civil war for six years; famine has taken 250,000 lives — 10 percent of its population.

Foreign investment on the rise in U.S.

Foreign investment in American companies climbed from $90 billion in 1980 to $304.2 billion in 1988 as a result of the weak dollar and a strong domestic market. Fears of job cuts and theft of valuable corporate research, however, have proved unfounded. Managers and money from overseas are actually re-energizing sluggish steel, tire, chemical and building material industries. Firms with no foreign investment, in fact, appear to be the big losers, facing stiffer competition on their own turf.

Soviet defenseman is signed by Devils

June 27. The New Jersey Devils of the National Hockey League have signed the U.S.S.R.'s Vyacheslav Fetisov, considered by many the world's finest defenseman. The Devils drafted Fetisov in 1983.

The 31-year-old captain of the Soviet national team will be joined in New Jersey next season by his countryman Sergei Starikov. They are the second and third Soviets ever to join an NHL team. Rightwinger Sergei Priaken, who signed with the Calgary Flames in March, was the first Soviet athlete permitted to play for a professional North American team.

Protestant churches losing flock in U.S.

After 300 years of domination, mainline U.S. Protestant churches are in a state of serious decline. Since 1965, the Congregationalists have lost 20 percent of their membership, the Presbyterians 25 percent and the Episcopalians 28 percent. These proud bastions of a quiet, conservative theology have fallen victim to rationalism on one side and an explosive evangelical fundamentalism guided by Madison Avenue marketing strategies on the other. As Presbyterian leader Isabel Rogers laments, the old churches are "no longer the primary shapers of values in American society."

Reclaimed from under 25 layers of paint and 95 years of history, the first-ever Coke sign is restored in Cartersville, Ga. It is indeed the real thing.

Su	Mo	Tu	We	Th	Fr	Sa
						1
2	3	4	5	6	7	8
9	10	11	12	13	14	15
16	17	18	19	20	21	22
23	24	25	26	27	28	29
30	31					

1. Athens: Greek Communists and conservatives of the New Democracy Party form a Cabinet to govern Greece.

1. Washington, D.C.: AT&T announces it will stop using chemicals that deplete the ozone (→ Sept 22).

2. New York City: Clare Booth Luce has left $70 million to the advancement of women's causes.

2. Hong Kong: British Foreign Secretary Sir Geoffrey Howe is booed by the people of Hong Kong who fear the colony's return to Chinese rule in 1997.

4. Washington, D.C.: Secretary of State James Baker calls for $1 billion in economic aid to the Philippines (→ Sept 27).

5. Mexico City: Mexico's ruling Institutional Revolutionary Party loses its first gubernatorial race.

5. Gallatin, Tenn.: Servpro Industries has capitalized on the flag-burning issue by inventing a spray which, when applied to a flag, makes it flame retardant (→ Sept 12).

6. Washington, D.C.: A new study shows that one-third of American adults have dangerously high cholesterol levels.

7. Pasadena, Calif.: Scientists confirm the discovery of a third Neptune moon.

8. Winnetka, Ill.: The town police department calls for Uzi machine guns for each officer in the wake of a schoolyard slaughter last year.

8. Buenos Aires: Carlos Menem sworn in as President of troubled Argentina (→ 14).

8. Johannesburg: South African President P. W. Botha meets with Nelson Mandela and then sends him back to jail (→ Aug 2).

DEATHS

3. Jim Backus, actor, voice of Mr. Magoo and the millionaire on *Gilligan's Island* (*1913).

6. Janos Kadar, former Hungarian leader who came to power after 1956 uprising (*May 26, 1912).

Colonel North fined for Iranscam role

A relieved colonel after sentencing.

July 5. Judge Gerhard Gesell today brought the latest chapter of the Iran-contra affair to a close by fining Lt. Col. Oliver North $150,000 and placing him on two years' probation. North will also have to perform 1,200 hours of community service. The key figure in the three-year-old scandal, North escaped a jail term because it "would only harden your misconception about government service," Gesell said. Looking directly at North, Gesell told the ex-Marine he still lacks "full understanding of how the public service has been tarnished." North, standing ramrod-straight, flushed when the sentence was delivered, then kissed his wife, smiled and left the courtroom (→ Sept 6).

July 2. *A match made in . . . Hef and bunny Kim Conrad are wed.*

Abortion rights limited

July 3. Outside the Supreme Court today, groups on opposing sides of the abortion issue shouted, waved placards and taunted each other; in the chambers, a tense silence hovered as onlookers awaited the decision. In a 5-4 ruling, the justices limited a woman's right to an abortion, provoking a mixed but hardly ambivalent reaction in the audience. The ruling upholds a Missouri law barring the use of state facilities for abortion and requiring tests to determine whether a 20-week fetus could live outside the womb. While the court did not reverse the 1973 Roe v. Wade decision, which established the right to an abortion, the majority is clearly moving in that direction, and has agreed to take on abortion cases next term.

Pro-choice advocates called the decision a major setback. "This is a sad day for freedom," said Planned Parenthood president Faye Wattleton. Pro-lifers, by contrast, were ecstatic. Archbishop John May of St. Louis said, "The biggest winners . . . are the tiniest people of all — children within the womb." Both sides promised a battle when the issue comes up in state legislatures. By the end of the day, protests had taken place across the nation (→ 10).

Runaway Soviet MiG crashes in Belgium

A red star fallen: the crumpled MiG lies near the Franco-Belgian border.

July 4. A Soviet MiG-23, pilotless and flying on automatic controls, flew over much of Western Europe today before crashing into a house on the border of France and Belgium. A 19-year-old Belgian man was killed. NATO officials said that two American F-15 fighters followed the jet before it ran out of fuel. It was hoped that the plane, clearly unmanned and unarmed, could be escorted over the English Channel. The Soviet news agency Tass reported that the Soviet pilot bailed out over Poland after experiencing a system malfunction.

Angered, Japanese women turn to politics

July 2. Japanese women, traditionally concerned with domestic or consumer issues, have angrily united in an attempt to reform their country's political life. They are trying to oust Prime Minister Sousuke Uno, who stands accused of conducting an extramarital affair with a part-time geisha. So today, in Tokyo, women are running in record numbers for the city assembly. According to Kii Nakamura, head of the Japan Housewives Association and leader of the anti-Uno effort, "It has suddenly become clear that someone who does not respect women is not fit to be Prime Minister of Japan" (→ 24).

Veteran Soviet aide Gromyko is dead

Gromyko, weathered by history.

July 2. Andrei A. Gromyko, 79, the former foreign minister whose dour face came to personify Soviet foreign policy, has died of a stroke. During his 35 years in the Foreign Ministry, Gromyko dealt with every American president from Franklin D. Roosevelt on. He won a reputation for loyalty so intense that Soviet leader Nikita Khrushchev once said of him, "If I tell my foreign minister to sit on a block of ice and stay there for months he will do it without back talk." Gromyko played a part in nearly every major East-West confrontation of the postwar era. He led the Soviet delegation to the U.N.'s founding conference; he helped talk the world through the Cuban missile crisis; and he presided at strategic arms negotiations. He was appointed to the ruling Politburo in 1973.

Bush, Gorbachev spar over proposals

July 6. The Gorby Guessing Game entered a new round yesterday as the Soviet leader once again caught the West off guard. On a state visit to France, Gorbachev offered a new timetable for cutting short-range nuclear weapons, thus leapfrogging NATO's insistence that conventional arms cuts must come first.

President Bush isn't having any of it. At the White House today, he told foreign reporters, "I see no reason to stand here and try to change a collective decision taken by NATO." bush noted the United States has "had encouraging sounds from the Soviets" on the NATO package, and said he simply does not want "to get off the track" (→ 21).

Gay couples given rights by N.Y. court

July 6. In what one lawyer called "a ground-breaking victory for lesbians and gay men," the New York Court of Appeals ruled today that a gay couple who lived together for a decade could be considered a family under New York City's rent control laws. The precedent-setting decision, which also applies to heterosexuals, protects the plaintiff from eviction, even though the apartment was in his deceased partner's name. In his opinion, Judge Vito J. Titone wrote that protection, "should not rest on fictitious legal distinctions or genetic history, but . . . should find its foundation in the reality of family life."

Israeli bus hijacked; Shamir unyielding

Violence overflows the West Bank: carrying bodies from the bus wreckage.

July 7. Middle East peace prospects suffered two setbacks this week. An Arab today seized control of a Jerusalem-bound bus and plunged it into a ravine, killing 14 and injuring 27. Prime Minister Yitzhak Shamir called the act "the fruit of a horrible mind full of hatred."

Two days earlier, Shamir, bowing to hard-liners in his Likud Party, agreed to impose four limiting conditions on talks with the Palestinians. These include a voting ban on the 140,000 Arabs in East Jerusalem and a pledge to keep the occupied territories out of "foreign" hands. Shimon Peres of the opposition Labor Party said, "What the . . . ministers suggested will not permit a peace process" (→ 9).

Black priest splits from Catholic Church

July 2. Catholicism got a dose of ethnic diversity at the Imani Temple on the campus of Howard University Law School, where 4,000 congregants gathered today to celebrate mass Afro-American style. The Rev. George A. Stallings Jr. conducted the service, which proudly celebrates black culture and history while practicing the conventional Catholic religious rituals. The Roman Catholic hierarchy is not at all pleased, and James Cardinal Hickey of Washington has threatened Father Stallings with suspension. Stallings has long spoken out about the need to include black culture in services.

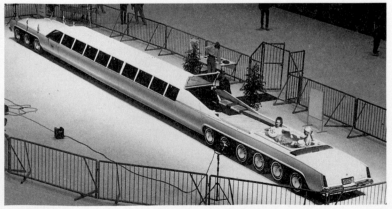

Take your pick; the car on the left may be the longest in the world, complete with Jacuzzi and other necessities of driving, but the car on the right, the new Mazda Miata, is proving to be one of the most sought-after new cars on the road — for those who live where parking may be scarce.

Su	Mo	Tu	We	Th	Fr	Sa
						1
2	3	4	5	6	7	8
9	10	11	12	13	14	15
16	17	18	19	20	21	22
23	24	25	26	27	28	29
30	31					

9. Detroit: NAACP leader Benjamin Hooks calls the Supreme Court a direct threat to blacks in light of recent rulings on affirmative action.

9. Jerusalem: Israeli government calls upon Jews to stop attacking Arabs (→ Aug 18).

10. New York City: Bertram M. Lee and Peter Bynoe are first blacks to own a major league sports team, announcing their purchase of the Denver Nuggets for $65 million.

10. Kabul, Afghanistan: Thirty die in rebel rocket attack (→ Oct 9).

10. Washington, D.C.: Gallup poll finds 53 percent of Americans oppose Supreme Court decision allowing states to restrict abortion (→ Oct 10).

11. Salt Lake City: Two Air Force officers charged with stealing three F-16 engines.

12. Washington, D.C.: Federal panel reports cold fusion cannot work and should receive little if any research money.

12. Washington, D.C.: Losses of $1 billion are estimated in the FHA (HUD) scandal (→ 22).

12. Washington, D.C.: NRA members now calling for President Bush's ouster from group due to his ban on assault rifles.

12. Dublin, Ireland: Charles Haughey elected Prime Minister for the fourth time, ending a political struggle.

13. Washington, D.C.: Two Americans and an Irishman are charged with supplying weapons to the IRA (→ Sept 22).

13. Cuba: Four former high-ranking military officers are executed after being found guilty of drug smuggling.

14. Washington, D.C.: Federal court holds industries responsible for full cost of cleaning up accidents.

15. Rome: Court has blocked exiled would-be King Victor Emmanuel from returning to Italy from Switzerland.

DEATHS

10. Mel Blanc, voice of notable cartoon characters, such as Bugs Bunny (*May 30, 1908).

A Kentucky county reaches a new high

The good people of remote Clay County, Ky., have never been known for their timidity. So when the local economy became so bad that they could barely make ends meet, many took matters into their own hands. Today, Clay County has a booming economy thanks to its newest cash crop — marijuana.

"The marijuana growers are the bootleggers of the '80s and '90s. We take no pride in that," says local banker Harvey Hensley. But whatever the moral reservations, few can deny that Clay County has not benefited. New cars and old shacks with satellite dishes mark the new prosperity. Heady days indeed.

Argentine Economy Minister Roig dies

July 14. The task of reviving Argentina's debt-laden economy appears to be too much for mere mortals. Only six days after joining the newly formed Cabinet of President Carlos Saul Menem, Economic Minister Miguel Roig has died of a heart attack. Menem's "exceptional and emergency" economic measures now rest in the hands of businessman Nestor Rapanelli — the country's fourth economic minister in as many months. He faces an inflation rate of 114 percent and a government deficit of $9.7 billion.

July 9. *The young German duo of Steffi Graf and Boris Becker rose to dominance at Wimbledon today, defeating Martina Navratilova and defending champ Stefan Edberg for the singles titles.*

Solo pilot flies 1,000 miles; found shot

A rough landing in high seas. The mystery of Thomas Root continues.

July 14. The mystery surrounding the case of Thomas L. Root and his errant airplane, which crashed into the Atlantic Ocean two days ago, continues to deepen. Root's leased private plane apparently flew for nearly 1,000 miles while Root was unconscious at the controls, until the Cesssna 210 Centurion ran out of fuel and crashed into ocean waters near Eleuthera in the Bahamas.

When he was almost three-quarters of an hour late for an early morning landing in Rocky Mount, N.C., air controllers had managed to contact Root by radio. After telling of chest pains and breathing difficulties, he was not heard from until a search team found the stricken pilot still alive in his plane.

Police today disclosed that medical investigators found a gunshot wound in Root's abdomen. Although Root maintains he did not shoot himself, other theories seem unlikely since he was alone in the plane. Root is a lawyer whose practice has recently run into legal trouble. He has also been suspected of smuggling drugs.

Soviet coal strike forces concessions

July 13. Striking workers in one of the Soviet Union's major mining centers have forced the government to capitulate to many of their demands. Some 12,000 mineworkers took part in the walkout, which shut down all five mines in the Siberian city of Mezhdurechensk. In addition to the usual demands for improved living conditions, the strikers also called for political reforms such as limits on the power of the Communist Party. They got a surprisingly warm reception. Press coverage was favorable; the official union offered its support; and the government responded to their demands quickly, promising pay raises and more time off. Moscow has not, however, addressed the political demands. This was the 12th miners' strike this year (→ 25).

Coal mines in U.S. rocked by violence

July 10. A "cooling-off" period called by the United Mine Workers was abruptly shattered today when gunfire erupted at a non-union mine. An explosion also damaged a coal company trailer. Over 30,000 union members in the coalfields of West Virginia, Virginia and Kentucky have been participating in a sympathy strike in support of 1,900 other miners engaged in a wildcat strike against the Pittston Coal Group. Government and industry officials fear that the work-stoppage and violence may cause Japanese steelmakers to look elsewhere for coal. "We cannot afford to allow the Pittston strike to jeopardize West Virginia's high standing in international coal markets," warns that state's junior senator, Democrat Jay Rockefeller.

France celebrates Revolution's 200th

July 14. Exactly 200 years after the fall of the Bastille, France's bicentennial celebrations have reached their climax. Joining the festivities today were 33 heads of state from four continents, many of whom are in Paris for a summit conference of leading industrial democracies. Celebrations began with the Bastille Day parade, powered by 300 tanks and 5,000 troops to commemorate the victory of the Allies in two world wars. As night fell, 6,000 performers in outrageous costumes poured into the streets, bringing the curtain down for the hundreds of thousands of revelers with a touch of 1980s avant garde.

The French love a great party.

Bush brings mixed blessing to East bloc

Bush and Polish leader Wojciech Jaruzelski at the site of the Nazi invasion.

July 12. President Bush's sweep through Poland and Hungary this week has offered East bloc citizens a glimpse of their future. Bush's visit not only highlights the improving relations between the United States and Eastern Europe, but his presence itself serves as a symbol of democracy and capitalism.

Poland and Hungary have been quick to take advantage of the opportunities for change offered by the more liberal policies of Soviet leader Mikhail S. Gorbachev. They have opened doors to the West both figuratively and literally. The Hungarians, in fact, began in early May to dismantle the barbed-wire fence on their Austrian border. As Bush told a Hungarian audience, "the

Iron Curtain has begun to part."

Symbolism aside, many people in Poland and Hungary were disappointed at the small amount of aid pledged by the United States. Bush offered $115 million to Poland, a country with a foreign debt of $39 billion, and $25 million to Hungary. In spite of a desire to see reforms succeed, the United States is reluctant to do anything that will provoke a crackdown by the Soviet Union. Some administration officials expressed concern that until changes are implemented, more aid would contribute to continued inefficient economic management. Others explain that the United States simply cannot afford to give any more assistance (→ 19).

Acting great Olivier dies at age of 82

July 11. Sir Laurence Olivier, one of the century's most respected actors, has died peacefully in his sleep at his home near London. He was 82 years old.

A performer of virtuosity and daring, truly a "princely lord" of his profession, he drew long lines as a Shakespearean actor, and made movie history in *Henry V, Wuthering Heights, Rebecca* and more. Lord Olivier never stopped working, in spite of cancer of the prostate, leg thrombosis, kidney obstruction, a deteriorating muscular disorder and pneumonia. Even last year, he played a cameo role in the movie *War Requiem.*

Good night, sweet prince.

Assaults on gays are on the rise

Reports from gay rights groups around the nation are painting an ugly picture of fear and hatred. A study by the National Gay and Lesbian Task Force reports 7,248 incidents of violence against gays in 1988, including slayings, and verbal and physical assaults. The increase in attacks by college students, right-wing groups and the general population was laid in part to the fear of AIDS. Some states have laws to monitor hate crimes, but there is no such federal legislation. Calling the violence "alarmingly widespread," the task force warned that "intolerance may be gaining ground."

For the second year in a row, major fires like this one in Nebraska are plaguing the western part of the United States. The damage is not as severe as last year's, but drought has turned firefighting into a Promethean task.

Violence rampant in nation's youth

Violent crimes in the United States, formerly the trademarks of mobsters, drug pushers and psychopaths, are committed increasingly by children under 18. From 1983 to 1987, arrests of minors jumped 22.2 percent for murder, 18.6 percent for aggravated assault and 14.6 percent for rape, while the number of teens in the total population declined 2 percent. Experts blame anything and everything, including abuse and neglect by parents; too few healthy role models in society; glorified sex and violence in the media; poverty; leniency in the courts, and chemical imbalances.

Saudi arms dealer extradited to U.S.

July 19. Adnan M. Khashoggi, the Saudi entrepreneur who helped finance arms shipments in the Iran-contra affair, seems to have a fetish for underground operations. Last October, a U.S. federal grand jury indicted Khashoggi for "illegal property dealings" that allegedly helped former Philippine President Ferdinand Marcos take more than $100 million from his country's treasury. The high-finance artist was extradited to the United States from Switzerland yesterday after his lawyers learned he would face prosecution only for obstruction of justice and mail fraud rather than conspiracy and racketeering.

Khashoggi arrives in New York.

Explosion on Iowa a possible suicide

July 22. A U.S. Navy study is now tentatively calling the April 19 explosion aboard the battleship Iowa one of the bloodiest suicides in history. They can't prove it, but investigators believe Clayton Hartwig, 25, used an electronic detonator to touch off the explosion and fire that took his life and the lives of 47 others manning the largest naval gun turret in the world. An earlier suspicion involving a 21-year-old man whom Hartwig had named as beneficiary of his $100,000 life insurance policy has been dropped with a quiet apology (→ Sept 7).

DC-10 crash-lands in Iowa; many survive

A section of the fuselage, amputated but intact, lies helplessly on the runway.

July 19. A United Airlines DC-10 with 298 people aboard crashed this afternoon in Sioux City, Iowa, just a half-mile short of its runway. It cartwheeled on impact and broke into flaming pieces. Miraculously, an estimated 150 people survived. The United jet, Flight 232, was flying from Denver to Chicago en route to Philadelphia when the pilot radioed just after 4 p.m. that the plane had sustained "complete hydraulic failure." This is the fifth major DC-10 crash since 1974. The ill-fated model has also had three engine failures without fatalities.

Ambassadors anything but diplomatic

Critics are jumping on President Bush for his ambassadorial selections. Of 37 nominations, less than a third have been Foreign Service officers; the rest are cronies and major contributors to Republican campaigns. Many of them, critics contend, employ little knowledge of the country where they will serve — and even less tact. Ambassador to the Bahamas nominee, ex-Nevada Sen. Chic Hecht, said life in Las Vegas prepared him well for life in the Bahamas. Peter Secchia, the new ambassador to Italy, joked that the new Italian navy uses glass-bottomed boats "so they can see the old Italian navy."

July 21. *The Truth hurts. Carl "The Truth" Williams is just the latest victim of "Iron" Mike Tyson, in one of the fastest title fights ever — 93 seconds.*

Congress hears tale of Soviet arms cuts

July 21. A high-ranking Soviet officer disclosed formerly secret information on tank production today to a packed hearing of the House Armed Services Committee. Marshal Sergei F. Akhromeyev, personal military adviser to Soviet leader Mikhail Gorbachev, told the panel that total Soviet tank output "will be reduced to the tune of 40 percent by the end of 1990." During his four and a half hours of testimony before a House committee that plays a key part in drawing up the military budget, Akhromeyev repeatedly warned that future arms control breakthroughs would be unlikely unless the United States took a more conciliatory approach. Akhromeyev pressed specifically for talks on naval reductions, which he said were "a major prerequisite for further improvement of Soviet-American relations" (→ Sept 19).

Reagan top cowboy

July 21. Another chapter was added to the Reagan legend today with the former President's induction into the Cowboy Hall of Fame. He takes his place beside Will Rogers, John Wayne, Gary Cooper and Teddy Roosevelt for his role in *The Santa Fe Trail*, and for his days as host of TV's *Death Valley Days*.

Threatening fans

When celebrities become objects of obsession, their lives may be in danger. The past is full of scary reminders, including John Lennon's death; President Reagan being shot at in a fan's bizarre bid for actress Jodie Foster's affection; the 5,000 threatening letters sent to Michael J. Fox; the shooting of two studio guards by a man demanding to see actor Michael Landon; the knifing of actress Theresa Saldana; and, most recently, the shooting death of actress Rebecca Schaeffer by a crazed fan. Psychologists are studying the warning signs of fatal obsession: incessant talk about an idol, a whole room made into a shrine, neglect of normal responsibilities and travel to be near an object of intense preoccupation.

Bush calls for moon base, Mars mission

Mars beckons, and Bush will heed the call. But is he ready with the cash?

July 20. "Back to the future" was President Bush's byword today in a speech marking the 20th anniversary of man's first moon landing. As he stood outside the National Air and Space Museum facing an audience crammed with big-name astronauts, the President called for a base to be built on the moon and for an expedition to Mars. He mentioned no timetable or costs, but said he was entrusting the details to the National Space Council, headed by Vice President Dan Quayle. If the President means business, he must orchestrate a huge buildup of the space program, at a cost, experts say, of about $500 billion, laid out over 30 years. NASA needs more rockets, a space station, plus new technology. It's a "daydream," scoffed Democrat Albert Gore, chairman of the Senate Committee on Space, Science and Technology.

Trial revealing U.S. espionage details

July 17. Details of highly secret U.S. intelligence operations based in West Berlin are emerging during the trial of Huseyin Yildirim, who is charged with conspiracy to commit espionage. Yildirim, a mechanic at a U.S. Army base in West Berlin, allegedly delivered classified material from James Hall, an analyst of intercepted communications at the base, to East German agents.

West Berlin is crucial to American espionage operations in the Eastern bloc, both for gathering intelligence for the ultrasecret National Security Agency, and as a base for CIA spy recruiting. In response to West German objections to the spy operations, the United States contends that information obtained from the base in West Berlin is needed to offset the Warsaw Pact's advantage in conventional forces.

Rabbi trading cards

Oy gevalt! What'll they think of next? Arthur Sugarman of Baltimore has created a series of rabbi trading cards to help Jewish youngsters learn about the religious leaders they study. Each card has a picture on the front and information about the rabbi's life and achievements on the back.

Hunting and slaughter of elephants draws worldwide attention

Last month, activists protested in front of one of Paris's largest ivory dealers.

July 18. In a burst of flames, 12 tons of elephant tusks went up in smoke today. The fire, lit by Kenya's President Daniel arap Moi and watched by diplomats, farmers and conservationists, was a gesture intended to persuade the world to stop the ivory trade. Since 1979, poaching has cut Kenya's elephant population from 65,000 to 17,000. "I appeal to people all over the world to stop buying ivory," Moi said. The tusks were collected from some 2,000 elephants that poachers had shot and left behind. According to experts, the majority of tusks were from females. Poachers wiped out most of the males, which have larger tusks, years ago. The burned tusks would have brought an estimated $3 million on the market.

23. Troon, Scotland: American Mark Calcavecchia wins the British Open golf tournament in a three-way playoff.

23. Paris: American Greg Lemond wins Tour de France bicycle race by 8 seconds.

24. New York City: Exxon estimates the cost of cleaning up the Valdez oil spill at $1.28 billion (→ Aug 15).

24. Wilmington, Del.: Court allows Time Inc. to buy Warner Communications Inc., forming one of the world's largest communications firms.

26. Washington, D.C.: Federal grand jury indicts Robert T. Morris for infecting federal computers with a "virus."

27. Moscow: Soviet legislature backs plan to allow Estonia and Lithuania to institute free-market economies independent of Moscow, beginning next year (→ Aug 9).

27. New York City: After 121 years, the New York Athletic Club votes to admit women.

27. Detroit: Workers at Nissan plant in Smyrna, Tenn., overwhelmingly reject U.A.W. bid to organize a union.

28. Chicago: First meeting of Congress of Chinese Students in the U.S. is held; 1,100 attend to address concerns over repression of pro-democracy movement (→ Aug 12).

28. Lebanon: Israeli commandos kidnap Sheik Abdul Karim Obeid, leader of radical Arab group (→ 31).

29. Geneva: World's largest accelerator, the Electron-Positron Collider, is activated.

29. Warsaw: Polish President Jaruzelski resigns as Communist Party leader (→ Aug 18).

29. Nicosia, Cyprus: H.H. Rafsanjani declared victor in Iran's presidential race.

30. New York City: New York Times/CBS poll finds 67 percent of Americans approve of Bush's presidency.

DEATH

31. Michael Harrington, leading socialist and author (*Feb. 24, 1928).

Hostage Higgins hanged by Beirut captors

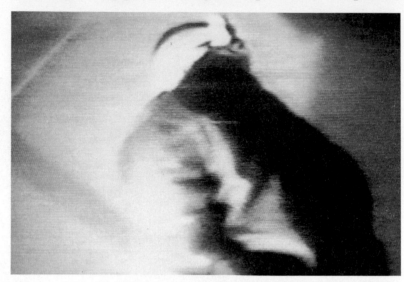

Higgins' ghostly figure hangs from a ceiling somewhere in the Arab world.

July 31. Lt. Col. William R. Higgins has been hanged by his Shiite Muslim captors in West Beirut. Although not confirmed, Higgins' killing was apparently carried out by a group called the Organization of the Oppressed of the Earth, one of the most violent of the pro-Iranian militia groups. Americans were "shocked right to the core," according to President Bush, to see a shadowy videotape showing Higgins hanging by a noose. His captors said the execution was in retaliation for the Israeli kidnapping of Sheik Abdul Karim Obeid, a leader of the pro-Iranian Party of God. Congressional leaders have expressed outrage and frustration at Higgins' murder (→ Aug 2).

"Indecent" art attacked by Senate critics

July 26. The Senate has passed a bill proposed by Republican Sen. Jesse Helms to bar federal arts funds from being granted to "promote, disseminate or produce obscene or indecent materials, including . . . depictions of sadomasochism, homoeroticism, the exploitation of children, or individuals engaged in sex acts." The move is a response to an outcry over Andres Serrano and Robert Mapplethorpe shows that were funded by the National Endowment for the Arts. The Serrano show featured a crucifix submerged in urine (→ Sept 13).

July 23. *Birdie May Vogt, seen here celebrating her birthday last year, was the oldest person in America until her death today at 112 years of age.*

Second Tokyo ado forces Uno to resign

July 24. The sky fell on Japan's Liberal Democratic Party today as voters swept the Socialists to victory, giving them near control over Parliament's upper house. Even coming on the heels of Noboru Takeshita's ouster for financial misdeeds, the setback was the worst in the LDP's 34 years as ruling party. Liberal Democrats still control the more powerful lower house, but Prime Minister Sousuke Uno is out, his stint of two months marred by a liaison with a geisha. "The entire responsibility for the defeat lies with me," said Uno. But pundits cite a campaign that never connected with restive voters (→ Aug 8).

Uno announces his resignation and brings the self-destructing ruling party a step closer to its demise.

KKK leader must attend race class

July 26. Roger Handley, a leader of the Ku Klux Klan, will soon begin a class in race relations. His new education is part of a settlement for his 1979 attack on black civil rights marchers in Decatur, Ala. Nine other Klansmen were also named in the lawsuit. Although Handley has agreed to attend the two one-hour workshops, he has promised the world, "I will leave with the same opinion I walk in here with." What opinion is that? "I don't believe God meant for any two races to live in one nation," says Handley.

Stealth and Midgetman fall to budget cuts

July 27. The Stealth bomber and the Midgetman nuclear missile have become casualties, not of war, but of the massive American budget deficit. With Republican senators deserting the Bush military program en masse, the Senate voted on Wednesday 98-1 against further purchase of the radar-defying B-2 Stealth bomber, unless the Pentagon can demonstrate that it fulfills its promise. The senators also asked the military to cut the proposed fleet of 132 by 50 percent.

According to Sen. Edward M. Kennedy (D-Mass.), "We are clearly going to cut back on the program. The questions are where, by how much and should the program survive at all." Secretary of Defense Dick Cheney countered, "There is a perception abroad in the land that peace is at hand because of the changes in the Soviet Union and that allows us to make changes in our military posture. I think that is not the case."

The Bush administration suffered a second setback today when the House of Representatives voted to cut $100 million in Midgetman funds from the 1990 budget. The Midgetman was defeated when a compromise for funding both that missile and the larger MX unraveled. In explaining his negative vote, Rep. William L. Dickinson (R-Ala.) said, "We don't need the Midgetman and I only supported it as part of the package" (→ Aug 2).

The B-2 flew for the first time last week, but it was shot down by a Congress that felt $500 million was too much for a plane that may soon be obsolete.

Suspect convicted in killing of Palme

July 27. The third time proved a charm for prosecutors in the 1986 murder of Swedish Prime Minister Olof Palme. First they suspected a right-wing teacher, then left-wing Kurds. Finally, today, they convinced lay jurors that a 42-year-old drifter did it, without motive. The conviction rests shakily on the testimony of Palme's wife, who only remembers seeing the suspect at the scene of the crime. With two professional judges dissenting, the court sentenced Gustav Christer Petterson to life in prison (→ Oct 13).

Marx is disavowed by Mozambique

July 28. Gone are references to "class struggle" and "proletarian internationalism" in the new program drafted by Mozambican President Joaquim Chissano and his ruling Liberation Front Party. Instead, the document soft-pedals communist ideology to appeal for foreign aid and national unity in the face of a costly civil war. Chissano, hoping to end the insurgency, has also offered to negotiate with the rebels if they mend their violent ways. The war has claimed nearly 100,000 lives to date.

Striking Ukrainian miners return to work

Soviet miners read the news while awaiting word of their strike's result.

July 25. Striking Ukrainian miners, appeased by Soviet leader Mikhail S. Gorbachev's pledge to democratize local elections, have decided to return to work. The remaining miners in the nationwide strike have also started to go back to their jobs now that Gorbachev has offered to let each republic design its own elections. Such revisions will almost certainly lead to reduced Communist Party influence.

In a risky move that may provoke future strikes, Gorbachev bypassed local authorities and dealt directly with the miners, who he praised as having legitimate grievances which have been overlooked by local entrenched interests. He promised the miners imminent assistance and called on them to implement his own political reforms when they design their elections.

Evidently unwilling to give Gorbachev a chance to have second thoughts, the miners immediately held a rally to discuss the implementation of his proposals. They agreed on several changes that would make elections more democratic and more frequent, among them proposals to place local candidates outside the authority of party vetoes and to reduce to 100 the number of signatures required to place a name on the ballot.

Although local leaders were alarmed by the miners' political militancy, most signs indicate that the miners' first concerns are economic. As one miner said, "People support Gorbachev, but they are tired of waiting for the improvements he promises."

July 30. *Cuban Javier Sotomayor clears the 8-foot mark in the high jump, breaking his previous world record jump of 7 feet 11 3/4 inches.*

Su	Mo	Tu	We	Th	Fr	Sa
		1	2	3	4	5
6	7	8	9	10	11	12
13	14	15	16	17	18	19
20	21	22	23	24	25	26
27	28	29	30	31		

1. Washington, D.C.: Senate Judiciary Committee rejects nomination of William Lucas for administration's top civil rights post (→ 11).

2. Chicago: Forty-six commodities traders indicted on fraud and racketeering charges following two-year FBI probe.

2. Washington, D.C.: Senate passes 1990 military budget consistent in large part with Bush administration plan (→ Sept 26).

2. Washington, D.C.: Soviet Union agrees to U.S. demand that inspections of chemical weapons be made before concluding agreement (→ Sept 25).

2. Johannesburg: Some 200 black patients seek admission to all-white hospitals, launching new civil disobedience campaign (→ 14).

2. Washington, D.C.: CIA concludes Colonel Higgins was killed before last Monday (→ 3).

3. Indianapolis: Federal judge orders an art dealer to return four rare Byzantine mosaics to the church in Cyprus from which they came, setting a precedent in the art world.

3. Beirut: Muslim terrorist group suspends death sentence of hostage Joseph Cicippio to give Israelis time to release Sheik Abdul Karim Obeid (→ 3).

3. New York City: ABC News refuses to release videotape of Cicippio pleading for his life, saying it would help cause of his captors (→ 5).

3. Portland, Maine: St. Paul's Church withdraws from Episcopal Church to protest ordination of women and consecration of first female bishop.

5. Havana: Communist Party bans distribution of two Soviet publications, *Moscow News* and *Sputnik,* because they justify bourgeois democracy and find fascination with American life.

5. New York City: Kevin Wasowski becomes 20 millionth visitor to World Trade Center observation deck.

5. New York City: Telephone workers across 15 states go out on strike; management fills in (→ 13).

Canada ravaged by relentless forest fires

Beating back the blaze in Manitoba, the worst in Canada's history.

Aug 1. The Canadian province of Manitoba is being ravaged by the worst forest fires in its history, part of an epidemic of fires raging across Canada this summer. More than 23,000 residents have been evacuated from 23 besieged communities in the north. While no deaths have been reported, the toll on the region's forests has been catastrophic. So far this year, 18,000 square kilo-meters have been destroyed — an area about the size of Lake Ontario.

Rain and cool temperatures have begun to make up for a summer-long drought, and have stabilized the situation somewhat in the past week. In Manitoba, 14,700 evacuees have returned to their homes. But major forest fires are also burning in the provinces of Quebec, Ontario and Saskatchewan.

Chicago study finds race relations poor

Aug 4. Has America given up on civil rights? A new study by the National Research Council entitled *A Common Destiny: Blacks and American Society* says that this is decidedly the case. "Since the early 1970s," the report declares, "the economic status of blacks relative to whites has, on average, stagnated or deteriorated."

Statistics show that black male college graduates earn just 74 percent as much as their white counterparts. The black middle class (those families with incomes over $35,000) has grown from 18 percent to merely 22 percent of all black families over 16 years. The per capita income of blacks in general is just 57 percent of whites. And there has been no measurable increase in housing integration since the 1960s.

While *A Common Destiny* asserts that "blacks and whites share a substantial consensus" on the abstract goal of "achieving an integrated and egalitarian society," the report concludes that whites are more often than not opposed to specific reforms that affect race relations.

Sandinista regime prepares to bring democracy to Nicaragua

Aug 4. Marking a major step along the way to ending the 10-year civil war in Nicaragua, President Daniel Ortega today signed an agreement with the opposition to disband the U.S.-backed contra rebels. In return, the Sandinistas agreed to several opposition demands, including the granting of unconditional amnesty to the contras and the lifting of all restraints on news reporting. One opposition leader called the accord "a great achievement, even though there are a lot of things to be resolved." The agreement is considered a setback for the Bush administration, which has wanted to keep the contras intact until the Nicaraguan elections scheduled for next February.

Ortega also announced yesterday the suspension of the army draft until after the elections. It will be the first time since military conscription was implemented in 1983 that no new Nicaraguan recruits will be added to the army ranks. The move is considered by many observers to be a step toward meeting U.S. and opposition demands for a democratic election process.

However, critics inside and outside Nicaragua say the action is a ploy to manipulate world opinion, and that by removing the unpopular conscription law, Ortega hopes to sway undecided voters to support the Sandinista Party (→ 7).

Preparing for elections, the Sandinistas and the opposition have agreed to disarm the contras. Wary, the contras (above) are still training.

AZT: Some hope for AIDS victims

Hemophiliac Ryan White has AIDS.

Aug 3. A new study provides strong evidence that the drug AZT can delay the onset of symptoms in AIDS victims. Until now, AZT, or azidothymidine, has been used only by some 25,000 patients afflicted with full-fledged symptoms. The study involved 713 patients with only mild immune system decline; half got AZT and the other half a placebo. So far, 36 members of the placebo group have developed full symptoms, while only 14 patients in the AZT group have been afflicted by an advanced condition.

AZT's advocates will seek reductions in its cost, which presently restricts treatment to a privileged few of the 100,000 to 200,000 Americans infected with AIDS (→ Sept 6).

Hostage crisis continues; some hope seen

Joseph Cicippio's brother keeps a vigil over the hostages' time in captivity.

Aug 5. The brutal murder in Lebanon last week of Lt. Col. William Higgins has lent a new urgency to the problem of freeing the eight hostages remaining in the war-torn country. America's angry reaction, which has included hints at bombing Party of God headquarters in Lebanon if any more Americans are killed, has precipitated a diplomatic crisis in the Middle East. Intermediaries for several Arab states as well as Iran appear to be engaged in efforts to exchange hostages for Palestinian or Shiite prisoners being held in Israel. Iranian President H.H. Rafsanjani yesterday indicated that "the freedom of the hostages is solvable." And the deadline set for American hostage Joseph Cicippio's execution has apparently passed without event.

But so far, only France has been successful in getting its hostages back safely. Paris openly negotiates with terrorists, and offers them large sums of money. Said one French official, "Are the American people ready to do that with Iran? I doubt it" (→ 8).

American South losing its economic edge

After 30 years of unprecedented prosperity, the South's economic growth has come to a virtual standstill. Job growth has dropped below the national average, while unemployment levels have soared higher than in any other region. According to economists, the low wages that originally attracted industry to the South have been matched by foreign competitors. "The South tried to benefit from the mobility of industry, and then it turned out to be far more mobile than anyone ever imagined it could be," explains James Cobb, a professor at the University of Tennessee. Most other experts seem to concur. As Jesse White, director of the Southern Growth Policies Board, explains, "The Era of the Sunbelt will come to a close by the end of this century, and in fact, has closed in much of the Deep South."

Japan best seller cites U.S. decline

The U.S. military is at the mercy of Japanese technology — specifically computer chips — according to the authors of a best-selling book in Japan. Shintaro Ishihara, a longshot candidate for prime minister, claims that if Japan sold its chips to the U.S.S.R. instead of the United States it "would instantly change the balance of military power."

Akio Morita, chairman of Sony Corporation and co-author of the book, *The Japan That Can Say No,* writes, "Americans do not manufacture any more. It is not that America does not have the technology." Noting that the United States has been "unable to mass produce goods by applying new technology," he suggests that it "abandon its superpower consciousness and rebuild its economy quickly."

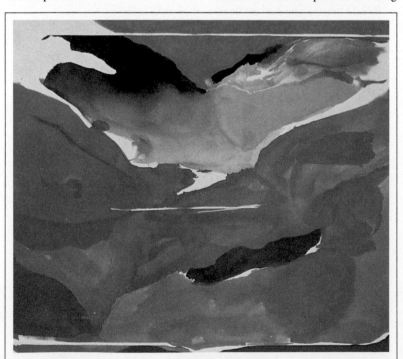

Helen Frankenthaler's Nature Abhors a Vacuum, *part of a retrospective of the artist's work at the Museum of Modern Art in New York City.*

U.S. arms sales up 66% in Third World

Aug 1. Last year, Third World nations bought more American weapons than ever before. Sales in 1988 rose 66 percent from 1987 levels, bringing the amount of arms sold nearly to the level of the Soviet Union, reports the Congressional Research Service. The United States and the Soviet Union together accounted for nearly two-thirds of all weapons sales to Third World nations, the American share jumping from 15 percent in 1987 to 31 percent in 1988, and the Soviet share falling from 50 percent to 33 percent. In dollars, that means $9.2 billion in sales for the United States and $9.9 billion for the Soviets. New orders from old customers — including a purchase of 40 F-18 aircraft by Kuwait — accounted for the increased American profits.

AUGUST

1989

Su	Mo	Tu	We	Th	Fr	Sa
		1	2	3	4	5
6	7	8	9	10	11	12
13	14	15	16	17	18	19
20	21	22	23	24	25	26
27	28	29	30	31		

6. La Paz, Bolivia: Formerly exiled revolutionary Jaime Paz Zamora is installed as Bolivia's President.

7. Tele, Honduras: Presidents of five Central American nations, in direct defiance of United States, set Dec. 8 as deadline for disbanding of contras (→ Oct 10).

7. Memphis, Tenn.: The latest in museums, one featuring Elvis Presley's automobiles, is drawing big crowds.

7. Wellington, New Zealand: Prime Minister David Lange announces resignation due to declining health.

8. Tokyo: Toshiki Kaifu becomes president of the ruling Liberal Democratic Party (→ 9).

8. West Point, N.Y.: Kristin M. Baker is the first woman in history to hold the position of first captain of the Corps of Cadets, the highest ranking cadet at the academy.

8. Cape Canaveral, Fla.: The original shuttle, Columbia, is successfully launched carrying an advanced spy satellite, after being grounded for three years.

8. Tehran: Iran says it will help free American hostages in Lebanon if U.S. will release frozen Iranian assets (→ Oct 23).

9. Washington, D.C.: President Bush signs savings and loan bill committing federal funds of $166 billion over 10 years to insuring American bank depositors (→ 21).

9. Estonia: Some 20,000 ethnic Russian workers walk off their jobs to protest new election law that will deny them right to vote or hold office (→ 10).

9. Panama: Authorities arrest two United States MPs in retaliation for the arrest of 29 Panamanians by canal authorities (→ 23).

11. Washington, D.C.: William Lucas, rejected for Justice Department's top civil rights post by Senate, is named Atty. Gen. Dick Thornburgh's personal representative.

11. Warsaw: Polish Senate formally condemns the 1968 invasion of Prague, in which Polish troops participated.

Estonia puts end to Russian strikes

Aug 10. Ever since their country was annexed by the Soviet Union in 1940, the Estonians have chafed under Russian rule. Recently the republic's government has been allowed to wield more power, and today it wielded it against the Russians. The Estonian government banned its Russian citizens from striking to protest a recently passed law that prevents much of the republic's Russian minority from voting in upcoming elections. The law, which requires voters to have lived for two years in a district or five years in the republic, may disenfranchise about 150,000 residents, most of them Russians (→ 23).

Two women named to Japanese Cabinet

Aug 9. After his predecessor Sousuke Uno resigned under heavy pressure from women's groups, Japan's new Prime Minister, Toshiki Kaifu, isn't taking any chances. He was formally sworn in today in Tokyo and announced the first Japanese Cabinet ever to include more than one woman. Mayumi Moriyama, 61, will be director general of the Environmental Agency, and economist Sumiko Takahara, 56, will head the Economic Planning Agency. Kaifu's Liberal Democratic Party has been jolted by the upper house's recent endorsement of Takako Doi for prime minister. Doi, head of the Japan Socialist Party, is the first woman in the country ever to lead a major party.

Doi, head of Japan's Socialists.

Soviet founder V.I. Lenin demythologized

Aug 10. In embracing Mikhail Gorbachev's "new thinking," the Soviet Union has laid the foundation upon which its old icons are being smashed. At the center of the onslaught is Vladimir I. Lenin, founder of the one-party Soviet state, whose legacy was once thought to be beyond the reach of glasnost. But a legal opposition, set up last week within the Communist Party, is now challenging Leninism itself.

The Interregional Group, composed of 388 deputies in the 2,250-member Congress of People's Deputies, has demanded a rewrite of the Soviet Constitution, which defines the party as society's "leading and guiding force." Seeking pluralism and civil rights, they want power to rest with elected officials. Even Gorbachev is too cautious for the legislative radicals. But, says Alexander Yakovlev, a close supporter of the Soviet leader, a "new world requires a new philosophy" (→ 17).

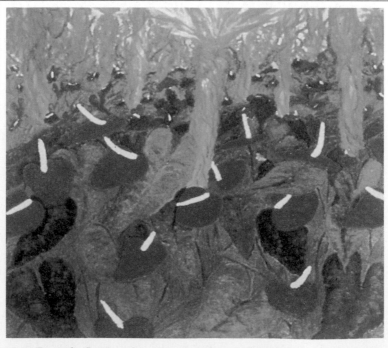

Heart Forest *by Patricia Gonzalez, in a show at the Brooklyn Museum.*

Adieu, Oh Calcutta!

Aug 6. It's all right, you can lower your hands from your eyes: *Oh! Calcutta!* cannot possibly embarrass you or anyone else again. The 20-year-old erotic stage musical gave its 5,959th and final performance tonight at New York's Edison Theater. Featuring dubious writing efforts by Sam Shepard, Jules Feiffer and John Lennon, *Oh! Calcutta!* bared bodies front and back in a series of skits purporting to be humorous and meaningful.

Americans seeking out urban life again

Aug 7. Americans may complain about the quality of big city life, but more and more of them seem to be seeking it out, according to the latest Census Bureau statistics. The bureau reports that nearly half of all Americans now live in areas with populations of one million or more. Since 1980, nearly 86 percent of population growth has been in 282 officially designated "metropolitan areas," reversing the suburban and rural boom of the 1970s. The 1987 statistics also reveal that nearly 90 percent of the country's growth took place in just 37 urban areas. In recent years, the South and West lead in growth, while the Midwest shows a net loss and the population drop in the Northeast has been halted.

20,000 shells fall on Lebanon; 27 die

Aug 11. There was no rest for the war-weary in this battle-scarred land as 20,000 shells and rockets rained death and destruction on one-third of Lebanon over the past 24 hours. The bombardment, which began Thursday afternoon and lasted until daybreak Friday, hit 100 towns and villages, killing 27 people and wounding 120.

The artillery duel was the latest chapter in the violent struggle between 50,000 Syrian troops and their Lebanese Muslim allies, and the 30,000-man Christian regular army. The conflict has cut the once-thriving city's population from 1.5 million to 250,000 (→ Sept 6).

Chinese education: 4 years plus labor

Aug 12. The government of China is giving a graduation present to its best college students: one or two years laboring on a farm or in a factory before going on to graduate school. The gift comes in repayment for the student unrest that rocked China in the spring.

Rural areas in China already suffer from a labor surplus, but officials insist the plan is a necessary tool in the fight against "bourgeois liberalization." Enduring the hardships confronted each day by China's rural population, they say, will rekindle the flame of Communist values in the students, and smother the spark of Western ways (→ 30).

Gen. Colin Powell will head Joint Chiefs

Security clique: Bush, Powell and Secretary of Defense Richard Cheney.

Aug 9. President Bush told reporters today that he will name Gen. Colin L. Powell to the nation's highest military post. Powell, 52, will be the youngest man — and the first black — to serve as chairman of the Joint Chiefs of Staff. A veteran of two combat tours in Vietnam, he was jumped over 32 other lieutenant generals to succeed retiring Adm. William Crowe. Like Crowe, Powell is considered by Pentagon associates to be an intellectual. He had close contact with Bush while serving as President Reagan's last national security adviser. Powell's nomination is expected to receive quick Senate approval.

Abortion in Canada

Aug 8. Canada's Supreme Court today granted Chantal Daigle the right to an abortion just hours after the Quebec woman ended her 22-week pregnancy. The decision climaxed a controversy that erupted 32 days ago when Jean-Guy Tremblay, Daigle's ex-boyfriend, obtained a court injunction forbidding her to seek an abortion. The ruling, considered an important precedent, highlighted the fact that Canada has had no abortion law since the Supreme Court scrapped the existing one in 1988.

Housework hubby?

Housework for husbands? Not on the ashes of your Maidenform. Women trying to balance family and work in the late '80s are finding themselves liberated — to work twice as hard. They handle housework, child care and career while most husbands still do little more than take out the garbage. These, at least, are the conclusions of sociologist Arlie Hochschild's new book, *The Second Shift*. Hochschild also discovered that the stresses of two-job living hurts most couples' sex lives, marriages and careers.

Women making gains in American politics

Aug 6. It isn't easy, but then it isn't as hard as it used to be. That is the conclusion of the National Women's Political Caucus, which met today to discuss the status of women in public office. Statistics show the likelihood of women being elected is rising: 16.9 percent of state legislators are women, up from 4.7 percent in 1971. Of the mayors in larger cities, 122, or 12.7 percent, are female. Caucus members noted the hurdles of their campaigns — proving they are as "tough" as men — as well as the advantages: voters perceive women as more honest.

Hollywood classics making a comeback

Crossing deserts and the dust of history, O'Toole as "Lawrence" is back.

Lawrence of Arabia was a huge hit when it premiered 27 years ago. And it still is today. Restored for $600,000 and re-released this year, the David Lean film has moviegoers flocking to see Peter O'Toole in his first major film role. Some $6.5 million worth of tickets have been sold over the last five months. *Wuthering Heights*, which opened in 1939, is again making women whisper "Heathcliff" with Laurence Olivier's image in mind. *Gone With the Wind* has also stood the test of time after Ted Turner's $250,000 restoration. *The Wizard of Oz*, however, did not fare well in movie houses, perhaps because Judy Garland fans cannot be torn away from their perennial feast in front of the living room TV.

Perestroika in action. A billboard in Moscow announces the Soviet Union's culinary event of the year, the arrival of McDonald's and the Bolshoi Mac.

Su	Mo	Tu	We	Th	Fr	Sa
		1	2	3	4	5
6	7	8	9	10	11	12
13	14	15	16	17	18	19
20	21	22	23	24	25	26
27	28	29	30	31		

13. Chicago: Midwestern telephone workers go on strike, joining their Eastern counterparts; 39,500 out (→ 30).

13. Los Angeles: Two recent studies show that legalized aliens are unprepared to enter mainstream America, both culturally and lingually.

14. United Nations: U.S. agrees to go to World Court over American downing of an Iranian jetliner last year.

14. Hawthorne Woods, Ill.: Payne Stewart wins the 71st PGA championship.

14. Budapest: West Germany closes its embassy because it is packed with East Germans trying to escape to the West.→

14. Washington, D.C.: President Bush selects Richard C. Breeden to head the Securities and Exchange Commission.

14. South Africa: P.W. Botha resigns as President as Cabinet members and party rebuff him (→ 15).

14. Chicago: All charges against Gary Dotson, found guilty of kidnapping and rape 10 years ago, are dropped four years after his accuser admitted her story was a hoax.

15. Washington, D.C.: ARCO announces that, to cut pollution, it will replace its leaded gasoline with a new blend, beginning in California.

17. Stockton, Calif.: Two people die as a six-hour hostage drama comes to an end and the gunman kills himself.

18. Jerusalem: Some 4,000 Gazans strike for a day as the Israelis introduce pass permits (→ Sept 18).

18. Warsaw: Senior Solidarity official Tadeusz Mazowiecki announces he has been nominated to be Poland's Prime Minister (→ 19).

19. Sri Lanka: Forty-five people are killed as political violence flares.

DEATH

17. Amanda Blake, best known as Miss Kitty on *Gunsmoke,* (*Feb. 20, 1929).

De Klerk becomes South African President

De Klerk (right) will preside over a cauldron of hope and anger.

Aug 15. "It is just a change of initials from P.W. to F.W.," said Anglican Archbishop and Nobel laureate Desmond Tutu about the changing of the guard in South Africa's presidency. Claiming that the nation was on the "threshold of a new era," F.W. de Klerk was sworn in today as acting president, replacing P.W. Botha, who recently resigned his post after leading the country for 11 years. De Klerk's post is a temporary one, pending parliamentary elections on Sept. 6. If de Klerk's National Party wins, as seems likely, he will remain as President of the racially divided nation. While de Klerk promises the end of the racist Apartheid system, black leaders note that he supports segregation in housing, education and politics (→ Sept 5).

Trotsky returns to Soviet Union, on paper

Aug 17. One of the key figures of the Russian Revolution, whose name and reputation disappeared from Soviet history books after Stalin exiled him and then presumably had him assassinated, is now being reintroduced to the Soviet people.

Thanks to Mikhail Gorbachev's decision to reassess Soviet history, an official Soviet magazine published an article today by Leon Trotsky, written in 1923, which criticizes the Communist Party for losing its revolutionary spirit (→ Sept 12).

Aug 13. *A music peace festival is held in Moscow. Glasnost Aid perhaps?*

East Germans flee to West in droves

An election is taking place in the Communist stronghold of East Germany that is as honest as any in the West; except that instead of using ballots, its citizens are using their feet to send a message of no-confidence to the governnment. Some 60,000 East Germans have fled to the West this year, 15 percent of them illegally, which is the highest rate of migration since the Berlin Wall was built in 1961. The exodus of the mostly young and educated has been fueled by East German leader Erich Honecker's refusal to experiment with the reforms being tried in Hungary, Poland and the Soviet Union (→ Sept 10).

Congressmen die

Aug 14. In less than a month, separate plane crashes have taken the lives of two U.S. congressmen. Larkin Smith (R-Miss.), a legislator who built his career on law enforcement, died Sunday night when his plane nosedived into the darkness of a Mississippi forest. And yesterday, after days of waiting, the friends of Rep. Mickey Leland (D-Texas) found their worst fears to be true. Leland, 44, perished in a plane crash in Ethiopia while trying to help the hungry of that nation. Under fire for devoting too much time to Africa, the former head of the Black Caucus once responded, "I am as much a citizen of this world as I am of my country."

Shuttle completes "secret" mission

Aug 13. The space shuttle Columbia successfully completed a top-secret five-day mission today. NASA officials would not give details of the flight, but space analysts believe the crew deployed a 10-ton spy satellite that is designed to observe Russian troop movements and monitor compliance with Soviet-American arms agreements. The oldest craft in the shuttle fleet, Columbia touched down at Edwards Air Force Base in California at 6:37 a.m. A NASA spokesman called it a "perfect landing."

Solidarity Cabinet to rule over Poland

Mazowiecki, new Prime Minister.

Aug 19. The man who once sought to crush Solidarity today nominated one of its members to be Poland's first non-Communist Prime Minister since the postwar years. Communist President Wojciech Jaruzelski chose 62-year-old editor Tadeusz Mazowiecki to form a government. In an official statement, Jaruzelski said the new government would be conducive to "satisfying the needs and aspirations of Polish society." Jaruzelski was forced to turn to Solidarity because the union's sweep of the June elections for Parliament made it impossible for his first choice to form a Cabinet. Solidarity has assured the party continued control of the Interior and Defense departments (→ 22).

Ethnic Turks flee Bulgarian repression

Turkish tents dot the border as Turks flee to preserve their ethnic identity.

In what has become one of the largest refugee movements since 1945, over 279,000 Bulgarians of Turkish descent have swarmed into Turkey. The refugees, almost all of whom are Muslim, claim the Bulgarian government has subjected them to a policy of forced ethnic assimilation, and systematically attacked their religious identity. The migrants report that they have suffered jailings and beatings and have been publicly humiliated by Bulgarian authorities. A former high school teacher, Avni Velioglu, says that the refugees "lived in a hell, and they're ready to give up everything to come here." Turkish officials are distressed by the influx, saying that it will be virtually impossible to find adequate housing and jobs for so many people.

Soviets construct first baseball stadium

Aug 15. "If the Soviet Union is to be competitive, we must hit the inside curveball." So said Aleksei L. Nikolov, a top Russian umpire, at the unveiling of his nation's first ballpark, built in the Lenin Hills near Moscow State University. The Soviet Baseball Federation plans to lay the groundwork, as well as the ground, for a medal in the 1996 Olympics. The stadium, still in need of finishing touches — like a pitcher's mound — will serve as the friendly home of a squad of handpicked "amateurs" all trained in the no-nonsense Soviet manner.

Bear blown away

Aug 14. A burned and bruised bear is resting today after climbing a utility pole, touching a live wire and plummeting 25 feet to the ground. Yesterday the bruin wandered into downtown Albuquerque, N.M., searching for a missing cub. Both bears are now at a local zoo and will be returned to the wild.

Jailbreak by copter

Aug 18. Two women freed a pair of inmates from a state prison today by flying them 35 miles away in a hijacked helicopter. The women, the wife of a prisoner and a former sheriff's deputy, had told the helicopter pilot they wanted to photograph real estate near the Arkansas Valley Correctional Facility, 50 miles east of Pueblo, Colo. When the pilot saw their gun, he knew they did not plan to shoot pictures. The two couples forced the pilot to land, bound him and left him behind as they drove off in a van.

Exxon's enemies mount as state of Alaska sues over oil spill

Aug 15. Alaska moved today to win billions of dollars from Exxon and six other oil companies for the March spill that became the worst in American history. In a lawsuit, the state charged that Exxon was responsible for the spill because it failed to adequately staff the Exxon Valdez and supervise the crew. The suit also claims that six other firms that manage the trans-Alaska pipeline misrepresented their abilities to clean up an oil spill. A state official called Alyeska, the pipeline company, a "sham . . . behind which these partners have been hiding for the last 12 or 15 years." The lawsuit seeks punitive damages, a negligence fine and monetary damages to repair the environment and restore the fishing industry.

The Exxon legacy in Alaska: the corporate giant is drawing the ire of a people who live or die by the land.

Su	Mo	Tu	We	Th	Fr	Sa
		1	2	3	4	5
6	7	8	9	10	11	12
13	14	15	16	17	18	19
20	21	22	23	24	25	26
27	28	29	30	31		

20. Colombia: Some 4,000 arrested after murder of a senator (→ 24).

21. Cambridge, Mass.: A Harvard study concludes that government policies have failed to stem marijuana use in U.S.

21. Washington, D.C.: It is announced that the nation's savings and loan industry lost $3.7 billion during the second fiscal quarter (→ Nov 3).

22. Warsaw: Soviet leader Gorbachev phones Polish President Jaruzelski, asking him to see to it that Poland's Communists cooperate fully with a Solidarity government (→ 23).

22. Pasadena, Calif.: Scientists say the partial ring around Neptune, found on Aug. 11, is in fact a complete ring (→ 27).

23. Washington, D.C.: Members of the OAS condemn U.S. military maneuvers in Panama, blaming them for failure of effort to oust General Noriega.

23. Brooklyn, N.Y.: A 16-year-old black youth is shot to death by a gang of 20 to 30 white youths (→ 26).

23. Angola: President Jose Eduardo dos Santos says Angolan truce is in danger because U.S. and South Africa continue to arm rebels (→ 27).

24. Warsaw: Polish Parliament elects Solidarity leader Tadeusz Mazowiecki Prime Minister, ending 40 years of one-party rule (→ Sept 14).

24. Lake Superior: Search team discovers wreck of the Edmund Fitzgerald, which sank in 1975 without a trace of the crew.

24. Kiev, U.S.S.R.: Club-wielding police break up demonstration marking 50th anniversary of Nazi-Soviet pact.

25. Washington, D.C.: Bush administration announces $65 million in aid to Colombia for war on drug trade (→ Sept 2).

DEATHS

22. Huey Newton, co-founder of the 1960s Black Panther Party (*Feb. 17, 1942).

26. Irving Stone, leading biographer (*July 14, 1903).

Killing of black youth sparks racial unrest

Black solidarity at the funeral of Yusuf Hawkins, the Bensonhurst victim.

Aug 26. Yusuf Hawkins and some friends were minding their own business earlier this week, shopping for a used car in the Bensonhurst section of Brooklyn. Suddenly, Hawkins and his friends were surrounded by an angry group of 10 or more white youths who carried baseball bats and at least one gun. There were four shots fired and Hawkins fell to the ground, fatally wounded.

The incident is an unfortunate reminder that a black person like the 16-year-old Hawkins cannot always travel freely in American cities. A study at Temple University has shown that most racially motivated violence occurs in lower-income white urban neighborhoods like Bensonhurst or Howard Beach, scene of a similar incident in 1986.

Only days after the death of Hawkins, scores of black protestors marched into Bensonhurst. They were greeted by an angry mob shouting racial slurs. Mayor Koch criticized the marchers for increasing racial tension, and the incident has become a major issue in New York's mayoral race. A grand jury has indicted two of the white youths for second degree murder, and a third has confessed to the shooting (→ 31).

Lion's friend Adamson is killed in Kenya

Adamson lived and died in what he considered his natural habitat.

Lion cubs have lost a good friend and foster father. George Adamson, 83, was murdered this week in the same way as some of the cubs he helped raise and return to the wild. During an attempt to rescue an employee and a guest who had been detained near his bush camp in Kenya, Adamson and two of his assistants were shot by poachers.

The former game warden gained international fame after his wife, Joy, wrote *Born Free* and *Living Free*, tales of their adventures raising captive and orphaned lions. She was killed in 1980 in a dispute with a servant. Her husband's murder is the latest in the battle between the Kenyan government and poachers trading ivory, rhinoceros horns and leopard and lion skins. Police have seized three suspects in the murder.

Polish leader calls for free enterprise

Aug 23. Echoing a recent statement by Solidarity leader Lech Walesa that the new government would pull Poland along the road "from a communist system of ownership to capitalism," Prime Minister-designate Tadeusz Mazowiecki today promised to open the country's economy rapidly to private enterprise. Ninety percent of Poland's industry has been nationalized since the Communists seized power in 1945. And although 75 percent of the land is farmed privately, state monopolies control the distribution of seed, farm machinery and fertilizers, as well as the food processing and distribution systems (→ 24).

Congressman Frank under fire for aide

Aug 25. Rep. Barney Frank says that playing Henry Higgins in his private life was his "biggest mistake." Frank's Eliza Doolittle was a male prostitute named Steven Gobie, whose services the congressman engaged in the spring of 1985. The Massachusetts Democrat then hired Gobie as his personal employee, hoping to encourage him to "change his life." Frank, the only admitted homosexual in Congress, says he had no idea his Washington apartment was used by Gobie to run a prostitution service.

Living a gay man's life in the public eye. Says Frank, "If I was planning [campaign] strategy, this is not one of the events I would propose."

Drug lords want absolute war on Colombia

Aug 24. The wave of violence that has engulfed Colombia in anarchy continues to rise. Drug traffickers have reacted to President Virgilio Vargas' recent crackdown by issuing a declaration of "total and absolute war on the government, on the industrial and political oligarchy, on the journalists who have attacked and ravaged us, on the judges who have sold out to the government, on the extraditing magistrates." The declaration concludes with the warning, "We will not respect the families of those who have not respected our families."

These are not idle threats. Over the past 10 years some 250 judges and judicial officials — including 11 of the 24 Supreme Court justices

— have been murdered, along with a justice minister, an attorney general, a newspaper publisher and several dozen journalists and police officers. The present attack on the drug lords was prompted by last week's murder of Sen. Luis Carlos Galan, the front runner in the presidential race and an outspoken foe of the drug trade.

As part of the crackdown, President Vargas has re-established an extradition treaty with the United States. The prospect of being tried by American judges and juries, who would be hard to intimidate, is particularly feared by drug traffickers. In fact, the group that issued the declaration of war signed themselves "The Extraditables" (→ 25).

Bogota: new front in the drug lords' battle to place themselves beyond the law.

Reds' Pete Rose gets professional bounce

Charlie Hustle has been run out of baseball on a rail — for life, no less.

Aug 24. Baseball great Pete Rose went down swinging today. He was banned permanently from the game by baseball Commissioner A. Bartlett Giamatti, who based the action on evidence that Rose had bet on baseball games, including those of the team he managed, the Cincinnati Reds. At a meeting with the press, Rose reiterated his denial that he bet on baseball. But he did acknowledge other betting. According to an agreement between lawyers for the two sides, Rose can apply for reinstatement after a year. Rose says he will do that, but of 14 persons previously banned, not one has been reinstated.

Thousands link arms for Baltic freedom

Aug 23. In a mass demonstration calling for independence from the Soviet Union, an estimated one million Baltic citizens linked arms today in a human chain that stretched for more than 400 miles. From the cobbled streets of Tallinn, the capital of Estonia, across Latvia to the Lithuanian city of Vilnius, the line held firm. The protest marked the 50th anniversary of the Stalin-Hitler pact, which cleared the way for Russian domination of the Baltic states (→ Aug 28).

50 Olympians show use of steroids

Aug 25. More than 50 male athletes in the 1988 Olympics used illegal anabolic steroids six months before the games, according to a report by the International Olympic Committee. While tests at the Games found traces of steroid use in the urine of only 10 athletes, the latest data, using more sophisticated tests, indicate more competitors had broken Olympic rules. No such test exists for female athletes. The new research shows that athletes were using the muscle-builders in training, and then removing traces of the steroids in time to prevent detection by on-site testing.

Stock market hits an all-time high

Aug 24. The Dow Jones peaked at an all-time high of 2,734.64 today, topping the record of 2,722.42 set nearly two years ago to the day on Aug. 25, 1987. Analysts say the most broad-based rally in three months is due to low interest rates, which have stimulated business and enticed individuals back into the market after the October 1987 crash. The upturn reflects investor confidence that the economy is steering clear of recession. But pre-crash enthusiasm is hard to find on Wall Street. Brokerage profits are down and institutional traders still dominate the market (→ Oct 13).

Calls for greater autonomy, even independence, continue in the Baltic states.

AUGUST
1989

Su	Mo	Tu	We	Th	Fr	Sa
		1	2	3	4	5
6	7	8	9	10	11	12
13	14	15	16	17	18	19
20	21	22	23	24	25	26
27	28	29	30	31		

27. Angola: Rebel leader Jonas Savimbi says he will resume truce signed two months ago (→ Sept 15).

27. Cape Canaveral, Fla.: Mc-Donnell Douglas becomes first private firm to launch its own satellite.

27. Pasadena, Calif.: Pictures received from the Voyager 2 show signs of volcanoes on Neptune's moon Triton (→ 29).

27. Paris: While negotiations continue on the future of Cambodia, Prince Sihanouk resigns as president of his political party (→ 29).

28. Washington, D.C.: Researchers from Cornell University and Puerto Rico announce they have been witnessing the birth of a new galaxy.

28. Warsaw: Poland's Catholic Primate, Josef Cardinal Glemp, criticizes Jews for opposing convent on site of Auschwitz concentration camp.

28. Los Angeles: Disney Productions purchases the Muppets for $100 million.

28. Estonia: Fearing crackdown from Moscow, Baltic leaders declare they will follow middle road to satisfy both nationalists and Kremlin (→ 29).

29. Biloxi, Miss.: Ex-HUD official Deborah Gore Dean says Reagan aides regularly used influence at HUD to gain contracts for friends (→ Sept 1).

29. Moscow: It is reported that Soviet leader Gorbachev personally helped prepare recent attack on Baltic independence movement (→ 31).

30. India: Anti-government riots leave at least 11 dead.

30. Washington, D.C.: Government orders airlines to install advanced bomb detectors.

31. Oneonta, N.Y.: Suspect in Bensonhurst racial killing turns himself in to police.

31. Denver: Light-skinned black woman wins court fight to change birth certificate, which lists her as white.

31. Riga, U.S.S.R.: Defying Kremlin, Latvian leaders call for "special status" for Latvia within Soviet Union (→ Sept 23).

Cambodian peace talks end in failure

Aug 29. Resumption of a shooting war between the factions vying for control of Cambodia appears likely following the collapse of peace talks held in Paris under the aegis of the French Foreign Ministry. With Vietnam scheduled to pull its 26,000 troops out of the beleaguered country by Sept. 27, the government of Premier Hun Sen and his army of 50,000 will stand alone against a guerrilla coalition headed by Prince Norodom Sihanouk and including the Khmer Rouge. Under Pol Pot, the Khmer Rouge ruled Cambodia from 1975 to 1979, and was responsible for the deaths of over one million people (→ Sept 25).

Secret executions reported in China

Aug 30. The world may never know how many dissidents are dying in China. Amnesty International said today that Chinese leaders have ordered the secret executions of "counterrevolutionaries." A government directive obtained by the group said that only a few death sentences should be revealed "in order to make examples." Amnesty International also reported that at least 1,000 civilians were killed in June's Tiananmen Square massacre. Some, said Amnesty officials, "were shot in the back" (→ Sept 16).

Aug 31. *Mick Jagger just won't go away. The Rolling Stones open their revival tour in Philadelphia.*

PTL founder Jim Bakker loses his cool

Out from under the couch: has he lost his marbles as well as his flock?

Aug 31. "I want to go to court. I want to be on trial." PTL founder Jim Bakker made this assertion while his body language dictated otherwise: as he spoke, he was curled up like a fetus in a corner of his attorney's office, his head under a sofa. Sobbing, "Please don't do this to me," the televangelist was taken to a federal prison 140 miles outside of Charlotte, N.C., for psychiatric evaluation. Bakker and other Praise The Lord leaders are currently being tried on charges of diverting some $4 million in PTL funds for personal use (→ Oct 5).

Studies find left-handers in deep trouble

Aug 29. After years of prodigious research, scientists have come to the conclusion that left-handedness may be harmful to your health. According to research statistics, southpaws are prone to accidents and, on average, die before their right-handed counterparts. Furthermore, among the mentally retarded, autistic, schizophrenic, dyslexic and diabetic, a significant number are left-handed. But not to fret, an unusually high percentage of those with I.Q. scores over 140 are left-handers. So if it's quiet mediocrity you want, lean to the right.

Listen to a story about rap's rise to glory

There's a new old sound that's going round; rap's the name and music's the game. It's 10 years old and the cuts are still bold. The people still listen cause the music still glistens. Some purists fear 'bout where the music is heading, but success is where the good money is still betting. And as for the rest, they say you should know that the music must grow. They have a message they want to deliver and to do this they have tapped into the river of black pride and history and it's no mystery that youth has helped put sales through the roof. D.J. Jazzy Jeff and the Fresh Prince won a Grammy and their videos on MTV sure are savvy.

NWA (Niggers With Attitude).

Space probe Voyager 2 answers key questions about Neptune

Aug 29. Nearing the end of an intrepid, if unmanned, journey of 12 years, the Voyager 2 spacecraft is sending back spectacular images and volumes of data from the distant planet Neptune and its moons. When the feeble but informative signals began to reach the Jet Propulsion Laboratory in Pasadena, Calif., the scientists and technicians who built and launched the robot craft in 1977 celebrated with cheering and champagne.

It is difficult to decide which is more amazing, the information being received through the huge radio telescopes of the Deep Space Network, or the fact the Voyager 2 is still functioning at all. Political and budgetary concerns in the 1970s had limited the Voyager program to two no-frills spacecraft intended to fly only as far as Saturn. But when the spacecraft was still functioning after its Saturn fly-by, NASA decided to take advantage of a rare planetary alignment and send the Voyager on to Neptune.

It will take years to sort through

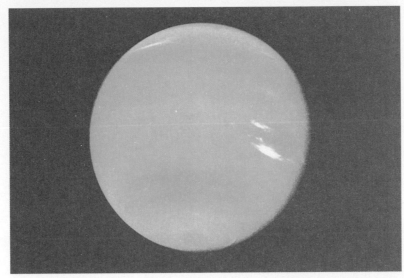

The planet Neptune as human eyes have never seen it before.

all the data being sent to earth by the robot's tiny 22-watt transmitter. But some incredible revelations are already evident. Voyager has charted previously unknown rings around Neptune, has clocked its rotation, identified its magnetic field and photographed what may be ice-volcanoes on the moon Triton. Voyager also filmed a violent storm dubbed the Great Dark Spot, which is nearly the size of the earth and races about the mid-section of the planet. The adventurous Voyager's next stop will be Barnard's star, in about 6,500 years.

Sawyer, Donaldson compete with news

As the TV news stakes climb, one network is banking on an odd coupling. ABC, which stole Diane Sawyer — the lanky blonde woman who dwarfs the stories she covers — from CBS' *60 Minutes*, has teamed her with Sam Donaldson (of the beetlebrows and bullying manners). They will host *Prime Time Live*, the latest entry in the flashy headlines-as-entertainment genre that is invading the airwaves.

The show, taped mostly live, is a gamble. But for Sawyer, who defected for $1.6 million per annum, the time is ripe for a run at the big time. "Look at the success that Barbara Walters has had," says ABC News chief Roone Arledge. "I think Diane will have that same kind of success." The Nielson rating will ride on the star chemistry. It's "a sonata for harp and jackhammer," Sawyer says of her pairing with hard-boiled Donaldson. Will he run roughshod over the ex-Junior Miss? No way, says Donaldson. "Diane is not going to be intimidated. I will probably get the sympathy votes."

Armenia facing civil war; tanks in streets

Ethnic and religious feuds between Christian Armenians and Muslim Azerbaijanis have cost hundreds of lives in sporadic outbursts of violence. Now the tensions have brought the mountainous region of Nagorno-Karabakh to the verge of civil war. Following the intervention of several thousand Soviet troops, backed by tanks, an uneasy truce prevails, but the two peoples are so closely intermingled that officials despair of finding a permanent solution. Says Arkady Volsky, the region's special administrator, "Only Allah or God knows the answer."

Horoscope of Iskandar Sultan, *at the Los Angeles County Museum of Art.*

Hotel queen Leona dethroned by court

Aug 30. Perhaps "only the little people pay taxes," as Leona Helmsley has said; but the big people sometimes pay the piper. Helmsley, 69, self-styled queen of the $5 billion Helmsley hotel chain, was found guilty today of tax evasion to the tune of $1.2 million. Sentencing, which could carry a maximum of 127 years in prison and over $7 million in fines, is slated for Nov. 14. The public has avidly followed the trial in Manhattan's Federal District Court, fascinated by tales of Helmsley's extravagant penny pinching. Example: she tried to claim the $58 she spent on leg waxing as a business expense.

Hard sell to federal cell?

Phone strike ends in five states

Aug 30. Residents of five Midwestern states can again reach out and touch someone. Some 37,000 workers at the Chicago-based Ameritech Company have ended their 17-day strike with a new contract that includes improved profit-sharing and health benefits, and higher pay. Theirs was one of four regional strikes that began in early August and affected more than 200,000 employees in 20 states. Bell Atlantic and Pacific Telesis have also come to terms, but 60,000 workers of the Nynex Corporation are still on strike. Nynex serves New York and most of New England.

Su	Mo	Tu	We	Th	Fr	Sa
					1	2
3	4	5	6	7	8	9
10	11	12	13	14	15	16
17	18	19	20	21	22	23
24	25	26	27	28	29	30

1. Bonn: West Germans mark 50th anniversary of beginning of World War II with caution and remorse.

1. Washington, D.C.: Former HUD official Deborah Gore Dean testifies that she and others shredded documents before they left their posts (→ 26).

1. Washington, D.C.: FDA reports it has discovered dioxin leaking from milk cartons into milk in small amounts.

2. Washington, D.C.: Government drafts plan to curb admission of Soviet Jews to U.S.

2. Bogota, Colombia: Drug ring sets off bomb at leading newspaper in retaliation for crackdown on drugs (→ 10).

4. Belgrade, Yugoslavia: Ninth non-aligned nations summit opens; shift away from anti-U.S. stand is apparent.

5. Washington, D.C.: Finding import fees cheaper than donation drives, Red Cross is seeking blood in Europe.

5. South Africa: Hundreds of thousands of black South Africans strike to protest tomorrow's whites-only vote (→ 7).

5. El Salvador: Rebel leaders say they will negotiate with government if U.S. ends aid to El Salvador (→ Oct 31).

6. Washington, D.C.: Journal of National Cancer Institute says fiber helps shrink enlarged colons and fight cancer.

6. Washington, D.C.: National Association of State Boards of Education releases report saying AIDS victims shouldn't be barred from school (→ Sept 18).

7. Washington, D.C.: Navy reports blast on USS Iowa was probably sabotage and blames top officers for failing to see potential personnel problem.

9. United States: Collegiate study shows only one in five student athletes ever graduates.

9. Flushing, N.Y.: Steffi Graf defeats Martina Navratilova to retain U.S. Open title.

DEATH

4. Georges Simenon, most widely published author of century (*Feb. 13, 1903).

South Africans protest vote; Tutu is held

Sept 7. "Whatever white government comes into power, this country is going to the dogs," said Archbishop Desmond Tutu before the election yesterday of F.W. de Klerk as President of South Africa. Election day lent credence to his words, as 29 people were slain by police while protesting the all-white vote. Tutu himself was arrested Sept. 1 during a protest over the beatings of church staff in recent demonstrations. The month-old "defiance campaign," which has been harnessed by police with tear gas and whips, is the most volatile outburst of dissent since the state of emergency was declared in 1986 (→ 11).

Tutu, prophet of non-violence.

Evert says goodbye

The first lady of the courts.

Sept 5. Chris Evert's professional tennis career ended abruptly today at the U.S. Open, where it all began 18 years ago. Zina Garrison disposed of Evert 7-6, 6-2 in their quarterfinal match on the stadium court. "The time is right," Evert said afterward. She had announced previously that the Open would be her swan song.

The first lady of tennis burst onto the scene at the 1971 Open, her hair in ribbons and two hands on her racket off the backhand. She made it to the semifinals before Billie Jean King stopped her. From there, Evert compiled an unmatched career record of 1,304-145, including 18 Grand Slam titles. And, as Garrison said, "She's been so much to the game. She's such a lady."

Somalia in turmoil

Sept 8. Reports from the war-torn interior of Somalia indicate that the army of President Mohammed Siad Barre is systematically attacking unarmed citizens. According to a U.S. State Department communique, some 5,000 civilians have been "purposely murdered" between June 1988 and March of this year. Most of the victims were members of the Isaak clan, who have been fighting the U.S.-backed Somali government. Washington recently denied Barre $2.5 million in military aid and $21 million in economic aid because of human rights abuses. Reports of torture have been denied by the government, but Western observers say the country is in a state of "disintegration."

Sept 3. *Near Toronto: a private plane frozen in a tragic moment.*

U.S. Embassy closed as Beirut war flares

Sept 6. A trio of American helicopters hovered over East Beirut today, finally plucking the 30-person U.S. Embassy staff out of harm's way. For the first time since 1975, the United States has no diplomatic presence in Lebanon. The Americans have long been caught between warring factions in Beirut. Iran and Syria want freedom to act without hindrance from Washington, while Gen. Michel Aoun's Christian Army has sought help in preserving its hold on East Beirut. On Tuesday, the last straw fell as 1,000 of Aoun's backers besieged Ambassador John McCarthy's residence, telling his staff they could enter or leave "at their own risk" (→ Oct 22).

Leaving Christian allies in the lurch?

Blind Cambodians

"I was just crying, crying, crying," she said, "and when I stopped crying, my eyes were swollen, and I couldn't see." With these words, a middle-aged Cambodian woman explained the cause of her blindness, a malady shared by about 150 Cambodian women now living in Southern California. New research reveals that nearly all of them had perfect vision until they witnessed atrocities — often the murders of their own husbands — committed by the Khmer Rouge, who ruled Cambodia with unparalleled ruthlessness from 1975 to 1979. Scientists believe that psychotherapy can restore their sight.

46 in crash saved after 2 days in Amazon

Crashing in one of the world's remotest regions, survivors are lucky to escape.

Sept 5. It began as a routine plane ride and ended up as an adventure worthy of Indiana Jones. On the last leg of a trip from Sao Paulo to Belem, a Brazilian jet faltered and disappeared into the Amazon jungle. Aerial searchers vainly combed the area; the entire nation despaired. Then came the news: a survivor of the crash, Epaminondas Souza Chaves, had trekked for two days and stumbled upon a remote ranch that, as one official said, "is not even on the map." By ham radio, Chaves reported that 46 of 54 people aboard the plane were alive. Rescue teams, wielding machetes, hacked through miles of jungle, reached the site and brought the amazing Amazon story to an end.

Virginia race riots draw National Guard

No fraternity prank, this; angered students fight for their right to party.

Sept 3. It is quite like martial law in Virginia Beach today. National Guardsmen patrol the streets after quelling riots between black college students celebrating their "Greekfest" and the mostly white store-owners and police. "We will not tolerate lawlessness," said Mayor Meyera Oberndorf. Police have arrested 160 people, and 100 stores have been seriously damaged. Two people were shot. Last night's debacle has been attributed to poor race relations between the students and Virginia Beach residents. One Howard University student commented, "When the stores won't let certain black people in, you get offended. All the prices doubled — not only to deter, but to get more money."

Moscow communists courting capitalists

"Leave it to the Russians to show Americans how to make a lot more dollars." It's not quite as catchy as "Workers of the world, unite," but Moscow's latest slogan is aimed at a different audience: the American businessman. Desperate for hard currency to support economic reforms, Moscow is now in the business of courting capitalists, The Soviet airline Aeroflot has launched a million-dollar ad campaign in the United States that promises such "Perestroika Perks" as free Mont Blanc pens. And the new Moscow Savoy, complete with casino and cable TV news, would make even Leona Helmsley feel at home.

President declares total war on drugs

Sept 5. America is being dosed into a narcotic stupor, and the President thinks he has a cure. Like his recent predecessors, George Bush has declared an all-out war on drugs. In his first televised presidential address, Bush today displayed a bag of crack purchased near the Oval Office and vowed that drug abuse in the United States will end. He outlined an $8 billion plan, but critics contend that the amount is too small. Only $1 billion is new money, the rest coming from existing programs. Many question whether a problem the public sees as the nation's most pressing will truly be the government's top priority (→ 26).

Reagan implicated

Sept 6. Lawyers for ex-national security adviser John Poindexter claimed in court today that former President Reagan ordered their client to lie to a congressional panel investigating the Iran-contra affair. In an effort to obtain certain presidential notes, defense lawyers asserted that Reagan met on several occasions with Poindexter concerning congressional hearings and directed him not to reveal the diversion of funds from Iran arms sales to the Nicaraguan rebels. When asked whether the President had explicitly ordered Poindexter to lie under oath, attorney Frederick Robinson replied, "Yes" (→ Oct 24).

Sept 1. *Libya, not usually noted for its wild celebrations, marks the 20th anniversary of dictator Muammar al-Qadaffi's reign in grand style.*

Yups hit the greens

Sept 4. The "greening of America" has finally come to pass, but with a rather bourgeois twist. The greens in question are dotted with golf balls and scored with cleat marks. "This is a way to be accepted," said 42-year-old Susan Mills, a television producer fresh from a week at golf school. Accepted, that is, by the crowd that closes its big-money deals over the front nine. Not that the golf craze is limited to yuppies. The laid-back form of exercise has caught on across the nation, among young and old, white and black. In fact, last year Americans spent twice as much money on the sport as they did in 1985.

SEPTEMBER
1989

Su	Mo	Tu	We	Th	Fr	Sa
					1	2
3	4	5	6	7	8	9
10	11	12	13	14	15	16
17	18	19	20	21	22	23
24	25	26	27	28	29	30

10. Budapest: Hungary grants permission to 7,000 East Germans to migrate to West (→ 11).

10. Flushing, N.Y.: Boris Becker beats Ivan Lendl 7-6, 1-6, 6-3, 7-6 for his first U.S. Open title.

11. South Africa: Officials say police will stop using whips against protesters (→ 15).

11. Washington, D.C.: FDA finds sloppy manufacturing and possible cheating at 11 of 13 generic drug companies.

12. Washington, D.C.: House votes 380-38 in favor of plan to make flag-burning a federal offense (→ Oct 19).

12. Dayton, Ohio: The Rev. Roger Griese of Roman Catholic Sacred Heart Church has instituted dress code for mass; no communion for those with bare legs.

13. Washington, D.C.: House rejects bill to ban government funding of "obscene" art.

13. New York City: David Dinkins defeats Mayor Ed Koch in Democratic mayoral primary; Rudolph Giuliani wins Republican race (→ Nov 7).

13. Paris: Ex-Vichy police chief Rene Bousquet charged with crimes against humanity in World War II deaths of 194 Jewish children.

13. United States: On average day in U.S., 169 women and 56 men get nose jobs.

14. Washington, D.C.: Under pressure from Congress, President Bush says he will double food aid to Poland (→ Oct 19).

14. Montreal: Researcher reports chicken embryos that flew on March shuttle mission have hatched into perfect birds; Kentucky Fried Chicken sponsored experiment.

15. Angola: Rightist rebel leader Jonas Savimbi cuts off talks with government.

16. Beijing: After three months in seclusion, Chinese leader Deng Xiaoping reappears and announces China will seek change (→ Oct 10).

16. Sri Lanka: Gunmen rampage through three villages, killing 82 people.

Blacks march in South Africa ... legally

Festooned with banners, South Africans march legally in Johannesburg.

Sept 15. Some 20,000 protesters marched unmolested through Johannesburg today, safely decrying the racist policies of the South African government. President F.W. de Klerk, elected last week amid widespread violence, has for the second time in three days given official permission for such an event. Thousands participated Wednesday in a legal demonstration in Cape Town. Never before in South African history has the government sanctioned a protest against itself.

The Rev. Frank Chikane, general secretary of the South African Council of Churches and organizer of the marches, presented the minister of law and order, Adriaan Vlok, with a memorandum defining the purpose of today's protest. "The brutality of the police on occasions such as the "elections" of last week must be seen in the context of our people striving to communicate . . . frustrations and political grievances through peaceful means."

Although no request was made for permission to march, Johannesburg's chief magistrate, Pieter Theron, phoned Chikane minutes before the march and granted official approval. The memorandum explained that since they cannot vote to implement changes, blacks can only make themselves heard through protests like today's. This week's concessions have left most South Africans wondering if other channels will soon be opened (→ 21).

Soviet Yeltsin is toast of the town

Sept 12. Boris Yeltsin, the leader of Moscow's unofficial opposition, met today at the White House with President Bush. Although the short meeting involved no more than a general discussion of the Soviet economy, it seemed certain to bolster Yeltsin's stature at home. Bush spokesmen said they kept official photographers out of the meeting to show that the renegade legislator was not getting "a platform for dissent." But in public, Yeltsin was outspoken in his criticism of Mikhail Gorbachev, at one point comparing the Soviet leader's approach to reform to that of a general who stations his soldiers a mile apart and still expects to seize land (→ 23).

Yeltsin and Secretary of State Baker.

Bush allows U.S. forces to expand their role in Latin drug war

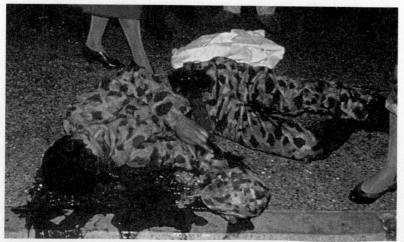

In Medellin, home of Colombia's most brutal drug lords, the body count rises.

Sept 10. United States military advisers in Colombia, Peru and Bolivia will be allowed to move outside their base camps into "secure areas" to train local forces in the war on drugs. "We're not going into combat zones," an administration spokesman promised. But officials acknowledge that the advisers will be vulnerable to attack by drug lords and leftist guerrillas; they can fire only in self-defense. The action drew criticism from Rep. Charles Rangel (D-N.Y.), who said, "It outrages me to think that every time there's an international problem we have to talk about the introduction of American troops" (→ 20).

Warren dies at 84; first poet laureate

Warren in 1986: a literary sage.

Sept 15. He was called America's greatest man of letters — a poet, novelist, scholar and teacher whose work stimulated high-brow critics and thrilled plain readers. After a bout with cancer, Robert Penn Warren, 84, died today at his summer home in Stratton, Vt., a long way from Guthrie, Ky., the town where he was born and raised. He was best known for the novel *All the King's Men* (1946), about the rise and fall of Huey Long, the Louisiana demagogue. It won Warren the first of three Pulitzer Prizes; two more came for verse (in 1957 and 1979). He was given many honors, but to him none quite matched his selection in 1986 as the nation's first poet laureate.

7 slain with AK-47

Sept 14. "I told them I'd be back," said 47-year-old Joseph T. Wesbecker before going on a spree that left seven of his former co-workers dead and 13 wounded, most of them felled by an AK-47 assault rifle. He then ended his own life with a 9-millimeter pistol. The gunman, who had been placed on permanent disability at the Louisville printing plant, had often talked of avenging himself against his employers. But when Wesbecker entered the plant at 8:30 a.m., he "couldn't find any of the bosses," in the words of one lucky survivor, who added, "He just shot anything that was close to him."

Exodus! East Germans flee to West

Sept 11. "It's like Christmas," said one East German, describing yesterday's decision by Hungary to allow 60,000 of his countrymen to cross its border into Austria and to freedom. Some 7,000 refugees poured across the frontier last night, almost all of them destined for West Germany, where they are entitled to automatic citizenship.

The exodus has its roots in an act that was primarily symbolic four months ago. On May 2, Hungary began tearing down the barbed-wire fence that has cut it off from Austria and the West since the end of World War II. To many young East Germans, disenchanted with the aggressively anti-reform government of Erich Honecker, Hun-

In a tent city, East German refugees wait patiently for deliverance.

Passports to freedom for a couple.

gary's action opened an escape hatch. They traveled there on vacation, and many refused to go home.

Hungary responded by stepping up its border patrols, in effect imprisoning the vacationers in Budapest until East Germany could get them to come home. But yesterday, officials decided the situation had become unbearable and temporarily suspended a 20-year-old pact with East Germany that bound each country to prevent refugees from fleeing west. "We cannot become a country of refugee camps," said the Hungarian foreign minister, adding that Hungary would not force East Germans to return home.

The Honecker government angrily criticized Hungary's move, im-

plying that Bonn had paid Budapest to violate its treaties. Moscow also disapproved, but took no action. Given the large number of legal exit visas East Germany has issued this year, many think that Honecker is actually glad to get rid of malcontents by migration.

As Germans on both sides of the Berlin Wall watched the drama unfold, many began wondering if yet another miracle is possible: the reunification of Germany. Although it has long been discussed, many observers in Europe and the United States find the thought of a single, powerful Germany less than heartening. As one French author put it, "I love Germany so much I am glad there are two of them" (→ 30).

Afternoon nap OK

Sleep researchers have let the cat-nap out of the bag. Evidence suggests that people have an innate urge to snooze in the afternoon. Separate studies by William Dement, head of the Sleep Disorders Clinic and Research Center at Stanford University, and Roger Broughton, professor of neurology at the University of Ottawa, show that the biological clock starts to run down daily at about 3 p.m., even in people who have had a good night's sleep. While the scientists cannot explain it, they do feel employers should take note: On-the-job accidents might decrease if workers were allowed to catch a daily 40 winks.

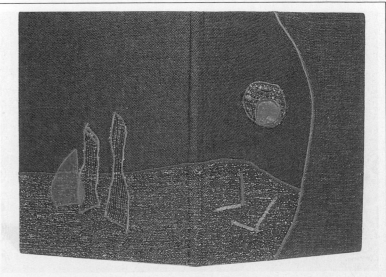

A Vincent Fitzgerald illustration in "Artists of the Book," in Toledo.

SEPTEMBER

1989

Su	Mo	Tu	We	Th	Fr	Sa
					1	2
3	4	5	6	7	8	9
10	11	12	13	14	15	16
17	18	19	20	21	22	23
24	25	26	27	28	29	30

18. Tokyo: Dai-Ichi Kangyo, world's largest bank, will buy into Manufacturers Hanover for $1.4 billion, largest amount spent on a U.S. financial firm by a Japanese bank.

18. Cairo: Israeli Defense Minister Yitzhak Rabin and Egyptian President Hosni Mubarak meet to lay groundwork for Middle East peace talks and devise voting plan for occupied territories (→ Oct 3).

18. McKee, Ky.: A 17-year-old who is upset with father holds school class hostage nine hours, then gives up.

19. Washington, D.C.: James Baker holds his first news conference as secretary of state, to counter charges of inaction on U.S.-Soviet relations (→ 23).

19. Rome: Vatican urges Polish church to remove convent at Auschwitz.

20. Washington, D.C.: Gen. Colin Powell, chairman of the Joint Chiefs of Staff, tells Congress that using U.S. troops in drug war would be risky, but would not lead to another Vietnam (→ Oct 29).

20. Huntsville, Texas: James Pastor, singer and Elvis impersonator, executed for murder.

21. South Africa: It is announced that 780 whites of draft age vow not to report for mandatory military service to protest draft (→ Oct 15).

21. Pakistan: Poll shows 31 percent of Pakistanis believe U.S. was behind last year's killing of President Muhammad Zia ul-Haq.

21. Nashville, Tenn.: Judge rules life begins at conception in awarding seven frozen embryos to mother after estranged husband fought to have them destroyed so children would not be born into broken home.

22. Pittsburgh: FAA suspends pilot and co-pilot of USAir jet that crashed into East River.

22. Antarctica: Researchers announce hole in ozone is growing at alarming rate.

23. Moscow: Working group in Soviet legislature drafts bill for debate which would legalize opposition parties (→ Oct 3).

Summit peaks in the Wyoming mountains

Baker, Shevardnadze and secret service: "openness and candor" in the wilds.

Sept 23. A lodge in Wyoming's Grand Teton National Park has for two days been the site of an amicable foreign ministerial summit that yielded impressive progress on arms control. The success of the meeting between Secretary of State James Baker and his Soviet counterpart, Eduard Shevardnadze, was all but assured yesterday when the Soviets dropped their insistence that the United States end its Star Wars program. That demand had been a major obstacle in strategic arms talks during the Reagan years. Pacts were then signed on monitoring chemical weapons and verifying strategic arsenals.

The summit's unusual location, so far geographically and spiritually from the usual foreign policy centers of New York and Washington, was chosen intentionally, Baker explained, to symbolize the "new openness and candor" in Soviet-American relations. Over the two days, the two officials held lengthy one-on-one meetings that ran over schedule, attended a barbecue and went fly-fishing.

The two men also announced that President Bush will meet with Soviet leader Mikhail Gorbachev next spring or summer, probably in Washington. Bush's critics hope that he will use that opportunity to advance some imaginative proposals and end what they believe is an overly cautious stance toward the Soviets (→ Oct 31).

Firm cuts price of anti-AIDS drug AZT

Sept 18. The Burroughs Wellcome Co., sole producer of the anti-AIDS drug AZT (azidothymidine), agreed today to reduce its cost by 20 percent. The only drug proven to slow the progress of the disease, AZT has cost patients between $8,000 and $10,000 yearly. Unfortunately, children suffering from AIDS cannot celebrate the price reduction. Burroughs Wellcome has not made the drug available in a pediatric dose, despite evidence that it can prolong children's lives and reverse some forms of mental deterioration (→ Oct 25).

Sept 17. *Fox nips at the heels of the big three networks, as Tracy Ullman celebrates her Emmy.*

Grand old American Irving Berlin dies

Sept 22. He could play the piano only in the key of F sharp — but it was the key to a treasure trove of great American music. Composer Irving Berlin, who died in New York today at the age of 101, seemed incapable of writing a forgettable song: *Alexander's Ragtime Band*, *White Christmas*, *God Bless America* and *Puttin' on the Ritz* were just a few of his 1,500 tunes. Born Israel Baline in a Russian village, Berlin came to New York at the age of 6. At 19, he published his first song, *Marie From Sunny Italy*. Surprisingly enough, he was not its composer, but its lyricist. His 19 Broadway shows, however, proved he had a way with a melody.

Berlin in This is the Army *(1943).*

French DC-10 found strewn over desert

Sept 20. Wreckage of a DC-10 airliner that disappeared yesterday en route from Chad to Paris was found in the Niger desert today. All 171 people aboard are presumed dead. The vast area over which the debris was spread and the lack of any emergency call from the crew lead officials to believe a bomb caused the explosion. Bombs have downed seven planes since 1970, the most recent a Pan Am 747 over Scotland late last year. While several groups have claimed responsibility for the latest incident, officials say they have no solid evidence yet.

IRA bomb kills 10 at Marine school

Sept 22. A powerful explosion ripped through Britain's Royal Marines School of Music in the village of Walmer today, killing 10 people and wounding 22. The Irish Republican Army, which had promised a "bloody summer," claimed responsibility for the blast. Most of the victims were musicians training to be members of the Marine staff band; the IRA considers them armed soldiers. The guerrillas released a chilling statement referring to a recent state visit of British Prime Minister Margaret Thatcher: "Mrs. Thatcher visited occupied Ireland with a message of war at a time when we want peace. Now we, in turn, have visited the Royal Marines."

Lithuania nullifies Soviet annexation

Sept 23. Lithuania's legislature formally challenged Soviet rule today by declaring Moscow's 1940 annexation of its country invalid. In a 274-0 vote that could pave the way for secession, the lawmakers adopted a report charging that the Baltic countries of Lithuania, Estonia and Latvia were annexed in accord with a secret pact between Stalin and Hitler. The report directly contradicts last week's assertion by Soviet leader Mikhail Gorbachev that the Baltic republics joined the Soviet Union voluntarily (→ 29).

Last-minute loan bails out Bloomies

Sept 19. The giant Canadian real estate and retail firm Campeau Corp. announced today that it has ended a week-long financial crisis by obtaining a $250 million loan to bail out its nine American department store divisions. Robert Campeau, the company's founder and chairman, will lose operating control of his U.S. retail branch. The firm, which owns such well known stores as Bloomingdale's, Abraham & Strauss and Stern's, was forced to restructure by Olympia & York Developments, which owns 24.5 percent of Campeau and arranged for the needed cash. The loan will allow the stores to meet demand over the Christmas season.

Hungary takes big step toward Israel

Sept 18. Hungary took one more step toward the West today when it became the first Communist nation to restore ties with Israel. Relations between the two countries were broken after the 1967 Arab-Israeli war. At a brief ceremony, Israeli Foreign Minister Moshe Arens said he expected his country would be able to help Hungary improve economic relations with the West. The United States took a step in that direction today, announcing it would negotiate a "comprehensive" business agreement with Hungary.

Hugo's horrible legacy

Wading down main street: Puerto Rico took the brunt of Hugo's fury.

As if huddling against the storm, boats on the coast lie blown into one mass.

Sept 22. Hurricane Hugo, the most destructive storm to hit the United States in 20 years, tore across the South Carolina and North Carolina coasts just after midnight yesterday. At least 10 people are feared dead and property damage is expected to climb into the millions.

Residents of Puerto Rico and other Caribbean islands are still reeling from Hugo's initial landing Sept. 17. Twenty-six people are reported killed on the eight largest islands, but radio and telephone damage has made accurate estimates scarce. Tourists in St. Croix report a lack of fresh water and mass looting by island residents. Uniformed National Guardsmen have also been seen robbing homes and stores. On Sept. 20, President Bush declared the Virgin Islands a disaster area and promised financial assistance to the region.

The people of Charleston, S.C., and Charlotte, N.C., huddled today in high schools and other public buildings to escape the 135-mph winds. High tide and winds combined to send 17-foot walls of water crashing over coastal homes. Boats were tossed from their moorings onto highways. In the fishing town of McClellanville, S.C., people seeking refuge in the local high school were forced to stand on tables and hoist children onto their shoulders when flood waters rushed in.

By 6 a.m., Hugo had slowed to 50 mph. Reclassified a tropical storm, it headed inland on a northwesterly course.

Sept 20. *A USAir 737 rests in the East River following an aborted takeoff from La Guardia Airport that killed two and injured many. Reports indicate that the pilot and co-pilot had little experience flying 737s.*

Su	Mo	Tu	We	Th	Fr	Sa
					1	2
3	4	5	6	7	8	9
10	11	12	13	14	15	16
17	18	19	20	21	22	23
24	25	26	27	28	29	30

24. New York City: *Seventeen* magazine survey finds most American teen-agers lose virginity by age 17.

25. Cambodia: Last of Vietnamese troops withdraw, ending 10-year occupation (→ 30).

25. Washington, D.C.: Doris Day Animal League, with 310,000 members, begins national boycott of Procter & Gamble to protest cosmetics testing on animals.

26. Washington, D.C.: Senate trims $800 million from Star Wars budget.

26. Washington, D.C.: Transportation Department reports half of nation's rural bridges are unsafe.

26. Athens: Prominent Greek politician Pavlos Bakoyannis is killed by leftist guerrillas.

26. Washington, D.C.: Keith Jackson, 18, is arrested for selling the crack that President Bush used as prop for Sept. 5 televised announcement of new anti-drug plan.

27. Washington, D.C.: Joint U.S.-Canadian report claims Canada has become major money laundering center.

27. Tusayan, Ariz.: Sight-seeing plane crashes while touring Grand Canyon; 10 die.

28. Washington, D.C.: United States informs Israel it plans to sell 300 tanks to Saudi Arabia.

29. Los Angeles: Largest American drug seizure ever nets huge amount of cocaine and $10 million in cash.

29. Lithuania: Legislature calls on Moscow to allow Lithuanian military recruits to serve only in Lithuania amid reports of torture and sexual abuse.

30. Minsk, U.S.S.R.: Thousands of Byelorussians march, urging further cleanup at site of Chernobyl nuclear accident.

30. Cambodia: Non-communist guerrillas claim to have captured three towns, largest conquest since withdrawal of Vietnamese troops (→ Oct 22).

DEATH

30. Virgil Thomson, American composer (*Nov. 15, 1896).

Deposed Philippine President dies in exile

Imelda received mourners in her Honolulu home, offering a Philippine buffet.

Sept 29. The man who for 20 years ruled the Philippines with an iron hand and a greedy fist is gone. Ferdinand Marcos died yesterday in exile in Honolulu of kidney, lung and heart ailments. He was 72 years old. The current Philippine President, Corazon Aquino, says she will not allow Marcos's body to be returned to Manila for burial.

A tough autocrat with a flair for the dramatic, Marcos imposed martial law on the Philippines from 1972 to 1981, before being deposed in 1986. He was a staunch ally of the United States. After becoming a trial lawyer in Manila, he served his country as a much-decorated officer in World War II. At the war's end, Marcos rose steadily in government, serving as a member of both the Philippine House of Representatives and the Senate. A convert to the Nationalist Party, he won election as President in 1965 and again in 1969. Marcos began his tenure with vast popular support, and gradually lost nearly all of it amid rampant corruption.

The beginning of the end came with the 1985 slaying of political rival Benigno Aquino Jr., whose martyrdom eventually catapulted his widow into the presidency. A civilian panel found Marcos guilty of masterminding the assassination.

His wife, Imelda, was criticized for outrageous spending habits, and both have been accused of robbing the government treasury. Mrs. Marcos is now on trial, accused of defrauding the U.S. government.

Sept 25. *A gory encounter at the annual French festival, Feria de Nimes.*

President calls for chemical arms cuts

Sept 25. President Bush received only polite applause today after telling the United Nations that the United States would destroy 80 percent of its chemical weapons. Bush said it was time to "rid the earth of this scourge," but added that America will act only if the Soviet Union also agrees to reduce its stockpile. Most of the delegates found Bush's praise for the flowering of Soviet democracy to be sorely lacking in substance. This is in sharp contrast to the enthusiastic reception given Soviet leader Mikhail Gorbachev when he announced cuts in conventional forces last year.

Philippine killings

Sept 27. Two American civilian employees of Camp O'Donnell, a U.S. air base in the Philippines, were shot to death today hours before the arrival of Vice President Dan Quayle on a state visit. According to Filipino police, the victims' car was blocked by a dump truck while six men riddled them with bullets. The assailants are believed to have been leftist guerrillas. Earlier in the day, a member of President Corazon Aquino's presidential guard was killed by gunmen just a mile from the presidential palace.

Quayle is in Manila to discuss the volatile issue of U.S. bases in the Philippines. Just hours before his arrival, protesters burned a flag and the vice president's effigy, shouting, "Bases out. Quayle go home!"

Senate odd couple

Sept 26. Politics makes strange bedfellows, but this pairing has even insiders scratching their pates. Sen. Jesse Helms (R-N.C.), long-time enemy of civil-rights legislation, has announced that joining his staff is James Meredith, 58, the black man who burst through the race barrier at the University of Mississippi in 1962. It seems that Meredith has made a U-turn; he now calls integration "the biggest con job ever pulled on anybody." He sent Helms some fan letters, the two became pals, and now the ex-activist has a new job.

Former HUD head Pierce takes 5th

Sept 26. It sounded like a replay from a bygone era. But this was no ''Red'' refusing to answer questions posed by a congressional panel. It was ex-Housing Department head Sam Pierce earning his nickname by exercising his Fifth Amendment rights. Three other officials besides ''Silent Sam'' have already opted to stay mum as Congress pursues the trail of wrongdoing that leads to Pierce's desk. At a closed hearing, the onetime federal prosecutor and New York State judge refused to answer eight detailed queries put to him by Rep. Tom Lantos (D-Calif.), who chairs the special panel.

House votes for cut in capital gains tax

Sept 28. The House of Representatives today approved a decrease in the capital gains tax, one of the cornerstones of President Bush's election campaign last year. The vote, a feather in the presidential hat, was not as close as the atmosphere in the House might have indicated. After all the arguing was done, 239 voted for the cut and 190 voted against it in favor of a Democratic alternative reintroducing IRAs. The capital gains cut would apply to income from the sale of real estate, stocks and bonds. It would be of greatest benefit to those in high income brackets (→ Nov 2).

East Germans in Prague, Warsaw freed

The West German Embassy in Prague, doubling as a campground.

Hollywood hunts for new nasty villains

Sly Stallone, in Rambo III, *left communists alone and went after terrorists.*

When strongman Manuel Noriega finally abandons his political aspirations, he might look for work in Hollywood. Film writers, surrounded by an increasingly democratic, kinder and gentler world, have difficulty creating bad guys these days, and the drug smuggler-cum-general just might be the inspiration they need.

Indeed, cocaine kingpins and other drug lords have been featured in many recent films, among them *Tequila Sunrise, Extreme Prejudice* and the latest James Bond picture, *License to Kill.* The enemies of yesteryear — Russian communists and Mafiosi — are no longer menacing enough; in fact, they often make

appearances as good guys. Glasnost gives us Arnold Schwarzenegger as a benign Russian detective in *Red Heat,* and *Saturday Night Live* spoofs of *The Godfather* have prepared us for Peter Falk's lovable Mafia pater in *Cookie.*

Hollywood's search for the uniquely and unequivocally nasty perhaps manifests itself best in the box office hit *Lethal Weapon 2,* starring Danny Glover and Mel Gibson. In that film, the bad guys are not just drug dealers but also white South African government officials. As long as apartheid and drug wars repel and fascinate the public, film writers will find work — with or without Noriega.

Sept 30. Thousands of East Germans who have been camping out in the West German embassies in Prague and Warsaw got an unexpected reprieve today when the East German government gave them permission to emigrate. The foreign minister in East Berlin said the act was a ''humanitarian gesture.'' One refugee said it was ''like Christmas and Easter'' at once. In fact, the liberation comes as something of a relief for the government of Erich Honecker as well. The summer-long occupation of the embassy compounds loomed as a major embarrassment for East Germany, which is preparing for an international celebration of its 40th anniversary next week.

According to a pact negotiated by the two Germanys, the refugees will be taken by train across East Germany to Hof, West Germany. Under the terms of the accord, they will be treated as legal emigrants, not fugitives. This is important since they will travel through East Germany, where they could be prosecuted for violating a law prohibiting ''flight from the republic.'' Aboard the trains, the hopeful travelers will give up their identity cards and receive documents verifying their legal exit as emigrants.

Before leaving the Prague embassy, many refugees filled plastic buckets with East German and Czechoslovak coins and bills for the West German Red Cross, which supplied food, tents, and medical aid over a total of 11 weeks (→ Oct 3).

Braque's Castle at La Roche-Guyon *and Picasso's* Woman in an Armchair, *in ''Pioneering Cubism,'' at New York's Museum of Modern Art.*

OCTOBER

1989

Su	Mo	Tu	We	Th	Fr	Sa
1	2	3	4	5	6	7
8	9	10	11	12	13	14
15	16	17	18	19	20	21
22	23	24	25	26	27	28
29	30	31				

1. Beijing: People's Republic of China celebrates 40th year, but high security bars citizens from Tiananmen Square (→ 10).

2. Washington, D.C.: House panel votes unanimously for bill to apply same strict auto emission controls as California.

2. Houston: Texas State Supreme Court rules financing of state schools unconstitutional due to "glaring disparities" between rich and poor districts.

2. Brighton, England: Labor Party, in attempt to broaden appeal, votes to reverse its long-standing support of unilateral nuclear disarmament.

2. Rome: Talks between Pope and Archbishop of Canterbury on reunifying two churches founder on Anglican policy of allowing women in clergy.

3. Prague: Czechoslovakia permits 11,000 East Germans to flee to West, then shuts its borders; East Germans outside West German Embassy scale compound walls in panic (→ 7).

3. Ramla, Israel: Israeli peace activist Abie Nathan given six months in prison for meeting with Yasir Arafat (→ Nov 16).

3. Washington, D.C.: Under pressure from Congress, administration says it will not let CIA play a role in upcoming Nicaraguan elections (→ 10).

3. Moscow: In defiance of Gorbachev, Soviet legislature votes to place limits, but not total ban, on labor strikes.

4. Washington, D.C.: Lebanese hijacker Fawaz Yunis given 30 years in jail for 1985 hijacking of Jordanian jetliner.

5. Oslo, Norway: Dalai Lama is awarded Nobel Peace Prize.

5. Hollywood: Panel of experts rates *Raging Bull* best movie of 1980s.

7. U.S.S.R.: En route to Korea, Pope sends Gorbachev a greeting; first time a pope has been allowed in Soviet airspace (→ Dec 1).

7. East Berlin: East Germans hold 40th anniversary celebrations under such tight control that most citizens cannot attend festivities (→ 13).

Hungarian Communists adopt a new label

Oct 7. Can a Communist party win free multiparty elections? With the embarrassing results of the Soviet and Polish elections in mind, the Hungarian Communists evidently decided the answer was no. So, with their own free elections only a few months away, delegates at an extraordinary party congress today approved a radical reform. They will rename themselves the Hungarian Socialist Party, and adopt an ideological position somewhere between doctrinaire Marxism and European democratic socialism. Prime Minister Miklos Nemeth, sounding like a true campaign manager, said of the party's new philosophy, "We don't want members, we want voters" (→ 18).

Delegates give their party a facelift.

Oldest known rocks found in Canada

Oct 4. Scientists have uncovered chunks of granite in northern Canada that may be the oldest rocks ever found. Dr. Samuel Bowring, who led the research team, estimates the rocks to be 3.96 billion years old. "There is nothing about these rocks that looks any different or says old rocks," explains Dr. Bowring, but according to the National Science Foundation, they are 100 million years older than any previously found. Dr. Bowring now predicts that the region's rocks may even date back 4.1 billion years.

Hollywood legend Bette Davis dies at 81

Oct 6. The often impersonated, always inimitable Bette Davis died in a French hospital tonight of breast cancer. She was 81. "Fasten your seat belts; it's going to be a bumpy night," her character Margo Channing had warned in the classic film *All About Eve*. Davis might have been referring to her own life. Among the "ups" were two Oscars (for *Dangerous* and *Jezebel*) as well as 10 nominations. But each of her four marriages ran into turbulence, and a daughter accused her of alcoholism. Davis once said she had been called "indestructible" — and she approved.

Bette Davis' eyes are forever closed.

Bakker is convicted of shearing flock

Oct 5. Disgrace turned into damnation today as federal court jurors in Charlotte, N.C., found television preacher Jim Bakker guilty on all 24 counts of fraud and conspiracy. During his days as head of the PTL (Praise The Lord) Ministry, the court decided, the evangelist bilked followers out of $158 million.

Bakker's setback underscores the hard times that have hit Jerry Falwell, Pat Robertson and other video messengers of God. Last year the Assemblies of God defrocked Jimmy Swaggart after his affair with a prostitute, and the Internal Revenue Service has rained audits down upon 23 other ministries (→ 24).

Atlantans re-elect Maynard Jackson

Oct 4. Maynard H. Jackson, mayor of Atlanta from 1974 to 1982, has been re-elected. The 51-year-old black lawyer returns to office with a landslide victory, polling over 79 percent of the vote. A controversial figure, Jackson alienated the white elite during his first two terms. But this time around, he toned down his combative image and received significant support from white voters, who comprise less than 40 percent of the city's population. Jackson's success running as a moderate may bode well for black candidates seeking election in November in New York City and Virginia (→ Nov 7).

Oct 6. *The AIDS quilt, a patchwork monument to the disease's victims, is on display for the last time in Washington, D.C. A gruesome reminder of the toll of AIDS, it has grown too large to show in its entirety.*

William Hurt wins a palimony battle

Oct 3. Actor William Hurt, who had memorable roles in *The Big Chill* and *Broadcast News*, completed his most stirring performance tonight when a New York judge ruled in his favor in a common-law marriage case. Hurt's former lover Sandra Jennings lost her suit for support payments when Judge Jacqueline Silbermann decided that the couple had not been married under South Carolina's common-law marriage statutes. The pair lived together for a few months, and Jennings has raised their 6-year-old boy. Her attorney accused the judge of being blinded by Hurt's shining Hollywood image.

Panama's Noriega survives coup; Washington admits active role

Oct 5. Aides to President Bush today admitted that the United States military played an active role in this week's military coup against Panamanian leader Manuel Noriega. The attempt by Panamanian dissidents to oust Noriega — the second in 18 months — nearly succeeded. The rebels, led by at least two of the general's closest military advisers, stormed into central military headquarters and for two hours held Noriega captive. But loyalist troops won Noriega's release and regained control of the army station.

Initially, President Bush said American forces stationed in Panama were in no way involved in the uprising. But now, White House officials admit that the U.S. Army barricaded roads to block any advance by troops loyal to Noriega, as requested by rebel leaders.

Noriega has transformed from a political ally of George Bush to one of his most hated enemies. Many believe the dictator's ruthless tactics and known involvement in the international drug trade should have precipitated an even larger role for U.S. troops. Sen. Jesse Helms (R-N.C.) blasted the administration for what he perceived as a botched effort, calling the officials in charge "Keystone Kops." While that characterization may seem harsh, evidence suggests that communication between the U.S. Army and the rebels broke down, allowing loyalists to regroup (→ 8).

Noriega celebrates his triumph, attended by a vigilant soldier from one of his loyal Dignity Battalions.

Butter meltdown strikes in Maryland

Oct 3. It was hardly a nuclear meltdown, but the disaster that struck Cambridge, Md., today has had far-reaching, and messy, consequences. Five million pounds of butter melted into a gooey fondue when a warehouse fire broke out, testing the skills of more than 300 firefighters, who battled for 21 hours to control the blaze while struggling for footing on a floor slick enough for a Paul Bunyan flapjack. Poland and the Soviet Union may not see the humor; both countries were awaiting shipment of the butter.

FBI seeking spies via the want ads

Oct 6. "Wanted: one brave comrade willing to snitch on another comrade . . ." Although it doesn't word its advertisement quite this way, the Federal Bureau of Investigation's want ad, which started running today in New York's Russian-language newspaper *Novoye Russkoye Slovo*, does indeed solicit the services of would-be spies. The director of New York's FBI office, James Fox, stated that not every former Soviet citizen will qualify, and that he will have to turn down a few KGB "ringers and plants."

NFL has first black head coach since '20s

Art Shell, the new Raider coach.

Oct 3. Hall of Famer Art Shell will be the National Football League's first black head coach since the 1920s. He was named today to be field boss of the Los Angeles Raiders, the team he played for throughout his pro career. The former all-pro defensive tackle was promoted to succeed Mike Shanahan, who had been coach since the start of last season. The NFL's last black head coach was Fritz Pollard, who led the Hammond, Ind., Pros in 1923-25, before the league stabilized. The NFL thus becomes the final major sports league to name a black to the top post on the field.

Gay couples recognized in Copenhagen

Oct 1. In a shower of rice and confetti, six homosexual couples took vows of fidelity today in Copenhagen and became the first legally recognized gay partners in the world. The civil ceremonies, sanctioned in May by a 71-47 vote in Parliament, endowed these "registered partnerships" with virtually all the rights and responsibilities of married heterosexual couples. They are not, however, recognized by the Danish People's Church, which is Evangelical Lutheran and serves 90 percent of Denmark's population. Nor can the couples adopt or obtain joint custody of a child. This last point troubles Danish lesbians, none of whom took part in the ceremonies.

Oct 4. *"He wasn't a horse. He was Secretariat," said one loving fan. And he will never race again. The 1973 Triple Crown winner, arguably the finest race horse in 40 years, was put to sleep today due to a painful hoof disease.*

United, with the sanction of the state.

OCTOBER
1989

Su	Mo	Tu	We	Th	Fr	Sa
1	2	3	4	5	6	7
8	9	10	11	12	13	14
15	16	17	18	19	20	21
22	23	24	25	26	27	28
29	30	31				

8. Washington, D.C.: Federal health experts find life expectancy of whites continuing to rise, yet dropping for blacks, as AIDS, drugs and alcohol take their toll.

8. Panama: Noriega orders execution of leaders of last week's failed coup (→ Nov 17).

9. Washington, D.C.: U.S. charges that Soviet military advisers are still fighting in Afghanistan, manning SCUD missile installations (→ 23).

10. Tallahassee, Fla.: State legislature rebuffs move to curb abortion rights (→ 11).

10. Beijing: Communist Party announces General Secretary Jiang Zemin will become supreme leader after Deng Xiaoping steps down (→ 30).

10. Nicaragua: Soviet cuts in aid to Sandinistas, announced by Foreign Minister Shevardnadze on recent visit, are said to be having an effect already (→ 21).

10. Victoria, Texas: Bodies of four illegal aliens found in trailer filled with fumigated flour.

10. Forked River, N.J.: Three of Donald Trump's top executives killed in helicopter crash.

11. Baku, U.S.S.R.: Azerbaijan Communist Party signs pact with nationalist Popular Front of Azerbaijan in effort to bring peace to the republic.

12. Washington, D.C.: State Department says it will reverse itself and begin hiring blind people as Foreign Service officers on case-by-case basis.

12. Palo Alto, Calif.: Stanford scientists announce they have concluded the universe is composed of only three basic types of matter, angering rival European researchers who were to release findings tomorrow.

13. Washington, D.C.: Reversing a nine-year policy, Bush administration announces it will let FBI seize U.S. fugitives in foreign countries without permission of host nation (→ 17).

14. San Francisco: Federal appeals court rules police can't search body cavities of people arrested on felony charges.

Shades of 1987: Dow plunges 190 points

Oct. 13. Friday the 13th brought the specter of 1987 to Wall Street today as the Dow Jones industrial average fell 190 points in less than an hour. Today's trading was a pale rerun of Oct. 19, 1987, which saw the Dow take its worst plunge in history, dropping 508 points in one afternoon. Most Wall Street executives quickly dismissed the eerie likeness of the dates as coincidence and urged investors not to panic. Treasury Secretary Nicholas F. Brady told the press, "Today's decline . . . should be viewed in the context of a 591-point rise since Jan. 1, 1989." Analysts attributed the market freefall to overspeculation and extravagant stock pricing in relation to corporate earnings (→ 16).

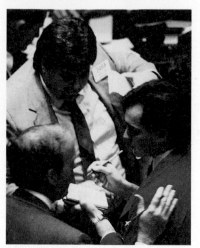

Concerned looks becloud the faces of Stock Exchange traders as the market makes its precipitous plunge.

Iowa cornfield yields missing DC-10 part

The missing piece is harvested.

Oct. 11. An Iowa farmer harvesting her fall corn crop has discovered what may be the key to last June's DC-10 crash in Sioux City, which killed 112 people. Janice Sorenson was driving her combine when it struck the United plane's 200-pound rotor fan disk. According to Jerry Clark, an investigator for the engine's builder, General Electric, the disk "will fill in the answers, as far as what precipitated the engine failure." G.E. officials believe that other engine parts may be found by local farmers. Mrs. Sorenson will receive a $50,000 reward for her fortunate discovery.

Canadian Mounties allow turban tops

Oct. 13. As part of an effort to recruit from Canada's growing Sikh community, the Royal Canadian Mounted Police have decided to allow the Indians to wear their turbans. In doing so they have raised a firestorm of controversy. The Mounties have traditionally topped their striking red uniforms with brown ranger hats, and Parliament member Barbara Sparrow says the hat should be preserved because "Canada has so little heritage left to protect." But Sikh spokesman Kulvinder Singh says the insistence on traditional dress is nothing more than "an excuse for racism."

Hispanic-Americans number 20 million

Oct. 11. The Census Bureau announced today that the Hispanic population of the United States has passed the 20 million mark, a 39 percent increase since 1980. Hispanics numbered 14.5 million as the 1980s began, but waves of legal and illegal migration have swelled that group from 6.5 percent of the nation's population to 8.2 percent. There is considerable debate in Congress as to whether the 1990 census should include illegal aliens. Bureau officials, whose statistics will be used for reapportioning federal funds, say they do not have the means to distinguish between legal and illegal immigrants.

Soviets now have new ethnic minority

Oct. 9. Tourism is on the rise in the Soviet Union, but things may be getting out of hand: Tass, the official Soviet news agency, reports that the town of Voronezh has just been visited by towering extraterrestrials. Apparently, witnesses saw "a banana-shaped object in the sky," and were "overwhelmed with a fear that lasted for several days." The aliens landed, promenaded their knobby little heads around a park, and left. "It is a serious dispatch," insisted one Tass official. Would the party's paper lie?

Oct. 13. *Students of the "Anti-American Crusade" undergo questioning in Seoul after vandalizing the home of U.S. Ambassador Donald Gregg. On the table are national flags, banners and petrol bombs captured by police.*

Palme murder suspect is freed by court

Christer Pettersson, just acquitted for the murder of Prime Minister Palme.

Oct 13. An appeals court in Stockholm today freed a 42-year-old drifter, drug addict and ex-convict who had been found guilty of the 1986 slaying of Swedish Prime Minister Olof Palme. The court cited a lack of evidence in the recent conviction and cleared Christer Pettersson of all charges, dealing a blow to authorities who had spent more than two years looking for the assassin. The main witness for the state was Palme's widow, Lisbeth, who picked Pettersson out of a videotaped police lineup. But a superintendent on the force admitted that when he first interviewed the "completely hysterical" Mrs. Palme, just after the killing, she "could not give any description of the killer."

Political winds begin to blow pro-choice

Oct 11. The debate on abortion, the most divisive social issue in America, has shifted from the streets in front of clinics and courthouses to the floors of state legislatures and the United States Congress.

Today, the House voted 216-206 to allow the use of federal money to fund abortions for poor women who become pregnant from rape or incest. The new bill is seen as a policy reversal and is the legislators' second recent move in favor of abortion rights. Last week, the House voted to approve the District of Columbia's budget, which included provisions to fund abortions for poor women.

On the state level, legislators in Florida yesterday rejected an appeal by Gov. Bob Martinez for tighter restrictions on abortion. Anti-abortion groups have vowed to mount a drive to elect candidates who oppose legal abortion. Ken Connor, head of Right to Life, told supporters, "In 1990, you'll have the right to choose. We want you to choose life. Put the Florida legislators under a microscope."

Abortion is already an election issue for several candidates in major campaigns, including the gubernatorial races in New Jersey and Virginia. Although it's too early to tell, it seems pro-choice candidates hold the edge. Rep. Les AuCoin from Oregon said, "The pro-choice side is active, they're making themselves felt at the ballot box" (→ 17).

Tutu, de Klerk talk about nation's fate

Oct 11. Three South African clergymen, including Archbishop Desmond Tutu, met today with F.W. de Klerk, President of the country's white government, to discuss the possibility of discussing broad-scale political change at a later date. The three-hour meeting focused on a list of reforms demanded by black leaders as a precondition to negotiations. The list was drawn up by the African National Congress, and if made into policy, would free the political voice of the nation's black majority (→ 15).

Oct 10. *New York City, home of Madison Avenue, hosts a unique promotion for the opera,* Aida.

Syrian visitor confounds Israeli military

This Syrian MiG 23 had no trouble penetrating Israeli airspace and landing.

Oct 12. Workers at a small crop-duster air strip near Meggido, Israel, were stunned yesterday when a Syrian pilot in a MiG-23 landed, got out of his plane, said in Arabic, "I have no hostile intentions," and asked for political asylum. Israel has offered no reason for the defection, and Syria claims the pilot made an emergency landing due to mechanical problems. It is not known how Maj. Adel Bassem, 34, flew 50 miles into Israeli territory without interception, a fact which has upset military officials enough for an investigation to be launched.

Educators urge liberal arts core in colleges

Oct 8. The education establishment has once again decided that Americans are fast on the road to ignorance. According to a recent Gallup Poll, over 40 percent of college seniors could not place the Civil War in time, and 25 percent failed to distinguish between the ideas in the American Constitution and those of Karl Marx. With the Cold War waning, this may not seem such a tragedy, but the National Endowment for the Humanities has sprung into action. Today, it urged colleges to institute a required 50-hour liberal arts core curriculum. The plan is to replace the 20-year tradition of hollow electives with a rigorous program in literature, philosophy, and, of course, history.

East German leader calls for changes

Oct 13. The leader of one of Eastern Europe's most hard-line Communist states has tentatively acknowledged a need to alter his nation's course. East German leader Erich Honecker said today that the Central Committee would make proposals "to the whole people" to reform the current policies on economic efficacy, consumer goods and travel. Coming only a week after he declared his government on the right path, Honecker's statement seems a direct result of a mass exodus of East Germans (→ 18).

Oct 14. *As F.W. de Klerk continues reforms, activists across South Africa press for the release of black leader Nelson Mandela.*

Su	Mo	Tu	We	Th	Fr	Sa
1	2	3	4	5	6	7
8	9	10	11	12	13	14
15	16	17	18	19	20	21
22	23	24	25	26	27	28
29	30	31				

16. Washington, D.C.: Secretary of State Baker says U.S. is willing to give technical aid to ailing Soviet economy (→ 31).

17. Washington, D.C.: President Bush announces he will veto bill that would publicly fund abortions for victims of rape and incest (→ Nov 9).

17. United Nations: For first time, Soviets abstain rather than vote with Arab nations to oust Israel from U.N.

18. Budapest: Hungary's Parliament revamps constitution, adding basic law requiring multi-party system (→ 20).

18. New York City: Cuba, Rumania and South Yemen elected to United Nations Security Council.

18. Pittsburgh: Researchers at University of Pittsburgh have found new drug that reverses organ rejection in transplants.

19. Washington, D.C.: In defeat for Bush, Senate, 51-48, rejects constitutional amendment to ban flag-burning.

19. Washington, D.C.: House votes three-year, $837.5 million aid package for Poland and Hungary aimed at developing free market (→ Nov 10).

19. Moscow: Brezhnev-era editor of *Pravda* is replaced by Ivan T. Frolov, a close aide of Soviet leader Gorbachev.

20. Budapest: A day after legalizing all opposition parties, Parliament votes to disband Communist Party militia (→ 23).

20. New York City: Congressman Robert Garcia, leading Hispanic lawmaker, and wife are convicted of extortion and conspiracy in Wedtech scandal.

21. Washington, D.C.: Pentagon report calls for end to ban on gays in U.S. military.

21. Nicaragua: Contras attack convoy of Sandinista troops, killing 18 (→ 28).

21. Honduras: Honduran 727 explodes in flight, killing as many as 144.

DEATH

20. Sir Anthony Quayle, one of Britain's leading actors and producers (*July 9, 1913).

GDR hard-liner Honecker out; Krenz in

Oct 18. East Germany's leadership has a new face today, though its personality is expected to remain the same. Ailing leader Erich Honecker, 77, was forced to resign in the wake of growing popular demands for reform. The Central Committee appointed his 52-year-old protege Egon Krenz as the new party leader. Krenz, who was the Politburo member in charge of security and youth, is said to share his mentor's hard-line approach to reform. For example, he has been outspoken in his support of China's crackdown on dissent. However, Krenz did promise in a televised speech tonight that, within certain bounds, "the door is wide open for earnest political dialogue" (→ Nov 4).

Egon Krenz, harbinger of change?

ANC chief Sisulu and 7 others released

Sisulu, walking free after 26 years.

Oct 15. "It was not possible to despair because the spirit of the people outside was too great." Thus spoke Walter Sisulu, former secretary general of the African National Congress, after his release from 26 years of confinement in a South African jail. He and seven other key political prisoners were freed today by President F.W. de Klerk, only a day after protests by 150,000 people hit over a dozen cities across the country. Nelson Mandela is said to have played an important role in the release of his fellow prisoners; they, in turn, called for his freedom as soon as they had their own (→ 29).

Rich-man's sport in a proletarian paradise

Oct 15. The "Lenin links" may sound like a secret arm of the KGB. But this is the Gorbachev era, and the links are actually nine holes in the middle of Moscow — 2,600 yards long and par 34. The Swedish investors who built the course hope it will become a key place for Western executives and diplomats to entertain their Soviet counterparts. While strolling across the green or dining in the clubhouse, the powerful putters will shape the post-Cold War world. Asked about golf's aristocratic image, one Muscovite noted that the Soviets already play baseball — capitalist America's national pastime. But with glasnost in the air, this is all par for the course.

Sean Connery, ready to tee off.

Galileo space probe sent off to Jupiter

Oct 18. It was clear skies and clear sailing this morning as the space shuttle Atlantis lifted off — after two postponements earlier this week — and embarked on a six-year, 2.5 billion-mile voyage to Jupiter. Thus began "the second golden age in the exploration of the solar system," in the words of a NASA spokesman. Scientists were just as elated by the long-delayed resumption of the mission to probe the atmosphere of the largest planet. The spacecraft Galileo will orbit Jupiter for at least 22 months and zoom in close to its four biggest moons, all the while recording data and taking highly detailed photos.

Atlantis takes off at Cape Canaveral.

Bush administration looks to unbind CIA

Oct 17. Despite the shadow cast on covert action by the Iran-contra affair, the Bush adminstration now claims the CIA is overly restricted. At issue is a 1976 executive order barring U.S. involvement in assassinations. CIA Director William Webster complains that U.S. advisers were unable to sufficiently support leaders of the recent coup in Panama because of the possibility that Noriega would be killed. Attempts to revise the order, however, may meet resistance in Congress. As Sen. William Cohen (R-Maine) says, "I don't want it to be open season on political enemies."

Gorbachev tries to oust defiant editor

Oct 17. Glasnost has its limits, as the editor of the Soviet Union's best-selling newspaper found out today. Vladislav A. Starkov, editor of *Argumenty i Fakty,* has been asked to resign for printing a poll that angered Soviet leader Mikhail S. Gorbachev. The offending poll ranked the members of the Soviet Parliament based on some 15,000 letters from readers. The top ratings went to legislators who have been critical of Gorbachev. Analysts speculated that Gorbachev may be growing concerned at the number of irreverent and critical articles being published. Starkov said he would not resign without a fight.

Justice speaks for "Afro-Americans"

Oct 16. Supreme Court Justice Thurgood Marshall has written a dissenting opinion in which he refers to Americans of African descent as "Afro-Americans." He is the first member of the court to use this term. The 81-year-old justice says he spent most of his life fighting to get Negro spelled with a capital "N," but then, "people started saying black and I never liked it." This usage is not an official ruling, says Justice Marshall. "It's like the old lady said when she kissed the cow — everyone to his own liking."

Bulls come charging back on Wall Street

Oct 16. The bulls came roaring back today, led by the blue-chip stocks, as the market regained almost half of what it lost last Friday. The Dow Jones industrial average gained 88 points, a 3.4 percent comeback against the 6.9 percent drop that ended last week's frantic selling spree.

Following a wobbly opening, the free-fall was stopped by the aggressive acquisitions of corporations that chose to buy back their own shares, and by institutions that bought stocks at bargain-basement prices. Overseas markets also rebounded healthily today.

Massive earthquake rocks Bay Area

Oct 21. It was not the "Big One" that California has feared, but the earthquake that struck the San Francisco Bay Area Tuesday was terrifying enough. At 5:04 p.m., the 15-second quake, measuring a powerful 6.9 on the Richter scale, shuddered through San Francisco, Oakland and Santa Cruz. Tremors were felt as far north as Sacramento and as far south as Los Angeles, the epicenter falling 10 miles northeast of Santa Cruz on the San Andreas Fault. There were 3,000 injuries, damages estimated at between $1 billion and $3 billion, and electrical outages affecting a million people.

As the week drew to a close, however, officials lowered their estimated death toll of 270. Fewer cars than guessed were found under a collapsed section of Interstate 880, where rush hour traffic had been racing along when the quake hit. Huge slabs of concrete buckled and fell, flattening some of the cars to a height of six inches. One 6-year-old boy, trapped under the body of his mother, had to have his right leg amputated before he could be freed. Nearly 90 hours later, in another miraculous rescue, Buck Helm, a 57-year-old longshoreman, was pulled from the wreckage in critical but stable condition.

Elsewhere in the Bay Area, newly erected skyscrapers wavered but stood, while older buildings crumbled to the ground. Homes in the Marina district tumbled, leaving thousands homeless. Broken gas mains ignited an inferno that took hours to contain. Traffic has been slowed to a crawl by the closure of the Oakland Bay Bridge, where a 30-foot upper section rippled and slid onto the lower level.

Having declared seven Northern California counties a disaster area, President Bush toured San Francisco Friday and stated he "would do what is necessary" to help the region recover. Californians, though left with plenty of emotional scars, have pulled through with pluck. When the quake hit, 58,000 were packed into Candlestick Park for the third game of the World Series. A silence fell as the seats rocked, light towers swept from side to side, and the earth rumbled. When the tumult stopped, the crowd cheered the victors: themselves (→ 22).

Buildings were severely shaken . . .   *. . . part of the Bay Bridge fell*

. . . the Nimitz freeway buckled and collapsed, leaving dozens trapped

. . . and the Marina district in San Francisco burned long into the night.

OCTOBER
1989

Su	Mo	Tu	We	Th	Fr	Sa
1	2	3	4	5	6	7
8	9	10	11	12	13	14
15	16	17	18	19	20	21
22	23	24	25	26	27	28
29	30	31				

22. Lebanon: Parliament passes charter to end civil war that gives more power to Muslims and recognizes Syrian role in nation's affairs; Christians say they will ignore pact (→ Nov 5).

22. Cambodia: Khmer Rouge has captured district capital of Pailin (→ Nov 14).

23. Tehran: President Rafsanjani says Iran will seek release of hostages if U.S. helps solve case of three Iranians kidnapped in Lebanon or releases frozen Iranian assets (→ Nov 7).

23. Budapest: Acting President Matyas Szuros declares Republic of Hungary as tens of thousands jam Parliament Square for 33rd anniversary of 1956 revolt (→ Nov 26).

23. New York City: Forbes lists media mogul John Kluge — worth $5.2 billion — as richest man in U.S.

24. Washington, D.C.: Judge in ex-national security adviser John Poindexter's Iran-contra trial rules Reagan must turn over personal papers (→ Nov 21).

25. Washington, D.C.: Federal officials announce anti-AIDS drug AZT will now be available to children.

26. Washington, D.C.: U.S. charges Israel has been helping South Africa develop mid-range missile.

28. Prague: Police use violence and mass arrests to disperse 10,000 protesters demonstrating for democracy (→ 30).

29. Colombia: Top Medellin drug cartel official Jose Abello Silva is extradited to United States to stand trial (→ Nov 26).

29. South Africa: Government allows 70,000 to march against apartheid; largest protest in history of ANC (→ Nov 16).

30. New York City: Japanese firm Mitsubishi Estates Corp. has bought controlling shares in Rockefeller Center.

31. Washington, D.C.: President Bush announces he will meet Soviet leader Gorbachev at sea in December (→ Nov 14).

31. San Salvador: Bomb explodes at leftist union hall, killing eight people (→ Nov 12).

Shevardnadze confesses past Soviet sins

Oct 23. Soviet Foreign Minister Eduard Shevardnadze conceded today that the 1979 Soviet invasion of Afghanistan was an illegal act. "We committed the most serious violations of our own legislation, our party and civilian norms," Shevardnadze told the Soviet legislature in what was otherwise an upbeat report on Soviet foreign policy.

The foreign minister also admitted that the Krasnoyarsk radar station in Siberia is in "open violation" of the Anti-Ballistic Missile Treaty with the United States, a point that Washington has been making since the radar was first noticed in 1983. The Soviets agreed last month to dismantle the station.

The unusually candid speech is part of a foreign policy reassessment mandated by Soviet leader Mikhail Gorbachev. "The main thing is not to conceal, but to acknowledge and correct mistakes," explained Shevardnadze — especially when the mistakes are the

Shevardnadze: Soviet confessional.

legacy of a previous era. Afghanistan and Krasnoyarsk are the work of the late Soviet leader Leonid Brezhnev, who Gorbachev has criticized for overseeing a period of "stagnation" (→ Nov 8).

Californians survey earthquake damage

Oct 22. The earthquake of Oct. 17 claimed lives, inflicted injuries and destroyed homes. Yet the Bay Area has even more to worry about — or look forward to. In order to avoid bankruptcy, many local insurers may have to raise premiums sky high to cover the quake damage. Larger insurance firms, still smarting from Hurricane Hugo, anticipate the industry's worst quarter in this century. That is, assuming no worse quake is looming; in fact, seismologists predict there is a 50 percent chance of a quake 30 times more powerful striking the Bay Area by the year 2020. As for the World Series, which was so rudely interrupted, it will continue with game three on Friday Oct. 27 at San Francisco's Candlestick Park. Play ball! (→ Nov 16).

Oct 23. *Fire strikes a Pasadena, Texas, petrochemical plant; 20 missing.*

Jim Bakker arrives at day of reckoning

Oct 24. Wearing handcuffs, leg irons and a weak grin, Jim Bakker was escorted out of a courthouse in Charlotte, N.C., today and sent to a federal prison in Alabama. There he will begin serving the 45-year sentence given him by Judge Robert (Maximum Bob) Potter, who declared himself "sick of . . . money-grubbing preachers and priests." Bakker swindled $158 million from his TV ministry flock. A harsh sentence was expected, but Bakker's lawyer pleaded for his client to get only probation. "Order him to complete the dream," he suggested. Bakker will get his chance — in 10 years, when he's eligible for parole.

Jim Bakker goes from pulpit to prison, where he can perhaps show his cellmates the error of their ways.

Leading novelist Mary McCarthy dies

Oct 25. Novelist Mary McCarthy did not credit her prodigious career to her unhappy childhood; nor, she once commented, did she "believe that artistic talent flowers necessarily from a wounding of the stem on which it grows." However, when she died today in New York at age 77, McCarthy left a series of memoirs and essays that reflect a difficult life. Such works as *The Groves of Academe* (1952), *Memories of a Catholic Girlhood* (1957) and *The Group* (1963) were among many praised for their cool analyses of herself and her times.

Richard Nixon lays it on line in Beijing

Oct 30. Former President Richard Nixon today confronted Chinese leaders on their own turf about their brutal repression of last June's student demonstrations. In a banquet speech before Chinese Prime Minister Li Peng and other top officials, Nixon referred to the violence as a "tragedy" and urged the government not to plummet into the "backwater of oppression and stagnation." The remarks will likely sting the Chinese, as official reports deny that any tragedy occurred in Tiananmen Square.

Nixon opened the door to restoring Sino-American relations with his historic trip to China in 1972. But the United States suspended official visits there after the crackdown. Nixon is visiting as a private citizen, but he will brief President Bush when he returns (→ Nov 9).

Oakland A's sweep "Subway Series"

Oct 28. Oakland's A's completed a sweep of their cross-Bay rivals, the San Francisco Giants, today in the first Subway Series since the 1950s. But their joy was muted. The quake that hit 11 days ago, killing 64 and leaving thousands homeless, not only interrupted the series, but also put major sports events into perspective. The A's cut fireworks and champagne from the celebration.

Despite the quake, the A's celebrate.

Ortega cancels truce with contras; demands U.S. cut off aid

Oct 28. Nicaraguan President Daniel Ortega announced yesterday that his country is suspending the cease-fire with the Nicaraguan rebels, the contras. The announcement came just prior to a meeting of 16 Western Hemisphere leaders in Costa Rica, taking most of them, including President Bush, by surprise. Bush denounced Ortega's decision and hurled insults at him, referring to him as "a little man" and "an animal at a garden party."

According to Ortega, the rebels have made several attacks, killing dozens of Nicaraguans. "We are facing a terrorist offensive from a counterrevolution financed by the United States," he said, adding that the attacks are threatening national elections scheduled for February. Members of the U.S. Congress are also concerned that resumption of open war will endanger the elections. Costa Rican President Oscar Arias, co-author of the Contadora peace plan that led to the cease-fire,

Bush and Ortega in a chance encounter that Washington had tried to avoid. The photo, released by Managua, was withheld from the press by Bush officials.

called Ortega's move "lamentable."

Today, however, Ortega softened his rhetoric, saying he will adhere to the cease-fire if the United States stops assisting the contras. The Bush administration has not responded to this condition. Congress will decide next month whether or not to continue sending humanitarian aid to the contras (→ Nov 1).

Czech regime crushes protest march; won't follow East Berlin

Oct 30. Czechoslovakia's hardline Communist government has sent a clear signal to its people that reform movements will meet a colder response in Prague than in East Berlin, Warsaw and Budapest. More than 300,000 people marched peacefully in Leipzig, East Germany today, but their Czechoslovak neighbors have not fared so well. On Saturday, some 10,000 Czechoslovaks, calling for freedom and democracy, were dispersed with extreme force by the Prague police.

The unrest in Czechoslovakia comes less than a month after large-scale protest marches and a mass exodus forced the resignation of long-time East German leader Erich Honecker. His successor, Egon Krenz, this week declared an amnesty for all those who have fled to the West. Without East Berlin as its ally against reform, the Czech government is clearly jittery, isolated within the Warsaw Pact. The protesters appeared optimistic that upheavals would soon shake the top rungs of the party. Said one, the leadership "is as alone as a slat in a fence. The slat must go."

The government had tried to forestall today's march by rounding up leading dissidents, among them Vaclav Havel, a prominent writer and human rights advocate. Despite the arrests, some 10,000 people gathered in Wenceslas Square this morning and started chanting, "Freedom!" and "We Want Democracy." When the crowd refused to disperse, policemen stormed the protesters, beating them with clubs and dragging them into waiting buses. The square was cleared within 10 minutes; some 250 people were detained and an unreported number injured.

Although the government was clearly the day's victor, it still faces some awesome challenges. The protests will continue, and small parties traditionally aligned with the Communists have begun to raise their voices for reform (→ Nov 1).

Gunter Schabowski, party chief in East Berlin, worries about job security.

Su	Mo	Tu	We	Th	Fr	Sa
			1	2	3	4
5	6	7	8	9	10	11
12	13	14	15	16	17	18
19	20	21	22	23	24	25
26	27	28	29	30		

1. Managua: President Ortega formally breaks 19-month cease-fire with contras, calls for new peace talks (→ Dec 3).

1. Czechoslovakia: Hours after East German government lifts travel ban, thousands swarm in, fleeing to West (→ 21).

1. Washington, D.C.: House votes 382-37 to raise minimum wage to $4.25 by 1991.

2. Washington, D.C.: Senate Republicans give up fight to cut capital gains tax.

3. Washington, D.C.: Senate panel asks five senators if campaign contributions from Lincoln Savings & Loan of Irvine, Calif., affected decision to support bailout of firm (→ Dec 4).

4. East Berlin: One million East Germans rally, demanding strict curbs on power of Communist Party (→ 10).

5. Beirut: Lebanese Parliament elects popular Maronite Catholic figure, Rene Moawad, President of Lebanon (→ 24).

6. Washington, D.C.: Convicted crack dealer testifies he sold drugs to Mayor Marion Barry.

7. U.S.S.R.: Bolshevik anniversary celebrations marred by demonstrations; parades canceled in Georgia and Armenia.

7. Washington, D.C.: President Bush announces U.S. will release some frozen Iranian assets and hold others to pay debts to Americans.

8. Afghanistan: Afghan secret police, the Khad, admits killing 11,000 during Communist coup of late 1970s (→ 28).

9. Beijing: Deng Xiaoping resigns as chairman of Central Military Commission, his last Communist Party post; he is replaced by heir-apparent Jiang Zemin (→ Dec 9).

9. Washington, D.C.: After election losses, Republican Party officials say party should tolerate candidates who support abortion rights (→ Dec 10).

10. Bonn, West Germany: Chancellor Helmut Kohl cuts short a visit to Poland after signing accord to give Warsaw $1.9 billion in aid, top amount yet from West (→ 15).

Elections a triumph for moderate blacks

Dinkins is the new Hizzoner . . .

and Wilder squeaks by in Virginia.

Nov 7. Several black candidates swept to victory today in local and state elections in what may prove to be a watershed in American politics. In the more notable races, Democratic Manhattan Borough President David Dinkins narrowly defeated popular former prosecutor Rudolph Giuliani for mayor of New York City, and Douglas Wilder of Virginia appears to have eked out a spot as the nation's first elected black governor.

Shunning the rhetorical flourish and left-leaning stance of Jesse Jackson, today's victors, graying and avuncular, opted for images of moderacy and competence. While none of the winning candidates gained a majority of white votes, Dinkins, who praised his city as a "gorgeous mosaic," garnered 27 percent of the white vote.

Wilder, who attracted voters, white and black alike, by coming out strong in support of abortion rights, may have tilted the political battlefield in another way. Liberal candidates who have treated the issue like it a handgrenade will be encouraged to embrace a pro-choice stance. Wilder's Republican rival, who lost by only 5,000 votes, has insisted on a recount (→ 26).

Local councils to run Chicago schools

Nov 3. Education begins at home, it is said, and in Chicago, the home seems to be gaining a powerful role at school. In a radical decentralization plan, 5,400 parents, teachers and community representatives today took an oath to "represent the interests of our children's education with respect and dignity." In order to administer Chicago's 540 public schools, a 10-person council was elected for each school in a transfer of power from the central Board of Education. Each council is composed of six parents, two community representatives and two teachers, with the chairman drawn from the ranks of the parents.

O Presidente, live!

Silvio Santos, Brazil's most popular TV personality, has announced he will leave the studio for the campaign trail. The country's first democratic vote since 1960 will be held in two weeks, and Santos' presidential bid has full-time politicians concerned: every Sunday he hosts a 10-hour variety show, and the exposure makes him a familiar face in a race crowded with over 20 candidates. A recent poll placed Santos well ahead of former front-runner Fernando Collor de Mello (→ 16).

Horowitz, greatest pianist of 20th century, is dead at 85

At last year's Grammys, Horowitz is hailed for his Moscow performance.

Nov 5. Vladimir Horowitz, whose electrifying virtuosity at the keyboard and eccentricity in the public eye made him the most celebrated pianist of the 20th century, died suddenly today of a heart attack.

The 85-year-old Russian emigre for years had challenged critics with highly personal interpretations of the classics and frustrated fans by retiring four times from public performance. He capped his career in 1986 with an emotional return to the Soviet Union after a 61-year absence.

Horowitz always reveled in his eccentricities and championed the emotional content of music, counseling others to simply "play from the heart." "I am a 19th-century Romantic," said the master. "I am the last."

East Germany cracks Wall as old order crumbles

East Germans hold a buoyant celebration atop the Wall at the Brandenburg Gate, turning that most visible symbol of political tyranny into a dance floor.

Nov 10. The Berlin Wall has been the world's most visible symbol of Communist oppression since its creation 28 years ago. Suddenly last night its specter dissolved. At the stroke of midnight, the East German government opened its borders, and the wall — actually two 8-foot-high concrete barriers that slice through Berlin — was transformed into a benign relic of a Cold War that has passed into history.

Within hours, thousands of East Germans poured across the border, eager to test their freedom and see how the prosperous other half lives. Thousands more spent hours dancing in joy atop the wall. Others vented years of anger with pickaxes, some picking up the pieces to sell as souvenirs. Many just stood and wept, perhaps in memory of those who died trying to cross over, perhaps just in overwhelming awe.

West Germans gave their compatriots a joyful welcome. Speaking outside West Berlin's city hall, Chancellor Helmut Kohl promised, "We're on your side; we are and remain one nation. We belong together." For many in the West however, joy was tempered by concern over their ability to handle the flood of refugees — 225,000 from East Germany and 300,000 from the Soviet Union and Poland in this year alone. Said West Berlin's mayor to those considering coming West: "Please do it tomorrow, do it the day after tomorrow. We are having trouble dealing with this."

In fact, only 1,500 of the many thousands who visited West Berlin so far have announced their intention to stay. Those who return to the East will find their country in the throes of major changes. East German officials have announced plans for free elections and new laws on freedom of association and the press. Last week the 21-member Politburo was replaced.

It was only nine months ago that long-time East German leader Erich Honecker predicted the wall would remain standing for 100 years. And indeed, most Western analysts agreed with Honecker that Stalinist East Germany was not likely to be swept up in the changes convulsing Eastern Europe.

But the Honecker regime fell on Oct. 18, pulled down by massive protests and the exodus to the West, which reached 300 an hour last week. The shortage of manpower got so severe that the government was forced to use soldiers to run trains and buses. The new regime of Egon Krenz recognized that only desperate measures could woo its citizens into staying. With Soviet leader Mikhail Gorbachev's blessing, and possibly his encouragement, Krenz announced the end to all restrictions on migration or travel to the West.

Washington's response to East Germany's sudden transformation was subdued. "We are pleased," said a quiet George Bush, adding, "We're handling it in a way where we are not trying to give anybody a hard time." But perhaps Bush's lack of eloquence could be forgiven. For what words could compete with the sight of a united German people dancing on the Wall (→ 12).

Su	Mo	Tu	We	Th	Fr	Sa
			1	2	3	4
5	6	7	8	9	10	11
12	13	14	15	16	17	18
19	20	21	22	23	24	25
26	27	28	29	30		

12. San Salvador: Leftist rebels launch full-scale assault on capital (→ 14).

12. East Berlin: East Germany cuts hole in Wall at Potsdamer Platz, center of old Berlin; mayors of two cities meet as 800,000 East Berliners visit West in one day (→ 17).

14. Moscow: President Gorbachev urges West not to gloat over communism's troubles or try to export capitalism, and urges continuance of NATO and Warsaw Pact (→ Dec 3).

14. Iraq: Thousands of Egyptian laborers have fled Iraq over past several days following reports of abuse and unexplained deaths.

14. Washington, D.C.: Congress curbs Bush administration's freedom to support noncommunist rebels in Cambodia to avoid American military involvement in the region.

15. Mobridge, S.D.: Over past week, town spends $8,500 to dig out from under 30 tons of tumbleweed, which actually buried some houses.

15. New York City: Picasso's *Au Lapin Agile* sells at Sotheby's for $40.7 million.

16. Brazil: Vote in yesterday's presidential election split between left and right; run-off expected (→ Dec 19).

16. South Africa: President de Klerk orders all beaches integrated, canceling 36-year-old law (→ Dec 15).

16. San Diego: California state legislator Lucy Killea, running for re-election in December, is barred from receiving communion because of her support of abortion rights.

16. Oakland, Calif.: More than 12,000 march across newly repaired Bay Bridge to celebrate its renewal after earthquake.

17. Washington, D.C.: Bush administration officials reveal U.S. is planning fifth "covert" attempt to oust Panamanian strongman Noriega (→ Dec 17).

18. Washington, D.C.: Star defensive end Dexter Manley of the Washington Redskins is barred from NFL due to repeated drug test failures.

SWAPO wins in Namibia's first elections

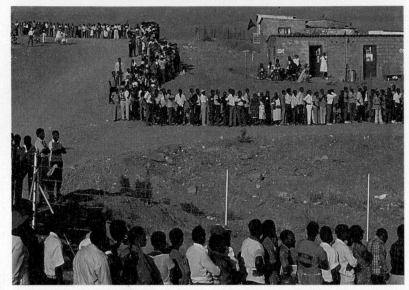

A passion for self-rule: lining up to vote in the Namibian countryside.

Nov 14. With recent elections certified "free and fair" by U.N. observers, the South-West Africa People's Organization (SWAPO) declared victory today in Namibia's first step toward national sovereignty. But the independence group, with 57.3 percent of the vote, failed to win the two-thirds majority necessary to gain full control.

SWAPO, which began its armed movement against South African rule in 1966, won 41 of 72 seats in the constituent assembly. This will give it the strongest voice when the assembly meets shortly to map out a constitution; but the failure to win a two-thirds majority denies the group a free hand in instituting its socialist agenda. The multiracial Democratic Turnhalle Alliance, which won 28.6 percent of the vote, is expected to pursue more moderate policies.

The transition to independence has been markedly smooth for this former South African colony, in large part because SWAPO has transformed itself from guerrilla force to political party with apparent ease. Despite an incursion into Namibia last April that led to clashes with South African troops, SWAPO appears to be satisfied with the power invested in it by electoral politics.

Pentagon strives to make tough cuts

Nov 18. Administration sources said today that the Air Force has proposed a cutback plan in response to a White House call to reduce Pentagon spending. The proposals come in the wake of Defense Secretary Richard Cheney's public request yesterday for $180 billion in cuts from the Pentagon budget over three years beginning in 1992. The federal deficit and changes in Eastern Europe have spurred officials to curtail defense spending.

The Air Force plan would close 15 air bases, retire Minuteman I missiles and disband five fighter wings. Stealth bomber purchases would also be stretched out. The other services have yet to respond.

Top award rejected

Nov 17. Leonard Bernstein was not among the recipients of the National Medal of Arts at the White House today. The composer and conductor was supposed to have received one of the 12 medals presented annually to those who have encouraged the arts in the United States, but he rejected the honor in protest over the withdrawal of a $10,000 National Endowment for the Arts grant to a show on AIDS at the Artists Space in New York City. The grant has since been reinstated.

The "German question" rears its head in councils of power

Breaking down walls . . . of all kinds.

Nov 17. When news that the Berlin Wall had fallen filtered through to the West German Bundestag, its members jumped to their feet and sang the rarely heard national anthem, whose lyrics include, "Unity and justice and freedom / For the German Fatherland." Their spontaneous display of national pride evoked the question that has found its way to the lips of political observers across the world. Are the two Germanys about to achieve a goal that for four decades has seemed like a dream: reunification?

East Germany has played down the idea, not surprisingly, since East Berlin would likely be dominated by the economically stronger Bonn. East Germany's Prime Minister, Hans Modrow, called today for a "new level" of relations with Bonn, but added that he hoped reforms within East Germany would end "unrealistic and dangerous speculation about reunification." Nonetheless, speculation continues.

"I love Germany so much, I'm glad there are two of them," novelist Francois Mauriac has said. In spite of the longstanding commitment of the United States and its allies to reunification, Mauriac's statement speaks for many. The division of Germany has coincided with 40 years of peace in Europe, albeit a cold peace. The challenge will be to ensure that their "unity and justice and freedom" apply to all of Europe (→ 21).

Walesa hailed as hero by Bush, Congress

Walesa signals victory in Congress.

Nov 15. The Polish electrician who went on to lead a labor movement that brought about the first democratic change of government in Eastern Europe received a triumphant reception in the U.S. Congress today. Solidarity leader Lech Walesa, who is visiting the United States for the first time to raise funds for his country, urged American legislators to pass a Marshall Plan for Eastern Europe. Two days ago, he received a Medal of Freedom from President Bush, who described him as "the spiritual godfather of a new generation of democracy." Walesa, in turn, said he hoped Poland would become "the America of the East," adding that he admired America's "human attachments to freedom" (→ Dec 13).

Rebels ravage Salvador

More trouble in Central America; Salvadoran troops take aim at the rebels.

Israeli heart for foe

Nov 16. A Palestinan gunman killed an Israeli soldier named Ze'ev Traum in Gaza on Monday, and today the soldier's family donated the dead man's heart to Hanna Khader, a Palestinian in need of a transplant. Khader was pronounced in stable condition after a four-hour operation at Hadassah Medical Center, and his wife then learned the identity of the donor. "He's a human being," she said, "and there is no difference between a Palestinian and an Israeli in such cases." In a land divided by the seemingly irreconcilable claims of Arabs and Jews, perhaps these are words of hope.

Pedal-pusher flies

Nov 12. Another page in aviation history was written today when students at California Polytechnic State University successfully tested the first human-powered helicopter. The pedal-powered aircraft, made of balsa wood, plastic foam and carbon materials, was "flown" four inches off the school's gymnasium floor by Greg McNeil for a breathtaking two seconds. Despite its brevity, the flight has been registered with the Federation Aeronautique Internationale, the organization responsible for keeping world aviation records. After all, cites one F.A.I. official, "It's never been done before."

Nov 14. Marxist rebels in El Salvador have launched a nationwide offensive, attacking targets across the country, including the private residence of President Alfredo Cristiani. Cristiani has declared the country under a "state of siege."

Government forces counterattacked today, and the United States Embassy estimated that 339 people have been killed and 373 wounded in two days of fighting. Battles have raged almost constantly and the government forces seem to be turning the tide against the guerrillas of the Farabundo Marti National Liberation Front. The FMLN has failed to capture strategic targets or to inspire a popular uprising in its biggest offensive since 1981.

Rebel leaders in the middle class suburb of Metropolis in San Salvador claim this is their "final battle," and their object is "to win or to die." So far they are doing far more of the latter.

The Salvadoran Army is using helicopter gunships against rebel strongholds where guerrillas are defending themselves from behind cobblestone barricades with rocket-propelled grenades. There is an eerie calm in neighborhoods not under attack. At least one American, whose name is being withheld, has been killed in the fighting (→ 17).

Six Jesuits butchered in San Salvador

Nov 17. United States officials have linked yesterday's murder of six Jesuit priests in San Salvador to "right-wing death squads." Witnesses said the brutal murders were carried out by a group of 30 men in military uniforms, who mutilated the priests with machetes before killing them. Bernard Aronson of the State Department said, "My guts tell me that they were killed by the right." Aronson told a Senate panel that leftist rebels have tried all year "to get the death squads to come out of the closet." Congressional Democrats, however, are outraged and maintain that provocation offers no excuse. Sen. Alan Cranston (D-Calif.) wants President Bush to cut off all aid to El Salvador (→ 19).

Praise the Lord and pass the pool cue. The sisters of London's Tyburn Convent have turned to snooker exhibitions to raise cash for renovations.

A prayer for the dead.

Su	Mo	Tu	We	Th	Fr	Sa
			1	2	3	4
5	6	7	8	9	10	11
12	13	14	15	16	17	18
19	20	21	22	23	24	25
26	27	28	29	30		

19. San Salvador: Archbishop Arturo Rivera y Damas blames military for last week's murder of six priests and two others (→ 22).

19. New York City: Steffi Graf beats Martina Navratilova in four sets to win Virginia Slims Championship.

19. Oakland, Calif.: "Lucky" Buck Helm, pulled from wreckage of I-880 after earthquake, dies suddenly of respiratory failure.

20. Bucharest: Rumanian leader Nicolae Ceausescu vows not to follow other nations in drive to "block socialism" (→ Dec 21).

20. Washington, D.C.: Sen. D.P. Moynihan rejects charge made in Indian newspaper that opposition leader V.P. Singh was paid CIA informant (→ 29).

21. Prague: With hundreds of thousands in streets, party leader Miklos Jakes appears on TV to warn protesters not to overstep their bounds (→ 25).

21. Washington, D.C.: In plea-bargain, Albert Hakim, financial organizer for Iran-contra scheme, pleads guilty to supplying Oliver North with home security system (→ 22).

21. Washington, D.C.: Hans-Dietrich Genscher, West German foreign minister, presents piece of Berlin Wall to President Bush (→ 26).

21. Seattle: Boeing machinists vote to end 48-day strike, accepting three-year package with 10 percent raise.

22. Washington, D.C.: Congress repeals Medicare provision covering long-term health costs for elderly, but promises new bill next year.

22. Cape Canaveral, Fla.: Space shuttle Discovery blasts off on secret mission; first night launching of a winged spacecraft in history.

22. Minneapolis, Minn.: Kirby Puckett signs three-year, $9 million contract, becoming first baseball player to earn $3 million a year.

DEATHS

22. C.C. Beck, creator of *Captain Marvel* (*1910).

Americans caught in San Salvador hotel

A fight to the finish: FMLN guerrillas fire rounds from behind a barricade.

Nov 22. A group of United States military advisers, including several Green Berets, are free following a brief, inadvertent siege in one of San Salvador's luxury hotels by guerrilla forces of the Farabundo Marti National Liberation Front (FMLN). About 15 rebels had fled into the Hotel El Salvador to escape an army patrol, only to run into the armed Americans. The Americans barricaded themselves at the end of a corridor, where they insisted they were not hostages. "We're doing fine," one of them said. "We just have our liberty restricted." No shots were exchanged between the two groups (→ 26).

Tokyo challenges Detroit ... yet again

Just when American car makers seemed to be winning back respect as well as customers, the Japanese competition has come up with a new edge: the multi-valve engine. Multi-valves burn fuel more efficiently than regular engines, and add power to a car without taking up more space. All this could cause more dark days in Detroit. Auto industry analysts predict it will cost millions and take from three to five years for domestic auto makers to convert to the new engines. Despite a recent upturn, Detroit's share of the domestic market has already dropped from 84 percent in 1978 to 69 percent last year.

It's not Lawrence of Arabia, but it could be Lawrence of Colorado; sand skiing seems to be catching on, among those who can't wait for winter.

Japanese lambast American economy

Nov 19. With a candor unusual even for an ally, Japan is telling the United States that it should put its own economic house in order before voicing its criticisms of Tokyo's trade policies. Japanese officials have recommended to Washington that schools be upgraded, the budget deficit be closed, more scientific research be funded and better worker training be undertaken. A "short-termist" mentality, according to the angry Japanese, places quarterly profits ahead of long-term investments and inhibits interest in upgrading American plants and equipment.

The sharp Japanese attack on American management and educational systems is part of ongoing negotiations aimed at resolving trade policy differences. Japan, however, is disturbed that most of the criticism was directed at Tokyo. As one spokesman declared, "We can't solve our trade imbalance looking at Japan alone."

Iran-contra trials impeded by Justice

Nov 22. The shroud of CIA secrecy has been extended to cover the activities of one of its high-ranking officials, on trial for complicity in the Iran-contra affair. Atty. Gen. Dick Thornburgh today refused to allow disclosure of classified information at the trial of J.F. Fernandez, ex-CIA chief in Costa Rica.

According to independent counsel and prosecuting attorney Lawrence Walsh, the information is already common knowledge. Thornburgh, however, contends that the data — locations of three CIA field offices in Central America and confirmation of three covert operations in the region — "would cause serious damage to the national security of the United States" if revealed.

Walsh's efforts in the ongoing court saga have already been severely hampered by official secrecy. He was forced to drop the two main charges against Lt. Col. Oliver North and accept plea bargains in the cases of retired Gen. Richard Secord and Iranian-born businessman Albert Hakim.

Lebanese President killed after 17 days

Moawad held a very dangerous job.

Nov 24. Observers are saying that more than lives were lost in Lebanon's latest round of blood-letting. When President Rene Moawad was assassinated by a car bomb two days ago — after but 17 days in office — the accord reached last month in Saudi Arabia providing for equal distribution of power between Muslims and Christians was severely wounded. Said Chawki Choueri, Lebanon's representative to the U.N.: "This is the major catastrophe of the years of catastrophies we have had so far. We may have lost one of the last opportunities to unite the nation." Twenty-three others died when the huge bomb exploded in Beirut. Today, Elias Hwari, also a Maronite Christian, was chosen to succeed Moawad as President (→ 28).

Czech regime totters as millions take to streets hailing Dubcek

Nov 25. Hungary. Poland. East Germany. And now Czechoslovakia? After eight days in which hundreds of thousands of Czechs demonstrated for democracy, the Communist Party has shuffled the membership of the Politburo and replaced hard-line General Secretary Milos Jakes, 61, with 48-year-old Karel Urbanek, a little-known Politburo member who described himself as "an honest man," open to dialogue.

But the party's measures were too halfhearted to quell the dissent of the hundreds of thousands who continued to gather in Wenceslas Square. As Czech human rights activist Vaclav Havel insisted, "The new leadership is a trick that is meant to confuse." The opposition was particularly angered by the continued membership of Miroslav Zavadil in the Politburo. Zavadil was involved in the suppression of the reform government of Alexan-

Dubcek gets a warm welcome from 350,000 protesters on an icy day in Prague.

der Dubcek 21 years ago.

Dubcek himself emerged this week from his years in the wilderness — he has been posted in the forestry department for two decades — to address a crowd of 350,000, braving the cold in Prague yesterday. "An old wise man said, *if there once was light, why should there be darkness again.* Let us act in such a way as to bring the light back," Dubcek urged (→ 28).

Altman's closes out

Nov 24. As they always do on the day after Thanksgiving, shoppers flocked to B. Altman & Co. today. But this visit may have no reprise. The 124-year-old New York store is on its last legs, ordered by a bankruptcy court to close after its final sale, the one that began today. "This is nostalgia," said Pamela Gordon, who came from Savannah, Ga., to wait in the cold with hundreds of others for doors to open.

Don't ask these people for directions ...

A nine-nation survey of geographic knowledge has provided evidence of common ground between the United States and the Soviet Union: ignorance. The results of the National Geographic Society survey show that the citizens of the superpowers have "an astonishing lack of awareness of the world around them." In scores on a 16-question map, Sweden ranked first, followed by West Germany, Japan,

France, Canada, the United States, Britain, Mexico, and the Soviet Union. The statistics are as embarrassing as they are disturbing: 13 percent of Soviets could not find their own country on a map, and 14 percent of Americans failed to locate the United States. They had even more trouble locating each other, lending new relevance to Kipling's "East is East and West is West, and ne'er the twain shall meet."

U.S. in World Cup

Nov 19. For the first time since 1950, the United States soccer team is going to play in the World Cup main round. A trip to the World Cup in Italy next summer was guaranteed today when the U.S. team defeated Trinidad and Tobago, 1-0, in a game the Americans had to win. A tie would have given the tiny Caribbean republic the entree to the main round. Paul Caliguiri, 25, of UCLA, injured much of this year, scored the game-winner in the 31st minute with a hard left-foot shot that found the upper right corner of the net. For the next 58 minutes, the Americans exercised patience and played tight defense.

Canaletto's San Marco: the Interior, *part of a show at the Metropolitan Museum of Art, N.Y.*

Nov 21. *With great pomp, Queen Elizabeth's crown is taken to Commons for the first-ever televised session of the venerable legislative body.*

Su	Mo	Tu	We	Th	Fr	Sa
			1	2	3	4
5	6	7	8	9	10	11
12	13	14	15	16	17	18
19	20	21	22	23	24	25
26	27	28	29	30		

26. San Salvador: El Salvador cuts ties with Nicaragua after crash of plane laden with arms for Salvadoran rebels (→ 26).

26. Colombia: Colombian 727 explodes in mid-air, killing all 107 on board; anonymous caller claims bombing for drug cartel (→ Dec 6).

26. Tokyo: American sumo wrestler Konishiki, weighing in at 490 pounds, is second foreigner to win Emperor's Cup.

26. Uruguay: Centrist Luis Alberto Lacalle wins presidency as Marxists gain control of Montevideo's city hall.

26. San Salvador: Witness to slaying of six priests testifies that killers appeared linked to armed forces (→ Dec 13).

26. East Germany: Free German Youth, Communist Party's two-million-strong youth organization, formally breaks all ties with party (→ Dec 1).

26. Richmond, Va.: Douglas Wilder is certified winner of the gubernatorial race by State Election Board, but rival still wants another recount.

26. Comoros Islands: European mercenaries launch coup, killing President Ahmed Abdallah Abderemane (→ Dec 15).

27. Budapest: Hungarians, in first free national vote in 42 years, reject ruling party plan to hold presidential elections on Jan. 7, before it has relinquished power.

27. United Nations: Bush administration threatens to cut off all American funds to U.N. if General Assembly recognizes a Palestinian state (→ Dec 5).

28. Moscow: Legislature pardons all Soviet soldiers for crimes in Afghanistan.

28. San Francisco: Crane topples from roof of building under construction, killing five and injuring at least 19.

29. Romania: Olympic gymnast Nadia Comeneci has reportedly defected to Hungary with six others (→ Dec 9).

30. San Francisco: Shell agrees to pay $19.75 million for spilling 400,000 gallons of oil in San Francisco Bay in 1988.

Troops revolt in Manila

Yet another country in turmoil; rebels in Manila take on the government.

Nov 30. Rebel forces of the Philippine military launched a major coup attempt today against the embattled government of President Corazon Aquino. The attack began at about 1 a.m., just after President Bush had left via helicopter for Air Force One on the way to his Malta summit with Soviet leader Mikhail Gorbachev. Since then, the rebels have bombed the presidential palace with four T-28 planes and seized the air force headquarters and two broadcasting stations.

With pitched battles raging all over Manila, President Aquino appeared on television at 4 a.m., urging the Filipino people to support her government "in this hour of challenge." As day broke, it remained unclear who was winning.

This fifth attempt to oust Aquino appears to be the best orchestrated and most threatening yet. Defense Secretary Fidel Ramos believes that the rebellion is being led by Col. Gregorio Honasan, who was instrumental in overthrowing Ferdinand Marcos, and failed in a coup attempt in August 1987. The rebels have yet to release a statement, but it is known that segments of the Philippine military are dissatisfied with Aquino's perceived weakness, particularly in the government's fight against leftist guerrillas.

The United States has yet to respond to the upheaval (→ Dec 1).

Highbrow refuse: A Hackensack, N.J., environmental museum turns garbage into art with trashy shows like "How Far Does Your Trash Travel."

Top terrorist Nidal under house arrest

Nov 27. Abu Nidal, leader of the world's most feared terrorist organization, is under house arrest in Libya, according to the PLO and Arab sources. "The man's time is over," a senior Arab envoy said. "He is becoming useless to all those who have used him." It is believed Egyptian President Hosni Mubarak put pressure on Libyan leader Muammar al-Qaddafi to restrain Nidal as a precondition for improved relations between Egypt and Libya. The two leaders met in October. With Nidal neutralized, most experts consider his organization on the verge of collapse. The group has killed or wounded 900 in 20 countries since it was formed in 1974.

Nidal in Baghdad in 1975.

Swiss Army knifed in national vote

Nov 26. In a country that values its soldiers almost as much as it does William Tell, it came as rather a shock to the Swiss military establishment that 35.6 percent of the population voted to abolish the army in a recent referendum. Those in favor of the move argue that the military can provide only imaginary defense against the most likely threats to the nation, such as nuclear war. However, the only major political group not to oppose the abolition bid was the Socialist Party. This has caused some politicians to urge the party's exclusion from the government's executive branch.

Lebanese general holds out in Beirut

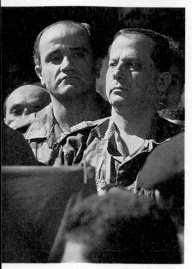

Michel Aoun, a maverick in Beirut.

Nov 28. Lebanon's Christian military leader, Gen. Michel Aoun, is refusing to yield power even in the face of Syrian tanks and a new successor named by Beirut's legitimate government. Aoun, who will not recognize the new Lebanese President, Elias Hwari, nor the accord last month that led to his election, remains at his stronghold with a force of about 15,000. The Syrian tanks lie within striking distance on the Damascus-Beirut road. In power only a week, Hwari replaced the assassinated Rene Moawad, also a Maronite Christian. The new government picked Emile Lahoud, 51, head of Lebanon's small navy, as Aoun's replacement (→ Dec 5).

Czech Communists lose leading role

Nov 28. Czechoslovakia's Communist Party caved in to the democratic opposition today and vowed to relinquish its 41-year monopoly on power. Following a two-hour meeting between Prime Minister Ladislav Adamec and opposition leader Vaclav Havel, government leaders announced that non-communists would be included in a new Cabinet to be named by Sunday. The regime also agreed to grant the opposition free access to the media, eliminate mandatory Marxist-Leninist instruction in universities, release all remaining political prisoners and form a commission to examine the Nov. 17 beating of protesters.

Minister Without Portolio Marian Calfa told reporters that Prime Minister Adamec would submit his resignation next Monday and that an interim government would be formed. Calfa avoided the issue of free elections, but it is widely understood that the loss of party monopoly paves the way for a multi-party

Prague's people hail their new freedoms, loudly, joyously and thankfully.

electoral system. The dominant opposition group, Civic Forum, seems poised to assume a role similar to that of Poland's Solidarity, which now governs that country.

Today's developments are a major step toward a freer Czechoslovakia but, as most Czechoslovaks know, the struggle is far from over. They now face the daunting task of building a democracy out of the carnage of one-party rule (→ Dec 1).

Roll it! Hollywood history lessons are telling it like it wasn't

We live in an age of mass-media education, when it is likely that more people learn about history from movie screens than books. A good story will sell, but should movie-makers tamper with facts in order to break box office records or moralize? The recent flood of historical dramas has many critics

concerned that we may be entertaining ourselves into ignorance.

In *Mississippi Burning*, for example, the 1964 murder of three civil rights workers is distorted and the role of the FBI practically invented for the film. In *Fat Man and Little Boy,* director Roland Joffe says he "tries to find the interior truth that

lics behind the often . . . superficial facts" of the Los Alamos atomic bomb project. In the process, he sometimes substitutes "metaphor" for fact, begging the question of whether film makers should be held to the same standards of accuracy as journalists or historians, or given the license of the artist.

Opposition ousts Gandhi, Congress Party

Singh, head of the National Front.

Nov 29. Following election losses, Rajiv Gandhi, grandson of Jawaharlal Nehru, has resigned as Prime Minister of India, a country which has been ruled by his family for all but five of its 42 years of independence. The often violent elections, however, left neither his Congress Party nor the opposition National Front with a majority. Both parties got harsh votes of no confidence in their respective regions of governance. The National Front, leading in votes, will turn to its leader V.P. Singh to form a government. But he will have to court the fundamentalist Hindu party, Bharatiya Janata, which has a new role as power broker in the divided nation (→ Dec 1).

Live-donor liver transplant makes history

Nov 27. In one of the most important transplant operations of recent years, doctors at the University of Chicago today took a section of liver from Teresa A. Smith and gave it to her 21-month-old daughter, Alyssa. What makes this operation special is that Teresa is a live donor. Since livers regenerate themselves if a not-too-large section is taken, the risk to the donor is not considered high, and the transplanted section will continue to grow with the child. The operation is being hailed by scientists as a major breakthrough because transplanting only a section enables a child to receive the organ much earlier than a full-organ transplant would.

Live liver is harvested for transplant.

Su	Mo	Tu	We	Th	Fr	Sa
					1	2
3	4	5	6	7	8	9
10	11	12	13	14	15	16
17	18	19	20	21	22	23
24	25	26	27	28	29	30
31						

1. Prague: New Czech Politburo formally condemns 1968 invasion by Warsaw Pact, which crushed Prague Spring reform movement (→ 9).

1. Manila: President Bush authorizes use of U.S. warplanes to help Aquino government crush coup attempt (→ 9).

1. India: V.P. Singh unanimously elected 11th Prime Minister of India.

1. East Berlin: Parliament amends constitution, stripping Communists of leading role in society (→ 9).

3. Bartow, Fla.: ACLU is challenging Florida sheriff's policy of making homosexual prisoners wear pink bracelets.

3. Nicaragua: Renegade Sandinista hero Eden Pastora returns from exile to participate in Nicaraguan politics.

4. Washington, D.C.: Danny Wall, head of Office of Thrift Supervision, resigns after coming under attack for savings and loan mess; calls House panel investigation unfair.

5. Beirut: Lebanese Muslim and Christian forces break a 10-week cease-fire.

5. United Nations: Arab countries agree to put off vote on Palestinian statehood to avoid U.S. suspension of funds to U.N.; assembly president scolds U.S. for using money to influence U.N. business.

6. Bogota, Colombia: Truck with half a ton of explosives blows up outside secret police headquarters, killing at least 35 and wounding hundreds (→ 15).

7. Miami: Police officer William Lozano found guilty in killing of two blacks that set off violent riots in January.

7. Covington, La.: Researchers report developing vaccine that has protected eight of nine monkeys from simian AIDS.

8. Washington, D.C.: Bush administration confirms Iraq has developed missile capable of launching satellite into space or nuclear warhead at enemy.

9. Beijing: Bush administration officials meet with Chinese officials on surprise visit (→ 11).

Castro vows to fight change to the death

Castro, still loyal to the cause.

Dec 8. Fidel Castro has never been a man to mince words. In a flat rejection of the reforms that are sweeping the communist world, the bearded one has sworn to defend Cuba's socialism "to the last drop of blood" against "the Yankee empire that has succeeded in embodying Hitler's dream of world domination." Cuba itself experimented with economic liberalization in the early '80s, but "rectified" that program when Castro decided that egalitarianism was eroding. His concern now is that changes in Moscow will affect the $5 billion in aid that is sent annually to Havana. "We can only expect negative economic consequences," he said.

Montreal massacre

Dec 7. He hated feminists and he blamed women for ruining his life. So Marc Lapin donned hunter's garb, took a rifle and slaughtered 14 women at the engineering school of the University of Montreal yesterday. Bursting into a classroom, Lapin first separated the men from the women and told the men to leave. He then proceeded through the rest of the building, shooting indiscriminately with a semiautomatic rifle. At the end of the worst mass killing in Canadian history, the gunman took his own life. In his pocket, police found a letter saying that if his life was ruined, it was because of women. They also found a list of 15 prominent women.

Philippine coup is ended with U.S. aid

Dec 9. An attempted overthrow of the Corazon Aquino government by Philippine rebel troops has been put down with the help of U.S. military intervention. On Dec. 1, with the coup in its infancy and most of the Philippine air force in rebel hands, President Bush authorized two F-4 fighters to fire on any Filipino military planes attempting to take off. The threat was enough to restrain the planes, and no American pilots had to fire. The coup ended today with the surrender of the last rebel holdout, Mactan Air Base in Cebu. Seventy-nine people were killed and over 500 wounded in the fighting. Many of the rebel military officers have escaped.

Alvin Ailey is dead

Ailey was a leader in modern dance.

Dec 1. Alvin Ailey has died at 58, and modern dance is the poorer for his passing. Ailey raised himself from an impoverished childhood to a radiant career as a dancer, choreographer and director. After gaining attention as a dancer with the Dunham and Horton companies, he began the Alvin Ailey American Dance Theater in 1958 and saw it grow into the most popular international touring company. When Ailey was criticized by fellow blacks for integrating his troupe, he said "I feel an obligation to use black dancers because there must be more opportunity . . ., but not because I am a black choreographer speaking to black audiences."

Romanian gymnast Comaneci defects

Comaneci and married boyfriend.

Dec 9. A matronly Nadia Comaneci, the gymnast who captured hearts around the world along with several gold medals at the 197 Olympics, has defected to southern Florida. She says she came to the United States to enjoy the freedom here, but her romantic interest in roofer, Constantin Panait (who married and has four children seems to have been a factor. She lived in relative luxury in her native Romania until she ended a relationship with the son of the head of state four years ago, at which point her fortunes declined. Comaneci relationship with Panait has caused a scandal in little Hallandale, Fla to which she appears oblivious.

Peace in Malaysia

Dec 2. Malaysian communists have agreed to a cease-fire after 41 years of armed rebellion. Their long "war of liberation" began in 1948, when "Malaya" was still a British colony. It took thousands of lives and at one point involved 70,000 British and Commonwealth troops. Now it is over, and 1,200 guerrilla fighters will leave their positions along the border with Thailand and go back to civilian life. In return, Malaysia and Thailand have promised the rebels fair treatment and full integration into political life. Analysts say that the changes in Eastern Europe and China's reluctance to give aid have caused the rebels to recognize the odds against winning.

East German party struggles to survive

Dec 9. In a desperate attempt to restore their credibility, delegates to an extraordinary congress of the East German Communist Party today elected 41-year-old attorney Gregor Gysi as their new chairman. Widely known as a reformer, Gysi built his reputation by defending dissidents in court. But with daily disclosures of corruption fanning public disillusionment into a firestorm of anger, even a saint would be overwhelmed by the task.

Former party leader Erich Honecker is now languishing under house arrest after it was revealed that he owned a $1.2 million seaside villa on an island once thought to be a deserted bird sanctuary. Other

Honecker, leading advocate of the classless society, enjoys a vacation.

party officials allegedly diverted to Swiss bank accounts tens of millions of dollars in proceeds from various illegal sales of arms and art.

Party officials have launched a tide of reform in attempt to quell the public outrage that has brought his country of over 16 million people to near collapse. On Dec. 1, Parliament voted to strip the party of its leading role in society. Three days later, the entire party leadership, headed by Egon Krenz, resigned. Last night, delegates voted to change the party's formal name, the Socialist Unity Party of Germany, when the congress meets next week. They also rejected reunification with West Germany, but expressed a readiness to explore "confederate structures." Elections have been scheduled for May 6 (→ 17).

Summit on the high seas

For Presidents Gorbachev and Bush, calm meetings in spite of stormy waters.

Dec 3. The Malta summit meeting came to a close today and a new era in Soviet-American relations appears to have dawned. President Bush and Soviet President Mikhail Gorbachev concluded their three days of talks aboard American and Soviet warships with a joint news conference far more friendly than the heavy seas on which they met.

Of course there were points of discord — Central America, Afghanistan and naval disarmament, — but both leaders clamored to minimize them. "The arms race, mistrust, psychological and ideological struggle, all those should be things of the past," the Soviet leader said. President Bush concurred.

"We stand at the threshold of a brand-new era of U.S.-Soviet relations," he stated proudly.

With a list of 18 proposals ranging from arms control to economic cooperation, Bush managed to dispel doubts about his enthusiasm for communist reform. Just two weeks ago, an exasperated Gorbachev adviser had wondered about the U.S. response to perestroika, "What do we have to do for you Americans to do something in return? Restore the Romanovs to the throne?" On Saturday, Gorbachev changed the tune: "I have heard you say that you want perestroika to succeed," he said, "but frankly I didn't know this. Now I know."

Gorbachev and Pope hold historic meeting

Dec 1. In a two-hour meeting held today at the Vatican, Soviet leader Mikhail Gorbachev and Pope John Paul II began to chip away at 70 years of philosophical and diplomatic animosity. The men agreed to establish diplomatic ties between their two states and, under pressure from the Pope to allow Ukrainian Catholics freedom of worship, Gorbachev promised to enact a new law guaranteeing freedom of religion. At the conclusion of the talks, Gorbachev extended an invitation to the Pope to visit the officially atheist Soviet Union. The Pontiff extended his thanks, but commented only that he hoped "developments would make it possible" to accept.

Gorbachev visits the Pontiff.

Czech leader Husak is forced to resign

Dec 9. Just a day after Czechoslovakia's acting Prime Minister, Marian Calfa, announced he would seek to create a Cabinet with a Communist minority, hard-line President Gustav Husak has promised to resign from office following the swearing in of the new government on Sunday.

The removal of President Husak has been a major demand of the opposition since the pro-democracy movement began earlier this year. A wave of street protests, threatened strikes, and the opposition group Civic Forum's rejection of a Communist-dominated Cabinet left government leaders with no alternative but to meet one of the

A bust of Stalin in Prague carries the words, "Nothing lasts forever."

opposition's most fervent demands.

The ouster of Husak will surely become one of the high points in the popular uprising that has brought this Central European country out of its Stalinist dark ages. Husak replaced Alexander Dubcek as party chief in 1968 following the crushing of the Prague Spring reform movement by Warsaw Pact troops, and he soon came to personify the shattering of democratic hopes.

Husak's exit now paves the way for final agreement between Prime Minister Calfa and Civic Forum leader Vaclav Havel on the formation of a new Cabinet. And while no final agreement has been reached, reports that the internal and/or foreign affairs posts will go to non-Communists illustrates the growing strength of the opposition (→ 11).

DECEMBER
1989

Su	Mo	Tu	We	Th	Fr	Sa
					1	2
3	4	5	6	7	8	9
10	11	12	13	14	15	16
17	18	19	20	21	22	23
24	25	26	27	28	29	30
31						

10. Washington, D.C.: Congressional report claims Reagan administration suppressed surgeon general's report showing abortion is safe and in best interests of women.

11. Prague: For five minutes at midday, millions of Czechoslovaks take to the streets to celebrate the formation of a predominantly non-Communist Cabinet yesterday (→ 23).

11. Washington, D.C.: Report by panel of National Geographic Society concludes Admiral Peary did reach North Pole, citing evidence such as angle of sun in 1909 photo.

11. Canada: Canadian destroyer fires warning shot at U.S. fishing boat refusing to stop on way out of Canadian waters; fishing boat had rammed destroyer three times.

12. Moscow: President Gorbachev musters enough votes to postpone debate on move to strip Communist Party of its monopoly on power.

12. New York City: Leona Helmsley sentenced to four years in prison and fined $7.1 million for tax fraud.

12. San Jose, Costa Rica: Five Central American presidents sign accord calling for disbanding of Nicaraguan contras and leftist rebels in El Salvador.

13. Brussels: Meeting of world's 24 leading industrial nations creates plan to lend Poland and Hungary $1 billion each to help them develop market economies.

13. San Salvador: American Jennifer Jean Casolo, arrested for harboring weapons for leftist guerrillas, is freed by Salvadoran judge for lack of evidence and deported.

13. South Africa: President de Klerk and imprisoned black leader Nelson Mandela meet to discuss future of country (→ 15).

15. Covenas, Colombia: Colombian troops kill Medellin drug boss Jose Gonzalo Rodriguez Gacha in shootout.

15. South Africa: Appeals court frees five dissidents, each in jail for treason or terrorism; anti-apartheid forces celebrate.

French mercenary force gives up Comoros

Modern mercenaries are just looking for a nice place to call their own.

Dec 15. French mercenary Col. Bob Denard and 21 of his confederates left Comoros today, just three weeks after they seized control of the tiny island nation. Denard and his men flew to South Africa after turning the islands over to French military authorities who had threatened to launch an assault if he refused to cede power. The mercenaries are expected to leave for France within 48 hours.

Denard overthrew and killed President Ahmed Abdallah Abdermane last month after a falling out between the two men. Ironically, it was Denard who helped Abdermane seize power in 1978.

Hong Kong ships 51 Vietnamese home

Dec 16. The hopes of 51 Vietnamese refugees were crushed and the fears of 44,000 others brought nearer to realization as Hong Kong began the forced return of its illegal immigrants to Hanoi this week. "The repatriation went very smoothly" said an official, "everyone was calm and went quietly." In the last 16 months, tens of thousands of boat people have come to the island to escape Vietnamese repression. The government expects that most of them will be denied asylum. As to who would monitor their safety after they are back in Vietnam, the same official reported: "We have no information on that."

Weary and destitute, the Vietnamese boat people can find no safe harbor.

Tibet's Dalai Lama accepts Nobel Prize

Dec 10. A peaceful man fighting tidal wave of violence and oppression in his homeland, the Dalai Lama has been awarded the Nobel Peace Prize for his continued attempts to find a tranquil end to the Chinese occupation of his native Tibet. The Buddhist monk, political and religious leader of his country until an uprising against Chinese rule forced him into exile in 1959, accepted the award on behalf of all oppressed peoples. The Chinese are less than pleased with the award, and the Dalai Lama contends that repression in his homeland has worsened since the Nobel committee announced its choice.

The Dalai Lama continues to press for the freedom of his homeland.

Film banned in U.K.

Dec 12. For the first time ever in England, authorities have banned a film for blasphemy. The offending material comes from director Nigel Wingrove's *Visions of Ecstasy*, an 18-minute film that attempts to address the relationship of religion to sexuality through a literal and psychological depiction of the "raptures" of St. Theresa of Avila. The 16th century Spanish nun, who left behind vivid reports of her intimate "mystical marriage" to Christ, is shown kissing and caressing Him. John Stephenson, the film's producer, called the ruling "a disgraceful act of censorship."

U.S. officials' China visit sparks criticism

The toast heard round the world; Scowcroft drinks with Premier Qian Qichen.

Dec 15. The Bush administration was still reeling from criticism today over a diplomatic trip to China made by high-ranking U.S. officials earlier in the week. The mission, led by national security adviser Brent Scowcroft, was intended to smooth strained Sino-American relations, but has instead fueled a heated political debate at home.

In an effort to stem the tide of growing criticism, the White House issued a statement arguing that "while the President deplores the tragedy of Tiananmen Square last June . . . [he] views China as an important country in world affairs." Congressional leaders have nevertheless been quick to condemn the President for opening a dialogue with Beijing only five months after the Tiananmen Square massacre. Representative Stephen Solarz (D-N.Y.), lamenting the administration's apparent disregard for human rights in China, declared that the trip "makes neither good moral or strategic sense."

The trip to Beijing was portrayed as a briefing session on the Malta summit, when in fact the purpose was to reopen friendly ties between the two nations. It is now apparent that the Bush administration grossly underestimated the extent of the moral outrage generated in the United States by the Chinese leadership's brutality.

Andrei Sakharov, voice of conscience, dies

Dec 16. Since Andrei Sakharov died two days ago the Soviet Union has been in a state of mourning and shock. Sakharov's chair in the Congress of Deputies is now filled only by flowers. And the great nuclear physicist and reformer, who spent seven years in political exile from Moscow, leaves behind more than an empty chair. Many wonder who will give voice to the nation's conscience? Even Mikhail Gorbachev, who Sakharov often criticized, recognized that, "This was not some political intriguer, but a person who had his own ideas . . . which he expressed openly and directly." The former dissident supported Gorbachev, yet felt that his reforms were but half measures of freedom.

Andrei Sakharov's battle is ended.

Reforms reach Bulgaria and Yugoslavia

Dec 15. The upheaval sweeping Eastern Europe has finally made it to both Bulgaria and Yugoslavia, leaving only Rumania and Albania untouched by the seachanges now underway in the East bloc.

In Bulgaria, demonstrations led by the new opposition umbrella, the Union of Democratic Forces, have brought swift changes to the hard-line regime. Five days ago, 50,000 people assembled in Sofia to demand faster democratic reforms and an end to the Communist Party's monopoly on power. By Tuesday, the party had promised to relinquish its absolute grip on power and hold free elections. The following day, the party, under Petar T. Mladenov, voted to expel Todor I. Zhivkov from its ranks. Zhivkov ruled Bulgaria with an iron fist for 35 years until his ouster last month.

And in Yugoslavia yesterday, the Communist Party released a draft declaration pledging to give up its monopoly on power, hold free elections and institute a free market system. "We are changing all of this now," the paper said, "in order that tomorrow it will not be too late for socialism in Yugoslavia."

Dec 14. *Czechoslovakia today voided the treaty allowing Soviet troops on Czech soil, saying it was made under duress after the '68 Warsaw Pact invasion (above), which has been condemned by the pact's member nations.*

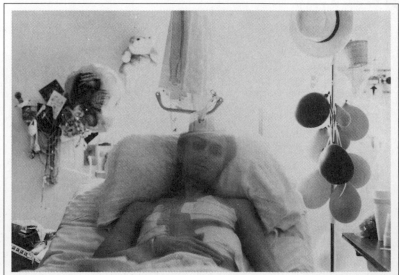

Phillip-Lorca diCorcia's Vittorio 1989, *in "Witnesses: Against Our Vanishing," an exhibit of AIDS-related art at Artists Space in New York. The show's federal grant was cut due to its controversial content, then restored.*

DECEMBER
1989

Su	Mo	Tu	We	Th	Fr	Sa
					1	2
3	4	5	6	7	8	9
10	11	12	13	14	15	16
17	18	19	20	21	22	23
24	25	26	27	28	29	30
31						

17. El Salvador: Lucia Barrera de Cerna, witness to slaying of six Jesuit priests, claims she was harassed into retracting testimony by FBI agents and a Salvadoran colonel in Miami.

17. Panama: U.S. condemns shooting of U.S. officer by Panamanian troops on Saturday, does not rule out military response (→ 23).

17. East Berlin: Communist Party announces it will dissolve secret police and is prepared to lose power in vote.

17. Stuttgart, West Germany: West Germany clinches Davis Cup as Boris Becker defeats Mats Wilander in straight sets.

18. Washington, D.C.: White House reports national security adviser Brent Scowcroft and Deputy Secretary of State Lawrence Eagleburger made trip to Beijing in July (→ 19).

19. Washington, D.C.: President Bush lifts some trade restrictions on China.

19. Brazil: Free-marketer Fernando Collor de Mello declared winner in presidential race.

20. Lithuania: Lithuanian Communist Party, ignoring Moscow, votes to split from Soviet party (→ 28).

20. United States: Researchers have discovered method to determine sex of fetus by doing blood test on mother.

20. New York City: *Pathfinder Mural* in Greenwich Village, depicting Lenin, Castro and Martin Luther King, is splattered with paint and defaced with swastikas.

21. Bucharest, Romania: After crowds shout down speech by President Ceausescu, at least 13 people are killed in clashes between protesters and troops; thousands have reportedly died in clashes in other cities (→ 23).

23. Israel: South African Archbishop Desmond Tutu backs Palestinian homeland on pilgrimage to Holy Land.

23. Prague: In accord between government and opposition, Vaclav Havel will become President, Alexander Dubcek chairman of Parliament (→ 29).

U.S. invades Panama to oust Noriega

Dec 23. At 1 a.m. on Dec. 20, Panama City was transformed into a war zone. The Bush administration, embarrassed by impotent attempts to oust Gen. Manuel Noriega, unleashed 24,000 U.S. troops to drive him from office and install the government of Guillermo Endara, who had been elected President by the Panamanian people in a contest voided by Noriega.

After the swearing in of the Endara government at an American military base, U.S. troops attacked simultaneously at three points in Panama City and gained control of much of the area. For three days, however, snipers and looters ruled the capital city as Noriega's fiercely loyal Dignity Battalions kept U.S. forces from establishing order.

Despite the relative calm that has now settled over the city, the strike forces have failed in one of their main objectives: the capture of Noriega himself. Following a misguided coup in October, the murder of an unarmed American officer by Panamanian troops this week, and a declaration of war against the United States, Noriega, no doubt, was well prepared for an action of this sort. Until American forces disabled the radio station, the dictator managed to broadcast a message urging the Panamanian people to resist their invaders. Noriega remains at large, somewhere in the Panamanian countryside (→ 23).

Invading soldiers tend to their captors — allegedly troops loyal to Noriega.

World responds to U.S. action in Panama

Dec 23. International reaction to the United States' invasion of Panama has been swift and predictable. Across Latin America, a region long sensitive to intervention from its northern neighbor, condemnation was quick and vehement. Peru recalled its ambassador to the United States. Nicaragua put its troops on alert. Venezuela, a regional leader in the attempt to convince General Noriega to step down, laid some of the blame for the U.S. action at the door of Latin America, citing "a lack of an effective and firm response by our countries" to the worsening situation in Panama.

In other areas, the Soviet Union urged the world to condemn the action, stressing that the situation should not be seen from the vantage point of an East-West confrontation, the norm during the Cold War. Spain, which in the past said it would provide asylum to Noriega, also reviled the action. The only unequivocally positive response came from Britain's Margaret Thatcher, who praised President Bush for a "courageous decision" (→ 29).

Marrow plus AZT may offer cure for AIDS

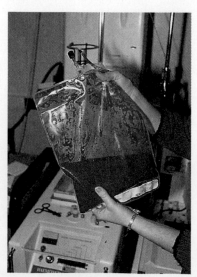

Slow progress against a killer.

Dec 19. For the first time since the disease was identified eight years ago, the AIDS virus has been completely eradicated from a patient's body. Researchers at Johns Hopkins University achieved the feat by combining a bone marrow transplant with doses of the drug AZT. The patient died of cancer 41 days after the operation, but his death was not caused by AIDS.

Doctors are cautiously optimistic. "It is certainly very intriguing," said Dr. Fredrick R. Appelbaum of the Hutchinson Cancer Center in Seattle, but "it is also just a single case." Bone marrow transplants carry a 25 percent risk of death and costs that may limit the treatment to only the wealthiest of patients.

Dec 18. *His name is Connery. Sean Connery. And "People" magazine has just named the 59-year-old the sexiest man alive.*

Romania in revolution; Ceausescu deposed, seized

Dec 23. It began six days ago when the Romanian government attempted to deport a dissident minister from Timisoara. Today, deposed Communist dictator Nicolae Ceausescu and his wife Elena wallow in custody while the nation drowns in a sea of blood.

The capture of the Ceausescus today is just one more in a series of startling events that has brought this paradigm of Stalinism crashing down. The Romanian revolution began last Sunday when authorities in the city of Timisoara, 250 miles northwest of Bucharest, moved against the Rev. Laszlo Toekes of the Reformed Church. Toekes is an ethnic Hungarian and a vocal supporter of Romania's two million-strong Hungarian community. It remains unclear precisely what happened after police officials arrived to take Toekes away, but within hours as many as 10,000 antigovernment demonstrators were met by tanks and security forces armed with guns water cannons. A bloodbath ensued. Troops loyal to Ceausescu mowed down thousands of unarmed men, women and children. A mass grave choked with 4,500 muddy corpses testifies to the brutality. One witness visiting from Hungary said, "It was like hell."

On Wednesday, President Ceausescu, who had just returned from a state visit to Iran, promptly addressed the nation to blame "fascists" and Hungarian agitators for the unrest in Timisoara. But the following day it became clear that the long-suffering Romanian people believed none of it. Before an enormous gathering outside the presidential palace in Bucharest, Ceausescu was speaking of "the freedom and life of our people, and the well-being of the whole nation" when he was interrupted by three minutes of hoots and jeers from the crowd. By nightfall, an estimated 15,000 people had assembled in University Square where, once again, heavily armed security forces attacked demonstrators, killing 13 people.

By Thursday it was evident that the end had come for the Ceausescu regime. Regular army troops were siding in force with the protesters and overwhelming the dreaded Securitat, Ceausescu's highly loyal militia, in bloody street battles. That day, a provisional government was formed under former Foreign Minister Corneliu Manescu.

The formal announcement made today that Ceausescu had been caught near Tirgoviste and would stand trial ends the wild speculation as to his whereabouts. It was believed for a time that he had escaped the country. Fighting between the army and the Securitat continues. But with their leader in custody, the pro-Ceausescu forces are fighting for their lives (→ 31).

Tanks, idle in the morning mist, heighten the surrealism of the last few days.

Dec 22. *At no point along its expanse was the Berlin Wall more a symbol of a divided Germany than at the Brandenburg Gate, just near the famed Checkpoint Charlie crossing between the two Berlins. Today, the countries' leaders, and huge joyous crowds, met to open the Wall at its symbolic center.*

Series of mystery bombings rocks U.S.

Dec 23. A judge and a lawyer have been killed and another judge injured by pipe bomb explosions in the past week. Two undetonated devices have also been found. The most recent attack came yesterday, when a blast seriously injured Judge John P. Corderman of the Washington County Circuit. It exploded in his apartment in Hagerstown, Md., at 2:30 p.m., damaging his eardrum and sending shrapnel into his stomach, abdomen and right hand. He was reported in stable condition last night by a spokeswoman for Washington County Hospital.

Federal agents involved with the case stress that no evidence exists to link the attack on Judge Corderman with the mail bombs that killed appellate court judge Robert S. Vance in Alabama on Saturday and Savannah lawyer Robert Robinson on Monday. The construction of those bombs, however, suggests that they are related to the two undetonated devices, which were found in Atlanta, Ga., and Jacksonville, Fla. FBI agents have also found links between the bombing spree in the South and an attack against the Atlanta office of the NAACP last August. Some say the bombs are the work of white supremacists; others suggest a drug cartel is responsible. Authorities are unsure, and neither suggestion has been linked to either the motive or the mechanism of yesterday's attack on Judge Corderman (→ 28).

DECEMBER
1989

Su	Mo	Tu	We	Th	Fr	Sa
					1	2
3	4	5	6	7	8	9
10	11	12	13	14	15	16
17	18	19	20	21	22	23
24	25	26	27	28	29	30
31						

24. United States: Doctors report crack use can lead to potentially fatal lung ailments similar to pneumonia.

24. Baton Rouge, La.: Massive explosion at Exxon oil refinery, nation's second largest, kills at least one and injures many.

25. Tehran: Iran releases 50 Iraqi POWs to the Red Cross as a humanitarian gesture.

25. Eastern Europe: For the first time in decades, Eastern Europeans celebrate Christmas freely and openly and for the first time in history church masses are broadcast live.

25. East Berlin: Leonard Bernstein conducts a performance of Beethoven's Ninth Symphony at the Berlin Wall in a plea for German unity.

26. Lebanon: Israel launches two attacks, one by air, one on ground, against communist bases in southern Lebanon.

27. Beijing: Chinese government is circulating memo to party members accusing Soviet President Gorbachev of "subversion of socialism."

27. India: Weeks after widespread rioting between Hindus and Muslims, government reports some 1,500 people have been found in mass graves.

27. Brazil: Heavy flooding in has killed 35 people and left as many as 200,000 homeless.

28. Atlanta: TV station gets letter from Americans for a Competent Federal Judiciary System, threatening to kill more judges and black leaders if justice continues to cater to blacks.

28. Australia: Earthquake kills 11 and injures 120; army protects Newcastle from looters.

29. Prague: Vaclav Havel sworn in as President of Czech republic, day after Alexander Dubcek is elected president of Parliament.

29. Warsaw: Polish Senate passes radical plan to institute free market.

30. Washington, D.C.: U.S. admits ransacking home of Nicaraguan ambassador to Panama; weapons were found.

Vatican harbors Noriega

Dec. 29. No sudden desire for absolution drove Manuel Noriega to see the Archbishop of Panama on Christmas: he came for sanctuary. "He simply drove up in a private car and asked for political asylum," said Archbishop Marcos McGrath.

General Noriega has been in hiding since the U.S. invasion began. He faces indictment in the United States on over a dozen racketeering and cocaine charges, and his flight to the Vatican embassy is obviously an attempt to gain a negotiated reprieve. The White House, which set Noriega's capture as a main objective of the invasion, is satisfied that his whereabouts are known and that he can not be a rallying point for his troops. Treating the events as a victory, Defense Secretary Dick Cheney said, "it is clear . . . that the Panamanian people have no use for him, that he had to take sanctuary in a foreign embassy."

For three days, American diplomats have been negotiating with the Vatican for Noriega's release, but no conclusion is in sight. A Vatican official today called the United States an "occupying power" and blamed Washington for the impasse. Noriega has said he wants to go to Cuba or Spain, and while Panama has no extradition treaty with the United States, it is unlikely that he has any desire to stay and face charges of narcotics trafficking and homicide. Once his location was made known, jeering crowds collected at the embassy. U.S. occupying forces set up speakers outside the compound to blare rock 'n' roll

One of the general's last triumphs: after the failed coup in October.

— songs like *I Fought the Law and the Law Won,* — a kind of music Noriega is known to detest.

Despite the highly visible presence of U.S. troops, daily life is settling down. The Panamanian Defense Forces have not resumed their role as the army and police of the nation, so U.S. forces are shouldering the task of rounding up Noriega's Dignity Battalions and imposing order. As for the new government, President Guillermo Endara has hastened to assure an anxious public that he will not purge former Noriega supporters. But he and his compatriots have yet to take charge of the country. As one Latin American diplomat pointed out, "So far, they are letting the Americans do their dirty work" (→ 30).

American troops found Noriega's private cache. In his office: 100 pounds of cocaine. At home: stacks of pictures of naked women, a framed picture of Adolph Hitler, $3 million cash and a veritable museum of modern weaponry.

Kremlin paralyzed over Baltic dissent

Dec. 28. Two days after a Central Committee meeting failed to reach the "ultimate decision" on the Lithuanian Communist Party's recent split with Moscow, the Latvian Parliament has voted to erase the local party's monopoly on power. This comes two days after Soviet President Gorbachev agreed to meet with Lithuanian party leaders and four days after the Congress of Deputies condemned the 1939 Hitler-Stalin Pact, which gave the Baltics to Moscow. Despite the constitutional crisis, Gorbachev has made clear that secession would "sow discord, bloodshed and death."

Beckett curtain call

His legacy of the absurd will live on.

Dec. 26. Samuel Beckett, whose *Waiting for Godot* set modern theater on a new course, was buried today in Paris, where he died last Friday at 83. *Godot,* about two tramps seeking a salvation that never comes, is credited with being the work that led later playwrights to experiment, among them Edward Albee, David Mamet, Harold Pinter and Tom Stoppard. Beckett also wrote poetry and fiction, the best known of the latter being a trilogy *Molloy, Malone Dies* and *The Unnamable.* Born and reared in Ireland, Beckett moved to France in 1932 and, with his wife, was active in the Resistance during the war. His wife died earlier this year.

Ceausescus are executed

Dec 31. Peace has finally returned to Romania. Five days after deposed Communist leader Nicolae Ceausescu and his wife Elena were summarily tried and executed for a series of crimes, including genocide, the Romanian people are awakening to a freer society.

The provisional government of President Ion Iliescu has been quick to dismantle the old regime. Today, the new leader announced that the Communist Party will soon meet to dissolve itself, and that free elections will be held in April. Among numerous other changes, typewriters no longer have to be registered, abortion is now legal, citizens are no longer required by law to refer to an official as "comrade" and the Communist emblem has been re-

Nicolae Ceausescu may be the least-mourned victim of the revolution.

moved from the nation's flag.

On Monday, Romanian television showed a tape of Ceausescu's two-hour trial, during which the ousted despot remained defiant to the end. A film of his bullet-riddled corpse was aired later during the same broadcast. The proof of Ceausescu's abrupt demise solidified the success of the two-week-old popular revolution, which has been the bloodiest in Eastern Europe. While Ceausescu lived, his brutal Securitat continued to fight, out of loyalty to Ceausescu and a desperate attempt to save their own lives. Over the past two days, however, the Securitat's armed resistance has withered. Nonetheless, estimates of the death toll over the past two weeks run from 10,000 to 80,000.

Funerals in Romania are an all-too-common sight. Thousands are dead.

1989: Sex, lies and the Satanic Verses

Top-grossing films:
1. *Batman* — $251 million; **2.** *Indiana Jones and the Last Crusade* — $196 million; **3.** *Lethal Weapon II* — $147 million; **4.** *Honey, I Shrunk the Kids* — $130 million; **5.** *Rain Man* — $127 million. Total box office receipts — $5 billion.

Top-selling albums:
1. *Don't Be Cruel* — Bobby Brown; **2.** *Hangin Tough* — New Kids on the Block; **3.** *Forever Your Girl* — Paula Abdul; **4.** *New Jersey* — Bon Jovi; **5.** *Appetite for Destruction* — Guns 'n' Roses.

Top-selling singles:
1. *Look Away* — Chicago; **2.** *My Prerogative* — Bobby Brown; **3.** *Every Rose Has Its Thorn* — Poison; **4.** *Straight Up* — Paula Abdul; **5.** *Miss You Much* — Janet Jackson.

Best-selling fiction:
1. *The Joy Luck Club* — Amy Tan; **2.** *The Satanic Verses* — Salman Rushdie; **3.** *While My Pretty One Sleeps* — Mary Higgins Clark; **4.** *Star* — Danielle Steel; *The Temple of My Familiar* — Alice Walker; *The Russia House* — John LeCarre; **5.** *The Cardinal of the Kremlin* — Tom Clancy; *Red Phoenix* — Larry Band; *The Negotiator* — Forsyth Frederick.

Best-selling non-fiction:
1. *All I Really Need to Know I Learned in Kindergarten* — Robert Fulghum; **2.** *A Brief History of Time* — Stephen W. Hawking; **3.** *Wealth Without Risk* — Charles J. Givens; **4.** *The Eight-Week Cholesterol Cure* — Robert E. Kowalski; **5.** *The T-Factor Diet* — Martin Katahn.

Steven Soderbergh, in his first effort as a director, parlayed a low budget into high praise and box office receipts. sex, lies and videotape *is a funny, intimate film about power and sincerity that won the Gold Palm at Cannes.*

Baseball's feisty Billy Martin dies in crash

Dec 25. Billy Martin, renowned as much for his off-field fights as his abilities as a baseball player and manager, died today as his pickup truck, driven by a friend, skidded off an icy upstate New York road and rammed into a culvert. Martin, 61, died of a broken neck and other injuries. The friend faces drunk driving charges. In an eight-year playing career with the Yankees, Martin starred in numerous World Series. He went on to manage the Yankees five separate times, in the meantime piloting Minnesota, Detroit, Texas and Oakland as well.

Martin: end of a tumultuous life.

Words of wisdom — or something like that

I don't want these. Give me big shoes. —**What the Kenyan native says in Maa in the Nike ad.**

Big deal, death always went with the territory. See you in Disneyland. —**Murderer Richard Ramirez, after receiving the death sentence.**

Outside of the killings, we have one of the lowest crime rates. —**D.C. Mayor Marion Barry.**

Hawaii has always been a very pivotal role in the Pacific. It is in the Pacific. It is a part of the United States that is an island that is right here. —**Dan Quayle in Hawaii.**

You all look like happy campers to me. Happy campers you are, happy campers you have been, and, as far as I am concerned, happy campers you will always be. —**Dan Quayle, to his Samoan hosts.**

I stand by all the misstatements. —**Dan Quayle, to the U.S. press.**

You go to bed every night knowing there are things you are not aware of. —**Reagan, on being President.**

How do you stop them from talking? —**Soviet official, after seeing Congress in action.**

We need spiritual values. We need a revolution of the mind. —**Mikhail S. Gorbachev.**

The nine months that shook the post-war world

The faces of change in Eastern Europe

Beginning in April with Poland's groundbreaking provisions for free elections and ending in Romania's bloody revolution, events in Eastern Europe have caught nearly all pundits off guard. At year's end we are left with a stream of new leaders, a blinding flurry of promises and policies — and a new world.

East Germany. *September: Exodus to West through Hungary begins. October: Protests force Communists to replace hard-line party chief Erich Honecker (left) with Egon Krenz. November: Massive purges fail to quell protests; government ends travel restrictions and Berlin Wall begins to fall. Party promises free elections and names Communist Hans Modrow (right) Prime Minister. December: Non-Communist Manfred Gerlach named President; reformist Gregor Gysi replaces Krenz as party chairman.*

Czechoslovakia. *October: Demonstrators meet with clubs and mass arrests. November: Government offers liberalization of travel regulations. As demonstrations swell to hundreds of thousands, party leadership resigns, leaving Karel Urbanek as party chief. With millions in streets denouncing new government, party gives up monopoly on power and promises free elections. December: Marian Calfa replaces Ladislav Adamec as Prime Minister; hard-line President Gustav Husak (left) resigns; playwright Vaclav Havel (right) chosen President.*

Poland. *April: Communist Party agrees to free elections after talks with Lech Walesa's Solidarity union. June: Vote hands Solidarity a resounding victory. August: Tadeusz Mazowiecki (right) becomes first non-Communist Prime Minister of an East bloc nation. Ex-Communist Party chief Gen. Wojciech Jaruzelski (left) remains as President.*

Hungary. *May: Border with Austria begins to open. June: Four-man presidency led by Rezso Nyers (right) chosen to head government. October: Karoli Grosz (left) ousted as party chief; party name changed to Socialist; social democratic platform adopted. November: Free vote allows new Parliament — to be elected in spring — to choose President.*

Bulgaria. *November: After initially rejecting glasnost, party suddenly ousts Todor Zhivkov (left) as party leader on day after opening of Berlin Wall; Petar Mladenov (right) becomes President and party chief. December: As demonstrators continue to press for change, Mladenov calls for end to party's monopoly; multiparty elections promised for spring; party congress set for March 26.*

A vicious tide of revolution and reaction

ROMANIA

"The sentence was death and the sentence was executed." With those words Romanian radio announced the end of dictator Nicolae Ceausescu's 24-year reign. It was a measure of the man that Soviet television could say of him, "In repressing his people he may have lagged behind our Stalin, but he nevertheless worked hard at it."

Surely few have had better reason to rebel than the Romanians. Ceausescu and his wife, Elena, led a hard line that demanded subservience so complete that typewriters had to be registered. Ceausescu's obsession with paying off the nation's $21 billion foreign debt led him to export food for currency even as his own people went hungry. "If we had a little more food it would be like wartime," went one joke. Ceausescu's family, however, escaped poverty. Some 300 of his relatives were on the government payroll, and he allegedly hid $1 bil-

Ceausescu: Fallen feudal lord.

lion in Swiss bank accounts.

For all that, up until late December, Ceausescu seemed to have hi[s] people under control. What turne[d] their fear into rage? Said one ana[lyst: they "faced at last the choic[e] to die fast or die slowly."

ALBANIA

Only one East European nation has so far eluded the reach of the "year of democracy." That is Albania, whose Stalinist leaders thought even the pre-Gorbachev Soviet rulers were too liberal and severed ties with the Soviets in 1961. With perestroika, Albania's relations with the Warsaw Pact grew so strained that when long-time leader Enver Hoxha died, Albania would accept condolences only from Romania.

Albania, where the Communists took power during a civil war in 1944, is arguably the most isolated country in the world. Its insistence on self-reliance is so great that it has banned cars rather than import them. The cost of xenophobia has been high: Albania has the lowest standard of living in Europe.

But it also has no foreign debt, and medical treatment and education are completely funded by the state. In search of the "new man," wholly devoted to the republic, the regime subjects secondary school students to a yearly regimen of seven months' study, two months' production work and one month of military training. Hoxha disciple Ra-

Alia: Reaction in a flood of reform.

miz Alia runs the country with [a] control that may make some of hi[s] neighbors nostalgic. There are n[o] street protests in Tirana.

Even Albania needs currency[,] however, and there are signs, in th[e] form of increased tourism and ne[w] commercial ties with Europe, tha[t] it is opening up slightly to get it[.] Still, perestroika is remote. "Eve[n] the turtles would run," said one ref[ugee, if Albania opened its borders.

And a "post-post-war" era begins to take shape

Now, what hath glasnost wrought?

He has been touted as the greatest statesman of the late 20th century, but Soviet leader Mikhail Gorbachev may have trouble getting through the next few months. His economy is gutted; one-party rule is under attack; and secessionist talk abounds. "Enough!" shouted Gorbachev recently at an unruly meeting of the Soviet Congress.

Gorbachev's reforms have unleashed forces that seem to be spinning the Soviet Union toward collapse. Goes one joke: "Brezhnev brought us to the edge of the abyss and Gorbachev is taking a giant step forward." Certain changes are probably inevitable. Article 6 of the Constitution, which guarantees one-party rule, will probably fall to pressure from the opposition. Independence for the Baltics is unavoidable. Each of these, however, would place Gorbachev in even greater peril with the party's hard-liners.

Tearing down the Wall may prove easier than building a new order in its place.

Washington strives to keep the pace

President George Bush is a lucky man. Events in Eastern Europe have presented opportunities that could ensure him a place in the history books. So far, he has moved cautiously, initially unconvinced that Soviet leader Mikhail Gorbachev really intended to reform, later afraid to push the reforms off track. But by the close of the Malta summit, Bush admitted that Gorbachev's handling of events "absolutely mandated new thinking."

Bush has definitely jumped on the Gorbachev bandwagon, prolonging the Soviet leader's job tenure by offering him economic aid. But beyond that, Washington has offered Eastern Europe only about $455 million, small change compared to the billions it spent on Western Europe after World War II. Secretary of State James Baker has also presented some proposals to show that the United States

Stumbling into the post-Cold War world

And then there were none.

The violent collapse of the Romanian regime in the waning days of 1989 completed the defection from communism of the six Soviet satellites in the Warsaw Pact. "The Cold War is over," declared Soviet Foreign Minister Eduard Shevardnadze, assuming, as did many, that with the pact toothless and its members embracing democracy, the superpower rivalry was at an end.

The most stunning thing about the upheaval was the ease with which it took place — as if millions collectively woke up from a long nightmare and said, "Enough!" In years past, the tide of reform would have brought tanks into the streets: But this time Soviet leader Mikhail Gorbachev refused to interfere. One Soviet official quipped that Gorbachev had instituted the Sinatra Doctrine: allowing Eastern Europe to do things "their way."

"When the ice breaks up, it can be very dangerous," British Prime Minister Margaret Thatcher has cautioned. Certainly, instability will grip Eastern Europe for years to come. Inexperienced new leaders will have to find ways to combine the socialist security net with capitalist productivity. Ethnic tensions are likely to erupt without the Soviets to suppress them. Still, there is good reason to hope that the "post-post-war" era will be a peaceful one. With the exception of Romania, the revolutions have been remarkably free of violence. The superpowers are united in supporting reform. And with one exception, no one is talking about the powder keg issue of redrawing boundaries.

The big exception, of course, is Germany. Reunification seems inevitable, and the resulting colossus will dominate its neighbors and disrupt the balance of power, a prospect that is unnerving to anyone whose memory goes back at least 40 years. "Germany's very size and location create problems even when the Germans behave well," said analyst Michael Mandelbaum.

The pace of reform has turned some observers into conservatives. Gorbachev spoke for many when he warned against "artificial acceleration" of the "process of change." What is certain is that the brave new world's leaders have yet to leap wholeheartedly into their future.

Gorbachev: Catalyst for change.

The economy, the nation's most pressing problem, needs a massive transfusion if Gorbachev is to avoid a revolt from below. Some are urging the President to impose emergency law and force reforms, but for now he is stalling, reluctant to jeopardize his chance to receive Western aid. In the end, the future of Soviet democracy may depend on whether Gorbachev can negotiate a route to a mixed economy.

Bush: A reluctant convert.

plans to stay active in "Europe's neighborhood," or as Bush said, "remain a European power."

Should Bush propose some brave new policy for the "post-post-war" world? It may not matter, since the thorniest issues will probably be resolved by European rather than super powers. "When the new shape of the world is decided," concludes Soviet expert Stephen Sestanovich, "it won't be one-on-one at all."

The World's Nations

This section gives brief updated facts on each nation's geographical location, population, area, language, religion, political status, and membership in international organizations. The head of state and head of government are also named. Figures provided for Gross National Product (GNP) and population are the latest available. Currency values are based on Sept. 30, 1989, indicative rates. The texts provide a short summary of the main events of 1989 up to early December. A list of abbreviations used is provided on page 123.

Afghanistan

Central Asia
251,773 sq. mi.
Pop: 10-12m.
UN

Capital: Kabul (Pop: 2m.)
Official languages: Pushtu, Dari (Persian)
Religion: Muslim (Shiite, Sunni)
Political status: People's republic
Head of state: Najibullah (since 1987)
GNP per capita: $250 (1985)
Currency: afghani ($1 = 63.02)

Despite the withdrawal of the last Soviet troops on Feb. 15, under the terms of the April 1988 U.S. and Soviet-guaranteed Geneva peace accords, war-torn Afghanistan continued to be rocked by major clashes between government forces and rebel fighters. Much of the bloodshed occurred around the strategic eastern city of Jalalabad, where Afghan rebels repeatedly tried to break the Soviet-equipped army's hold on the town. Mujahedeen guerrillas also repeatedly launched rocket attacks on the capital, often causing heavy civilian casualties. In February, President Najibullah declared a state of emergency, appointing a 20-man Supreme Military Council to replace Prime Minister Hasan Sharq. The Council took over full control of economic, political and military policy. In July, U.S. free-lance photographer Tony O'Brien was released after having been held for six weeks by the security forces.

Albania

Southeastern
Europe
11,101 sq. mi.
Pop: 3.08m.
UN

Capital: Tirana (Pop: 206,000)
Official language: Albanian
Religion: officially atheist
Political status: Socialist people's republic
Head of state: Ramiz Alia (since 1982)
Head of government: Adil Carçani (since 1982)
GNP per capita: $930 (1986)
Currency: lek ($1 = 6.50)

Tensions with Belgrade over the presence of some 1.7 million ethnic Albanians in Yugoslavia's Kosovo Province remained high in 1989. Albania, in June, welcomed China's crackdown on student demonstrators.

Algeria

North Africa
919,595 sq. mi.
Pop: 23.85m.
UN, AL, OAU,
OPEC

Capital: Algiers (Pop: 1,721,607)
Official language: Arabic
Religion: Sunni Muslim
Political status: Socialist republic
Head of state: Chadli Bendjedid (since 1979)
Head of government: Mouloud Hamrouche (since 1989)
GNP per capita: $2,570 (1986)
Currency: Algerian dinar ($1 = 8.15)

The adoption in February of a new constitution paved the way for a multi-party system after some 25 years of rule by the socialist FLN party. By year's end, Algeria was, however, faced with a severe economic crisis.

Andorra

Southern
Europe
180 sq. mi.
Pop: 51,400

Capital: Andorra la Vella (Pop: 15,639)
Official language: Catalan
Religion: Roman Catholic
Political status: Co-principality
Heads of state: The Spanish Bishop of Urgel, Msgr. Joan Marti y Alanis, and French President François Mitterrand
Head of government: Josef Pintat Solans (since 1986)
GNP per capita: $9,000
Currencies: franc and peseta

Andorra's 6,500 voters were voting in late December to elect the 28 members of the ruling body, the General Council, and nationalist candidates seemed well-placed to win.

Angola

Southwestern
Africa
481,351 sq. mi.
Pop: 9.39m.
UN, OAU

Capital: Luanda (Pop: 1.2m.)
Official language: Portuguese
Religions: Roman Catholic 55%, Protestant 9%, animist 34%
Political status: Socialist people's republic
Head of state: José Eduardo dos Santos (since 1979)
GNP per capita: $500 (1985)
Currency: kwanza ($1 = 30.85)

After 14 years of civil war, a cease-fire came into force in June following the reconciliation between President dos Santos and Jonas Savimbi, leader of the South African-backed, pro-Western UNITA rebel forces. More than 70,000 civilians died in the conflict, while some 400,000 Angolans were forced to flee abroad. The cease-fire came after the start of the pullout of an estimated 50,000 Cuban troops sent in to support Luanda's Marxist regime. The withdrawal is due to be completed by July 1991. However, the cease-fire accord was violated by both sides. In October, President Mobutu of Zaire tried to bring the two sides back to the negotiating table, while U.S. envoys sought to foster a settlement of the conflict that has devastated the country.

Antigua and Barbuda

Caribbean
171 sq. mi.
Pop: 81,500
UN, OAS,
Caricom, CW

Capital: St John's (Pop: 30,000)
Official language: English
Religion: Christian (mostly Anglican)
Political status: Constitutional monarchy
Head of state: Queen Elizabeth II
Head of government: Vere C. Bird (since 1981)
GNP per capita: $2,380 (1986)
Currency: Eastern Caribbean dollar ($1 = 2.72)

The Conservative Party won 15 of the 17 parliamentary seats in a March vote, despite gains by centrist candidates. In September, the country was badly hit by Hurricane Hugo.

Argentina

South America
1,073,358 sq. mi.
Pop: 31.06m.
UN, LAIA,
OAS

Capital: Buenos Aires (Pop: 9,927,404)
Official language: Spanish
Religion: Roman Catholic 92%
Political status: Federal republic
Head of state: Carlos Menem (since 1989)
GNP per capita: $2,350 (1986)
Currency: austral ($1 = 654.76)

From the time he took office as President on July 8, Peronist leader Menem battled against the country's worst economic crisis ever. A policy of wage freezes succeeded in cutting inflation to 9 percent in September from 200 percent in July. Relations with Britain, broken off after the 1982 Falklands war, improved in 1989.

Australia

South Pacific
2,966,200 sq. mi.
Pop: 16.25m.
UN, ANZUS,
CW, OECD

Capital: Canberra (Pop: 285,800)
Official language: English
Religions: Anglican 36%, other Protestant 25%, Roman Catholic 33%
Political status: Federal constitutional monarchy
Head of state: Queen Elizabeth II
Head of government: Robert Hawke (since 1983)
GNP per capita: $11,910 (1986)
Currency: Australian dollar ($1 = 1.33)

The country's Labor government in serious electoral trouble since the middle of the year, suffered a stinging rebuff in crucial November state elections in South Australia. The vote marked a 5 percent swing away from the Labor Party. The result was seen as a sign of trouble for the government of Prime Minister Bob Hawke and of growing discontent with high interest rates resulting from Canberra's efforts to slow down an overheated economy. This setback came as Hawke mapped out his strategy for general elections, due by the middle of 1990. Hawke, who turned 60 in December, will be seeking a record fourth term. In May, the country's foreign debt crossed the psychological threshold of 100 billion Australian dollars. In August, a pay dispute led to the resignation of 1,645 airline pilots, plunging air travel into chaos. Military planes were used to ferry stranded passengers. By year's end, the dispute was close to a final settlement.

Austria

Western Europe
32,376 sq. mi.
Pop: 7.58m.
UN, EFTA,
OECD

Capital: Vienna (Pop: 1,479,841)
Official language: German
Religions: Roman Catholic 84.3%, Protestant 5.6%
Political status: Federal parliamentary republic
Head of state: Kurt Waldheim (since 1986)
Head of government: Franz Vranitzky (since 1986)
GNP per capita: $12,297 (1986)
Currency: schilling ($1 = 13.13)

In July, Austria asked to join the EEC, but by year's end the issue seemed unlikely to be decided until 1993. Thousands of East German refugees poured into Austria from Hungary in September and October.

Bahamas

Caribbean
5,353 sq. mi.
Pop: 236,171
UN, OAS, CW,
Caricom

Capital: Nassau (Pop: 135,437)
Official language: English
Religions: Baptist 29%, Anglican 23%, Roman Catholic 22%
Political status: Constitutional monarchy
Head of state: Queen Elizabeth II
Head of government: Sir Lynden O. Pindling (since 1967)
GNP per capita: $7,190 (1986)
Currency: Bahamian dollar ($1 = 1)

In January, the destroyer USS Spruance ran aground in heavy weather on Andros Island. A member of the Bahamian parliament was indicted in the U.S. in March on charges of conspiring to launder illegal drug money.

Bahrain

Middle East
265.5 sq. mi.
Pop: 421,040
UN, AL, GCC

Capital: Manama (Pop: 151,500)
Official language: Arabic
Religion: Muslim 85%, Christian 7.3%
Political status: Emirate
Head of state: Isa bin Sulman Al-Khalifa (since 1961)
Head of government: Khalifa bin Sulman Al-Khalifa (since 1973)
GNP per capita: $8,530 (1986)
Currency: Bahrain dinar ($1 = 0.377)

The end of the Iran-Iraq war led to hopes that Bahrain would quickly reclaim its position as the Gulf's main banking center. The drop in oil revenues affected the economy in 1989.

Bangladesh

Southern Asia
55,598 sq. mi.
Pop: 104.1m.
UN, CW

Capital: Dhaka (Pop: 3,440,147)
Official language: Bengali
Religions: Muslim 83%, Hindu 16%, Buddhist, Christian
Political status: Presidential republic
Head of state: Hossain Mohammad Ershad (since 1983)
Head of government: Moudud Ahmed (since 1988)
GNP per capita: $140 (1986)
Currency: taka ($1 = 31.24)

The disastrous floods that killed some 2,000 people in late 1988 led the government to take steps such as reforestation and improved inland water drainage aimed at preventing future disasters. However, malnutrition and disease remained problems. In November, a dysentery epidemic left some 350 people dead.

Barbados

Caribbean
166 sq. mi.
Pop: 253,881
UN, CW, OAS,
Caricom

Capital: Bridgetown (Pop: 7,466)
Official language: English
Religions: Anglican 70%, Methodist 9%, Moravian, Roman Catholic
Political status: Constitutional monarchy
Head of state: Queen Elizabeth II
Head of government: Erskine Sandiford (since 1987)
GNP per capita: $4,668 (1987)
Currency: Barbados dollar ($1 = 2.02)

In February, former Finance Minister Richard Haynes set up the National Democratic Party and became opposition leader. Despite a poor sugar-cane harvest, the economy remained healthy due to a tourist boom.

Belgium

Western Europe
11,778 sq. mi.
Pop: 9.88m.
UN, EEC,
NATO, OECD

Capital: Brussels (Pop: 970,346)
Official languages: French, Dutch, German
Religion: mostly Roman Catholic
Political status: Constitutional monarchy
Head of state: King Baudouin I (since 1951)
Head of government: Wilfried Martens (since 1981)
GNP per capita: $9,230 (1986)
Currency: Belgian franc ($1 = 39.14)

Plans to liberalize an 1867 law on abortion sparked an uproar that nearly toppled the government. Abortion foes failed to block debate in Parliament on the controversial issue, which remained unresolved at year's end. In October, a leader of Belgium's Jewish community was murdered, just six months after the killing in Brussels of a Muslim dignitary.

Belize

Central America
8,866 sq. mi.
Pop: 176,000
UN, Caricom,
CW

Capital: Belmopan (Pop: 3,500)
Official language: English
Religions: Roman Catholic 62%, Protestant 28%
Political status: Constitutional monarchy
Head of state: Queen Elizabeth II
Head of government: George Price (since 1989)
GNP per capita: $1,170 (1986)
Currency: Belize dollar ($1 = 2.01)

Center-left candidate George Price beat incumbent Democrat Manuel Esquivel in September elections seen as vital for the consolidation of democracy in the former British colony.

Benin

West Africa
43,483 sq. mi.
Pop: 4.44m.
UN, OAU

Capital: Porto Novo (Pop: 208,258)
Official language: French
Religions: Mainly animist; Christian, Muslim
Political status: Socialist people's republic
Head of state: Mathieu Kérékou (since 1972)
GNP per capita: $270 (1986)
Currency: franc CFA ($1 = 316.90)

President Kérékou's hard-line government in December officially renounced the Marxist-Leninist ideology that had dominated the country's politics and economics since 1974.

Bhutan

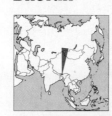

South Asia
18,000 sq. mi.
Pop: 1.4m.
UN

Capital: Thimphu (Pop: 15,000)
Languages: Dzongkha, Lhotsam (Nepali), English
Religions: Buddhist 75%, Hindu 25%
Political status: Monarchy
Head of state: Jigme Singye Wangchuk (since 1972)
Head of government: Council of ministers
GNP per capita: $160 (1987)
Currency: ngultrum ($1 = 16.70)

In April, a royal decree made the wearing of Bhutan's colorful national dress compulsory for all citizens as part of a plan to "preserve and promote" the tiny Himalayan kingdom's national identity.

Bolivia

South America
424,165 sq. mi.
Pop: 7m.
UN, LAIA,
OAS

Capital: Sucre (legal), La Paz (de facto) (pop: 992,592)
Official languages: Spanish, Quechua, Aymara
Religion: Roman Catholic 95%
Political status: Presidential republic
Head of state: Jaime Paz Zamora (since 1989)
GNP per capita: $540 (1986)
Currency: boliviano ($1 = 2.89)

Barely three months after his inauguration, President Paz Zamora was forced to declare a nationwide state of emergency in mid-November as large-scale social unrest and labor disputes threatened to plunge the country into a crisis. This move came barely a month after the World Bank agreed in principle to provide Bolivia with a $2.175 billion loan over three years, on condition that the country remained stable and its government took steps to reduce public spending. The President rejected huge wage demands by teachers, some 2,000 of whom responded by going on a hunger strike.

Botswana

Southern Africa
220,000 sq. mi.
Pop: 1.21m.
UN, CW, OAU

Capital: Gaborone (Pop: 110,973)
Languages: English (official), Setswana
Religions: Bahai, Muslim, Hindu, Christian
Political status: Presidential republic
Head of state: Quett Ketumile Joni Masire (since 1980)
GNP per capita: $840 (1986)
Currency: pula ($1 = 1.97)

In July, specialized units of the U.S. armed forces staged a series of joint exercises in an operation launched to improve the capability of Botswana's army to cope with a major disaster such as a drought or an epidemic.

Brazil

South America
3,286,487 sq. mi.
Pop: 144.3m.
UN, LAIA, OAS

Capital: Brasilia (Pop: 410,999)
Official language: Portuguese
Religion: Roman Catholic 89%, Protestant 6.6%, Spiritualist
Political status: Federal republic
Head of state: José Sarney (since 1985)
GNP per capita: $1,740 (1986)
Currency: new cruzado ($1 = 4.28)

Mired in its worst-ever economic crisis and facing triple-digit inflation and a crushing foreign debt, the country sought desperately in 1989 to find lasting solutions to the problem. Wage freezes and public spending cutbacks sparked a wave of strikes that culminated in a two-day general strike in March. In a November poll, Workers Party candidate Luis Ignacio da Silva won the right to run for the presidency in a mid- December runoff election against center-right candidate Fernando Collor de Mello. Da Silva promised to trim government bureaucracy, remove barriers to foreign investment, promote free-market policies and tax the rich to help the poor. He also vowed to reduce payments on the $110 billion foreign debt.

Brunei

Southeast Asia
2,226 sq. mi.
Pop: 226,300
UN, CW, ASEAN

Capital: Bandar Seri Begawan (Pop: 63,868)
Languages: Malay (official), Chinese, English
Religions: Muslim 63%, Buddhist 14%, Christian 10%
Political status: Sultanate
Head of state: Sir Muda Hassanal Bolkiah Mu'izzadin Waddaulah (since 1967)
Head of government: Sir Muda Hassanal Bolkiah Mu'izzadin Waddaulah
GNP per capita: $15,400 (1986)
Currency: Brunei dollar ($1 = 1.96)

With a fortune estimated at more than $25 billion, Brunei's ruler in 1989 remained by far the world's wealthiest individual, thanks largely to the small Asian monarchy's enormous oil and natural gas reserves.

Bulgaria

Southeastern Europe
42,823 sq. mi.
Pop: 8.97m.
UN, CMEA, Warsaw Pact

Capital: Sofia (Pop: 1,128,859)
Official language: Bulgarian
Religions: Orthodox 85%, Muslim 7%
Political status: Socialist people's republic
Head of state: Petar Mladenov (s. 1989)
Head of government: Georgi Atanasov (since 1986)
GNP per capita: $6,460
Currency: lev ($1 = 0.85)

In May, Sofia strongly denied Western charges that it was heavily involved in the international drugs traffic, while in August the U.S. recalled its ambassador to Sofia as a protest against repeated human rights violations. Tensions with neighboring Turkey remained high as Ankara accused Bulgaria of forcing its ethnic Turkish inhabitants to "Bulgarize" their names. In an unprecedented mid-November shake-up, hard-line leader Todor Zhivkov was ousted and replaced by the pro-Gorbachev Petar Mladenov.

Burkina Faso

Western Africa
105,839 sq. mi.
Pop: 8.53m.
UN, OAU

Capital: Ouagadougou (Pop: 442,223)
Official language: French
Religions: animist 45%, Muslim 43%, Christian 12%
Political status: Presidential republic
Head of state: Blaise Compaoré (since 1987)
Head of government:: Blaise Compaoré
GNP per capita: $150 (1986)
Currency: franc CFA ($1 = 316.90)

Burkinabe leader Blaise Compaoré further consolidated his hold on power in September when he ordered the execution of two senior army officers who had tried to oust him.

Burma

Southeast Asia
261,228 sq. mi.
Pop: 39.84m.
UN

Capital: Rangoon (Pop: 2,458,712)
Official language: Burmese
Religion: Buddhist
Political status: Socialist people's republic
Head of state: Saw Maung (since 1988)
Head of government: Saw Maung (since 1988)
GNP per capita: $200 (1986)
Currency: kyat ($1 = 6.84)

In August, a government-decreed amnesty led to the release of nearly 19,000 prisoners, many of whom had been jailed for taking part in banned political activities. In November, martial law was lifted in several northern provinces and the year-old military regime announced that the country's first general elections since 1960 would be held in May 1990.

Burundi

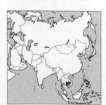

Central Africa
10,759 sq. mi.
Pop: 5.13m.
UN, OAU

Capital: Bujumbura (Pop: 272,600)
Official languages: Kirundi, French
Religions: Roman Catholic 60%, traditional tribal beliefs 32%
Political status: Presidential republic
Head of state: Pierre Buyoya (since 1987)
Head of government: Adrien Sibomana (since 1988)
GNP per capita: $240 (1988)
Currency: Burundi franc ($1 = 160.79)

Burundi in September celebrated the second anniversary of the founding of the country's third republic and the government appealed to citizens to help get the hard-hit, agriculture-based economy back on its feet.

Cambodia

Southeast Asia
69,898 sq. mi.
Pop: 6.23m.
UN

Capital: Phnom Penh (Pop: 500,000)
Official language: Khmer
Religions: Theravada Buddhism, Roman Catholic and Muslim minorities
Political status: People's republic
Head of state: Heng Samrin (since 1979)
Head of government: Hun Sen (since 1985)
GNP per capita: no accurate estimate available
Currency: riel ($1 = 150)

The last Vietnamese soldiers withdrew from Cambodia in late September, 10 years and nine months after they were sent in to topple the Khmer Rouge regime led by Pol Pot, held responsible for the massacre of hundreds of thousands of Cambodians between 1975 and 1978. Vietnam's troops, which suffered casualties estimated at well over 50,000 dead, pulled out after failing to defeat the well-armed, Chinese-backed anti-communist guerrillas, of which Khmer Rouge forces remained the chief component. Attempts to reach a lasting peace settlement failed due to disagreements within the anti-communist alliance. Following the Vietnamese pullout, Cambodian government troops appeared ill-prepared to cope with the guerrilla forces and there were fears among the population and in the West that the Khmer Rouge, which in November scored major military victories in the south and southwest, would succeed in making a comeback.

Cameroon

Western Central Africa
179,558 sq. mi.
Pop: 11m.
UN, OAU

Capital: Yaounde (Pop: 435,892)
Official languages: French, English
Religions: animist 39%, Roman Catholic 21%, Muslim 22%, Protestant 18%
Political status: Presidential republic
Head of state: Paul Biya (since 1982)
GNP per capita: $910 (1986)
Currency: franc CFA ($1 = 316.90)

Cameroon reported a good cotton crop and sought to persuade Canadian and Western European businessmen to invest in the country. Despite an anti-AIDS program, the disease claimed nearly 100 lives in 1989.

Canada

North America
3,553,357 sq. mi.
Pop: 25.6m.
UN, NATO, CW, OECD, OAS

Capital: Ottawa (Pop: 819,263)
Official languages: English, French
Religions: Roman Catholic, Protestant
Political status: Parliamentary monarchy
Head of state: Queen Elizabeth II
Head of government: Martin Brian Mulroney (since 1984)
GNP per capita: $14,100 (1986)
Currency: Canadian dollar ($1 = 1.18)

During a February visit to Ottawa, his first abroad since taking office, U.S. President George Bush agreed to open bilateral talks on the controversial acid rain issue that had severely strained relations between the two nations. In April local elections, Newfoundland's Liberal Party put an end to 17 years of conservative rule in the province. The same month saw the printing of Canada's last one-dollar bill. These are being phased out, to be replaced by coins. Montreal police in April seized half a ton of Colombian cocaine in Canada's biggest-ever drug bust. Also in April, budgetary constraints led to the cancellation of plans to spend an estimated 8 billion Canadian dollars on French or British-built nuclear submarines. The country's huge foreign debt remained a major problem, forcing the government to cut military spending and raise taxes. At the July summit meeting of leaders of the world's seven richest countries, Mulroney expressed satisfaction over plans to fight growing threats to the Earth's ecology. Also in July, devastating forest fires spread through Manitoba, Saskatchewan and Ontario, leading to the evacuation of tens of thousands of inhabitants. In September, Quebec's liberal Prime Minister Robert Bourassa was re-elected for a fourth term, despite gains by the pro-independence candidate. In October, Canada joined the OAS, thus paving the way for closer ties with Latin America. Mulroney in November made a successful five-day visit to the Soviet Union.

Cape Verde

Atlantic Ocean
1,557 sq. mi.
Pop: 359,000
UN, OAU

Capital: Praia (Pop: 37,676)
Official language: Portuguese
Religion: Roman Catholic 98%
Political status: Republic
Head of state: Aristides Maria Pereira (since 1975)
Head of government: Pedro Verona Rodrigues Pires (since 1975)
GNP per capita: $460 (1986)
Currency: escudo Caboverdiano ($1 = 82.73)

The country continued to rely heavily on international aid and the U.S. increased its economic assistance in June. The government also sought to provide incentives for foreign investment programs.

Central African Republic

Central Africa
240,324 sq. mi.
Pop: 2.86m.
UN, OAU

Capital: Bangui (Pop: 596,776)
Official language: French
Religions: animist beliefs 57%, Roman Catholic 20%, Protestant 15%, Muslim 8%
Political status: Presidential republic
Head of state: Gen. André Kolingba (since 1981)
GNP per capita: $290 (1986)
Currency: franc CFA ($1 = 316.90)

The re-scheduling under favorable conditions of the country's foreign debt burden considerably eased economic hardships, although General Kolingba in 1989 stressed the need for further budgetary efforts.

Chad

Central Africa
495,752 sq. mi.
Pop: 5.4m.
UN, OAU

Capital: N'Djaména (Pop: 511,700)
Official languages: French, Arabic
Religions: Muslim 44%, animist 38%, Christian 17%
Political status: Presidential republic
Head of state: Hissène Habré (since 1982)
GNP per capita: $88 (1984)
Currency: franc CFA ($1 = 316.90)

After talks between Chad's leader and Libya's Colonel Qaddafi, the two nations in August signed an accord aimed at ending fighting over a strip of desert that has been the focus of 16 years of bloodshed.

Chile

South America
284,520 sq. mi.
Pop: 12.68m.
UN, LAIA, OAS

Capital: Santiago (Pop: 4,858,342)
Official language: Spanish
Religions: Roman Catholic, Protestant, Jewish
Political status: Presidential republic under a military regime
Head of state: Augusto Pinochet Ugarte (since 1974)
GNP per capita: $1,320 (1986)
Currency: Chilean peso ($1 = 319.78)

In mid-December, Chileans were poised to vote in historic presidential and legislative elections. Prior to the ballot, General Pinochet and senior military officers vowed that the ballot would be free and promised to abide by the result. In October, the President disbanded the political police force, CNI, but warned that he would not stand by if a new civilian government were to take action against the military establishment. Christian-Democrat opposition leader Patricio Aylwin was favored to win the presidential elections.

China

East Asia
3,682,131 sq. mi.
Pop: 1,072.2m.
UN

Capital: Beijing (Pop: 5.86m.)
Official language: Chinese
Religions: officially atheist; Confucianism, Buddhism, Taoism
Political status: People's republic
Head of state: Yang Shangkun (since 1989)
Head of government: Li Peng (since 1987)
GNP per capita: $250 (1986)
Currency: yuan ($1 = 3.74)

The brutal crushing in June of the pro-democracy movement, which sent shock waves around the world, cast a shadow over the historic reconciliation between China and the Soviet Union, sealed during a May visit to Beijing by Soviet leader Mikhail Gorbachev. The visit was aimed an ending a 30-year rift between the two communist nations. The June events, which left hundreds if not thousands dead, led to an unprecedented wave of repression and dozens of executions. The Communist Party's reformist leader Zhao Ziyang was ousted and replaced by hard-liner Jiang Zemin. Tensions with the U.S. increased after a Chinese dissident and his wife were granted refuge inside the American Embassy in Beijing. International condemnation of the regime's actions was nearly unanimous, with only Albania and East Germany expressing approval. The U.S. and other Western governments froze their relations with China and applied wide-ranging economic and other sanctions, thus deepening the country's economic woes. The repression in China sparked grave fears among the people of Hong Kong, a British colony due to come under Chinese control in 1997. In November, China's paramount leader Deng Xiaoping resigned from his last post in the party leadership and was replaced by Jiang. During a November visit aimed at halting the deterioration in U.S.-China relations, former President Richard Nixon warned his hosts against further repression.

Colombia

South America
440,829 sq. mi.
Pop: 27.9m.
UN, LAIA, OAS

Capital: Bogota (Pop: 3,982,941)
Official language: Spanish
Religion: Roman Catholic
Political status: Democratic presidential republic
Head of state: Virgilio Barco Vargas (since 1986)
GNP per capita: $1,129 (1986)
Currency: peso ($1 = 410.73)

As the drug crisis worsened dramatically, the government launched an all-out offensive against traffickers, who responded by assassinating judges, forcing Justice Minister Monica de Grieff out of office and, in August, gunning down Sen. Luis Galan, a leading presidential candidate. U.S. aid and equipment to fight the drug lords was sharply increased.

Comoros

Indian Ocean
719 sq. mi.
Pop: 422,500
UN

Capital: Moroni (Pop: 20,112)
Languages: French, Arabic
Religions: Muslim (Sunni) 99%, Christian
Political status: Federal Islamic republic
Head of state: Vacant
GNP per capita: $280 (1986)
Currency: Comorian franc ($1 = 316.90)

President Abderemane, in power since he set up an Islamic republic in 1978, was assassinated in November shortly after winning a referendum that would have allowed him to stay in office until the mid-1990s.

Congo

Central Africa
132,046 sq. mi.
Pop: 2.27m.
UN, OAU

Capital: Brazzaville (Pop: 585,812)
Official language: French
Religions: Roman Catholic 54%, Protestant 24%, animist 19%, Muslim 3%
Political status: People's republic
Head of state: Denis Sassou-Nguesso (since 1979)
Head of government: Ange-Edouard Poungui (since 1984)
GNP per capita: $1,040 (1986)
Currency: franc CFA ($1 = 316.90)

In February, the country marked 10 years of Colonel Sassou-Nguesso's rule amid continued economic difficulties. In September, the Labor Party won parliamentary elections with more than 99 percent of the vote.

Costa Rica

Central America
19,730 sq. mi.
Pop: 2.81m.
UN, OAS

Capital: San José (Pop: 241,464)
Official language: Spanish
Religion: Roman Catholic
Political status: Democratic republic
Head of state: Oscar Arias
Sanchez (since 1986)
Head of government: Rodrigo Arias
Sanchez
GNP per capita: $1,420 (1986)
Currency: colone ($1 = 83.12)

The worsening economic situation, repeated charges of widespread government corruption and his failure to push forward his regional peace plan in 1989 considerably eroded President Arias' popularity.

Cuba

Caribbean
44,206 sq. mi.
Pop: 10.24m.
UN, CMEA

Capital: Havana (Pop: 2,014,800)
Official language: Spanish
Religions: Roman Catholic, Methodist, Baptist
Political status: Socialist republic
Head of state: Fidel Castro Ruz
GNP per capita: $2,696 (1981)
Currency: peso ($1 = 0.77)

Marking the 30th anniversary of the Cuban revolution, Fidel Castro lashed out against the Soviet government's reform policies in January and vowed to stand firm against any attempts to spread "perestroika" or "glasnost" to his country. Relations between Havana and Moscow remained chilly despite an April visit by Soviet leader Gorbachev. In February, the U.N. criticized Cuba for continued human rights violations. The year also saw the start of the withdrawal of Cuban troops from Angola, where some 5,000 Cubans were reported to have died.

Cyprus

Southern Europe
3,572 sq. mi.
Pop: 680,400
UN, CW

Capital: Nicosia (Pop: 164,500)
Official languages: Greek, Turkish
Religions: Greek Orthodox 80%, Muslim 19%
Political status: Republic
Head of state: George Vassiliou (since 1988)
GNP per capita: $6,831 (1987)
Currency: Cyprus pound ($1 = 0.50)

Despite repeated diplomatic efforts spearheaded by the U.N., tensions between the island's Greek and Turkish communities remained strong and little concrete progress was made towards a pull-out of Turkish troops and reunification of the divided country.

Czechoslovakia

Central Europe
49,383 sq. mi.
Pop: 15.5m.
UN, CMEA,
Warsaw Pact

Capital: Prague (Pop: 1,194,000)
Official languages: Czech, Slovak
Religion: Roman Catholic 67%
Political status: Federal socialist republic
Head of state: Gustav Husak (since 1975)
Head of government: Marian Calfa (since 1989)
GNP per capita: $8,700 (1985)
Currency: Czech koruna ($1 = 9.90)

The wind of change that roared through Eastern Europe in late 1989 did not spare Czechoslovakia. As millions of people took to the streets in November to protest Communist Party domination and demand free elections, President Husak and Prime Minister Ladislav Adamec suffered humiliating setbacks in late November when they were ousted from the Politburo. Party leader Milos Jakes stepped down and was replaced by Karel Urbanek. After 20 years of political oblivion, Alexander Dubcek, leader of the failed 1968 "Prague Spring" movement, made a triumphant return to the capital in November. In December, Adamec was replaced by Marian Calfa, a 43-year-old lawyer.

Denmark

Northern
Europe
16,631 sq. mi.
Pop: 5.13m.
UN, EEC,
NATO, OECD

Capital: Copenhagen (Pop: 619,985)
Official language: Danish
Religion: Lutheran 90%
Political status: Constitutional monarchy
Head of state: Queen Margrethe II (since 1972)
Head of government: Poul Schlüter (since 1982)
GNP per capita: $12,640 (1986)
Currency: krone ($1 = 7.25)

In mid-August, Prime Minister Poul Schlüter met President Bush during a visit to the U.S. In October, Denmark became the first nation to grant full rights to homosexuals, including the right to wed.

Djibouti

Northeastern
Africa
8,960 sq. mi.
Pop: 484,000
UN, AL, OAU

Capital: Djibouti (Pop: 290,000)
Official languages: French, Arabic
Religion: mostly Muslim
Political status: Presidential republic
Head of state: Hassan Gouled Aptidon (since 1977)
Head of government: Barkat Gourad Hamadou (since 1978)
GNP per capita: $760 (1984)
Currency: Djibouti franc ($1 = 177.14)

The closure of Ethiopia's border with Djibouti in May did little to slow the flood of refugees from that famine-stricken country. This added a new burden to Djibouti's economy.

Dominica

Caribbean
290 sq. mi.
Pop: 94,191
UN, CW, OAS,
Caricom

Capital: Roseau (Pop: 20,000)
Official language: English
Religion: Roman Catholic 80%
Political status: Republic
Head of state: C.A. Seignoret (since 1983)
Head of government: Mary Eugenia Charles (since 1980)
GNP per capita: $1,210 (1986)
Currencies: French franc, pound sterling and East Caribbean dollar ($1 = EC$2.72)

Hurricane Hugo in mid-September caused severe damage to the country, wiping out 80 percent of the banana crop and wrecking fishing boats.

Dominican Republic

Caribbean
18,700 sq. mi.
Pop: 6.7m.
UN, OAS

Capital: Santo Domingo (Pop: 1,313,172)
Official language: Spanish
Religion: Roman Catholic
Political status: Presidential republic
Head of state: Joaquin Balaguer (since 1986)
GNP per capita: $710 (1986)
Currency: peso oro ($1 = 6.75)

Tensions with neighboring Haiti grew despite attempts to settle a dispute over compensation for the accidental death in January of 50 Haitians.

Ecuador

South America
104,505 sq. mi.
Pop: 9.64m.
UN, LAIA,
OAS

Capital: Quito (Pop: 1,110,248)
Languages: Spanish (official), Quechua
Religion: Roman Catholic
Political status: Presidential republic
Head of state: Rodrigo Borja Cevallos (since 1988)
GNP per capita: $1,160 (1986)
Currency: sucre ($1 = 575)

Marking his first year in office, President Borja vowed in August to press ahead with democratic reforms. In September, he declared a state of emergency after widespread strikes threatened the ailing economy.

Egypt

North Africa
386,900 sq. mi.
Pop: 49.28m.
UN, AL, OAU

Capital: Cairo (Pop: 6,325,000)
Official language: Arabic
Religions: Sunni Muslim 90%, Coptic Christian 7%
Political status: Presidential republic
Head of state: Hosni Mubarak (since 1981)
Head of government: Atef Mohamed Naguib Sidki (since 1986)
GNP per capita: $760 (1986)
Currency: Egyptian pound ($1 = 2.6)

Israel handed back the tiny Taba enclave to Egypt in March after a lengthy dispute. The visit to Cairo of Foreign Minister Eduard Shevardnadze led to closer Soviet-Egyptian ties. In 1989, Egypt restored relations with many Arab nations who had broken off links after the Camp David accords. In July, a U.S. citizen was jailed for five years on charges of spying.

El Salvador

Central America
8,236 sq. mi.
Pop: 5.48m.
UN, OAS

Capital: San Salvador
Official language: Spanish
Religion: Roman Catholic
Political status: Presidential republic
Head of state: Alfredo Cristiani (since 1989)
GNP per capita: $820 (1986)
Currency: colon ($1 = 4.99)

Alfredo Cristiani, the leader of the right-wing Arena Party, won February elections with 53.8 percent of the vote and took office on June 1. His efforts to restore stability suffered a setback in late October when leftist, Soviet and Nicaraguan-armed rebels launched a large-scale offensive that left hundreds dead. Press freedom was suspended during the crisis and government troops raided church groups and humanitarian organizations. The November murder of six Jesuit priests was attributed by the Roman Catholic Church to far-right death squads. The rebels failed to spark a national insurrection. U.S. economic and military assistance remained high, at around $500 million.

Equatorial Guinea

West Africa
10,831 sq. mi.
Pop: 336,000
UN, OAU

Capital: Malabo (Pop: 10,000)
Official language: Spanish
Religions: mostly Roman Catholic; Protestant
Political status: Presidential republic
Head of state: Teodoro Obiang Nguema Mbasogo (since 1979)
GNP per capita: $420 (1983)
Currency: franc CFA ($1 = 316.90)

President Nguema, who ran unopposed in June presidential elections, won a new seven-year term with 99.96 percent of the vote. Only 69 voters cast their ballots against him.

Ethiopia

Northeastern Africa
471,800 sq. mi.
Pop: 46m.
UN, OAU

Capital: Addis Ababa (Pop: 1,412,575)
Languages: Amharic (official), Galla
Religions: Muslim 45%, Ethiopian Orthodox 40%
Political status: People's democratic republic
Head of state: Mengistu Haile Mariam (since 1977)
GNP per capita: $120 (1986)
Currency: birr ($1 = 2.07)

The regime survived a May coup attempt. In September and November, former President Jimmy Carter chaired talks between the government and the rebel Eritrean People's Liberation Front aimed at ending the 28-year conflict in northern Ethiopia, Africa's longest war. Threats of a famine were reported in November.

Fiji

South Pacific
7,076 sq. mi.
Pop: 715,375
UN

Capital: Suva (Pop: 71,608)
Official language: English
Religions: Christian 42%, Hindu 33%, Muslim 6%
Political status: Republic
Head of state: Sir Penaia Ganilau (since 1987)
Head of government: Sir Kamisese Mara (since 1987)
GNP per capita: $1,810 (1986)
Currency: Fiji dollar ($1 = 1.53)

In April, the country's 68-year-old Prime Minister said he planned to retire from politics in late December, at the end of his term. Fiji's current Finance Minister, Josevata Kamikamica, was set to succeed him.

Finland

Northern Europe
117,615 sq. mi.
Pop: 4.94m.
UN, NC, OECD, EFTA

Capital: Helsinki (Pop: 490,034)
Languages: Finnish and Swedish (official), Lappish
Religions: Lutheran 89.2%, Greek Orthodox 1.1%
Political status: Democratic parliamentary republic
Head of state: Mauno Koivisto (since 1982)
Head of government: Harri Holkeri (since 1987)
GNP per capita: $18,118 (1987)
Currency: Finnmark ($1 = 4.27)

In May, Finland officially became the 23rd member state of the 40-year-old Council of Europe. During a mid-October visit to Helsinki, Soviet leader Mikhail Gorbachev vowed to withdraw his nation's few remaining nuclear-armed Golf-class submarines from the Baltic Sea.

France

Western Europe
211,968 sq. mi.
Pop: 55.84m.
UN, EEC, OECD, NATO

Capital: Paris (Pop: 2,188,918)
Official language: French
Religion: Roman Catholic 76%, Muslim 4.5%, Protestant 1.4%
Political status: Parliamentary republic
Head of state: François Mitterrand (since 1981)
Head of government: Michel Rocard (since 1988)
GNP per capita: $10,740 (1986)
Currency: French franc ($1 = 6.34)

1989 was above all the year of the bicentennial of the French Revolution, which was celebrated spectacularly on July 14, Bastille Day. The event, attended by President Bush and many other world leaders, was followed by some 800 million television viewers worldwide. The festivities brought an unprecedented tourist boom, as millions came to attend the Bastille Day parade and the 100th anniversary of the Eiffel Tower. The year was also marked by local elections in March that brought gains for conservative candidates, for the extreme-right National Front, a major setback for the once-powerful Communist Party. In a June ballot for the European Parliament, the newly formed pro-ecology Green Party made a good showing. The government's attempts to bring lasting peace to the French South Pacific territory of New Caledonia suffered a setback in May when a moderate local leader was assassinated. In September, a terrorist bomb ripped apart a French DC-10 airliner over Africa, killing all 171 people on board. By year's end, France was reveling in what was said to be the best wine vintage in over a century, due to exceptional weather conditions.

Gabon

Central Africa
103,346 sq. mi.
Pop: 1.22m.
UN, OAU, OPEC

Capital: Libreville (Pop: 350,000)
Official language: French
Religions: Christian 84% (mostly Roman Catholic), animist
Political status: Presidential republic
Head of state: Omar Bongo (since 1967)
Head of government: Léon Mébiame (since 1975)
GNP per capita: $3,020 (1986)
Currency: franc CFA ($1 = 316.90)

President Bongo reshuffled his cabinet in August, cutting the number of ministers from 46 to 42. In early October, authorities said they had foiled a plot to assassinate the president and seize Premier Mébiame.

Gambia

West Africa
4,127 sq. mi.
Pop: 788,163
UN, OAU, CW

Capital: Banjul (Pop: 44,188)
Official language: English
Religions: Muslim 70%, Christian, animist
Political status: Republic
Head of state: Dawda Kairaba Jawara (since 1970)
GNP per capita: $230 (1986)
Currency: dalasi ($1 = 7.71)

The country celebrated the 24th anniversary of its independence in February. In mid-May, Gambia's leader met in Washington with President Bush to discuss an increase in U.S. economic aid to his country.

Germany (East)

Central Europe
41,827 sq. mi.
Pop: 16.6m.
UN, CMEA, Warsaw Pact

Capital: East Berlin (Pop: 1,223,309)
Official language: German
Religions: Protestant 80.5%, Roman Catholic 11%
Political status: Socialist republic
Head of state: Egon Krenz (since 1989)
Head of government: Hans Modrow (since 1989)
GNP per capita: $10,400 (1985)
Currency: GDR mark ($1 = 1.87)

For East Germany, 1989 was the most momentous year since the country's birth, as its citizens watched one of the most powerful symbols of the postwar division of Europe crumble before their eyes. Already jolted by the ousting in October of hard-line leader Erich Honecker, replaced by the younger Egon Krenz, East Germans reacted with an unprecedented surge of joy to the start of the dismantling of the Berlin Wall, on Nov. 9. This historic event, which allowed hundreds of thousands of exultant East Germans to flood into West Berlin, was almost universally welcomed in the West, although many of Western Europe's leaders warned about the possible effect of the rapid changes in East Germany on the postwar European order.

Honecker's downfall and the opening of the Berlin Wall came after the country had been rocked by repeated and massive pro-democracy demonstrations, and by an unprecedented wave of migration to the West. The exodus of tens of thousands of East German refugees began during the summer. It became a flood after Hungary opened its border with Austria on Sept. 10 to allow East German refugees to reach the West. East Germany's new leader and his reformist Prime Minister, Hans Modrow, acted quickly in November to defuse growing tensions, marked by persistent calls for reform and even for the government's resignation. Krenz was criticized in particular for having praised the Chinese leadership after the June crushing of the pro-democracy student movement in Beijing. Krenz responded by promising free elections and steps aimed at putting the country's economy back on its feet. Modrow vowed to introduce a radical decentralization of the economy by abolishing more than half of the state-decreed plans for industry. The government, however, stressed that it had no intention of restoring capitalism, adding it would act quickly to curb black market currency trading, a problem that had contributed to East Germany's decision to build the Berlin Wall. A special Communist Party congress was scheduled for mid-December, amid intense speculation over whether Krenz would succeed in staying in power, a prospect that appeared increasingly unlikely.

Germany (West)

Central Europe
96,025 sq. mi.
Pop: 61m.
UN, EEC,
NATO, OECD

Capital: Bonn (Pop: 291,400)
Official language: German
Religions: Protestant 49%, Roman
Catholic 44.6%
Political status: Federal republic
Head of state: Richard von Weizsäcker
(since 1984)
Head of government: Helmut Kohl (since
1982)
GNP per capita: $12,080 (1986)
Currency: deutschemark ($1 = 1.87)

The historic events in Eastern Europe, particularly in neighboring East Germany, profoundly affected West Germans, who were faced in September and October with the problems caused by the sudden influx of tens of thousands of East German refugees. These problems became more acute after the breaching in November of the Berlin Wall, which had divided the city since Aug. 13, 1961. The need to find housing and jobs for the refugees soon became the top priority for West Germany's government. By year's end, Turkish and other immigrant workers were complaining that East German job-seekers were being given preferential treatment. In West Berlin, the authorities, already faced with 100,000 unemployed, attempted to cope with thousands of new arrivals from the East. Chancellor Kohl, meanwhile, sought to reassure his country's neighbors, several of whom had expressed reservations about the possibility of German reunification. He reaffirmed his government's commitment to the EEC and NATO after several EEC leaders had voiced fears that West Germany would gradually turn toward the Eastern Bloc and away from its Western allies.

Ghana

West Africa
92,010 sq. mi.
Pop: 13.8m.
UN, CW, OAU,
ECOWAS

Capital: Accra (Pop: 867,459)
Official language: English
Religions: Christian 52%, Muslim 13%,
traditional beliefs
Political status: Republic
Head of state: Jerry John Rawlings (since
1981)
GNP per capita: $390 (1986)
Currency: cedi ($1 = 285.25)

The number of AIDS victims in Ghana rose by more than 35 percent in 1989 despite a government-sponsored anti-AIDS program. In March, Ghana signed an agreement aimed at increasing British investment.

Greece

Southeastern
Europe
50,949 sq. mi.
Pop: 9.99m.
UN, EEC,
NATO, OECD

Capital: Athens (Pop: 3,027,331)
Official language: Greek
Religion: Greek Orthodox 98%
Political status: Democratic parliamentary
republic
Head of state: Christos Sartzetakis (since
1985)
Head of government: Xenophon Zolotas
GNP per capita: $4,710 (1987)
Currency: drachma ($1 = 164.94)

A political crisis stemming from two inconclusive elections, in June and early November, was resolved when the three main parties agreed in late November to an all-party government that would rule until new elections could be held in April 1990. A former governor of the Bank of Greece, 85-year-old Xenophon Zolotas, was appointed to head the six-month interim coalition government.

Grenada

Caribbean
120 sq. mi.
Pop: 88,000
UN, CW, OAS,
Caricom

Capital: St George's (Pop: 4,788)
Official language: English
Religions: Roman Catholic, Anglican,
Methodist
Political status: Constitutional monarchy
Head of state: Queen Elizabeth II
Head of government: Herbert Blaize (since
1985)
GNP per capita: $1,240 (1986)
Currency: Eastern Caribbean dollar
($1 = 2.72)

Despite continued U.S. development aid and attempts to modernize the island's vital cocoa industry, Grenada was forced to turn to the IMF and Western Europe for aid.

Guatemala

Central America
42,042 sq. mi.
Pop: 8.99m.
UN, OAS,
Caricom

Capital: Guatemala City (Pop: 1.5m.)
Official language: Spanish
Religion: Roman Catholic
Political status: Presidential republic
Head of state: Vinicio Cerezo Arevalo
(since 1986)
GNP per capita: $930 (1988)
Currency: quetzal ($1 = 2.84)

President Cerezo survived a military coup attempt in May and the U.S. praised the officers who remained loyal to him. Vice President Dan Quayle visited the country in June.

Guinea

West Africa
94,926 sq. mi.
Pop: 6.53m.
UN, OAU

Capital: Conakry (Pop: 705,280)
Official language: French
Religions: Muslim 69%, tribal beliefs 30%,
Christian 1%
Political status: Presidential republic
Head of state: Lansana Conté (since 1984)
GNP per capita: $320 (1985)
Currency: Guinea franc ($1 = 301.90)

In April, Brig. Gen. Lansana Conté marked the fifth anniversary of his inauguration. He did not rule out a gradual return to a civilian regime.

Guinea-Bissau

West Africa
13,948 sq. mi.
Pop: 932,000
UN, OAU

Capital: Bissau (Pop: 109,214)
Language: Portuguese (official), Crioulo
Religions: Muslim 30%, Christian 5%
Political status: Republic
Head of state: Joao Bernardo Vieira (since
1980)
GNP per capita: $170 (1988)
Currency: peso ($1 = 654.13)

The tiny West African nation, one of the world's poorest, continued to rely heavily on Western and Soviet economic assistance in 1989.

Guyana

South America
83,000 sq. mi.
Pop: 812,000
UN, Caricom,
CW

Capital: Georgetown (Pop: 188,000)
Official language: English
Religions: Christian 52%, Hindu 34%,
Muslim 9%
Political status: Presidential republic
Head of state: Hugh Desmond Hoyte
(since 1985)
Head of government: Hamilton Green
(since 1985)
GNP per capita: $500 (1986)
Currency: Guyana dollar ($1 = 30.03)

At a White House meeting in June, President Bush welcomed Guyana's economic reform program and its efforts to fight against drug traffickers using Guyana as a staging-post.

Haiti

Caribbean
10,700 sq. mi.
Pop: 5.3m.
UN, OAS

Capital: Port-au-Prince (Pop: 449,831)
Official language: French
Religions: Roman Catholic, Voodoo
Political status: Presidential republic
Head of state: Prosper Avril (since 1988)
GNP per capita: $330 (1986)
Currency: gourde ($1 = 5.03)

Marking the end of his first year in power, General Avril, who crushed a coup attempt in April, said in September that he remained committed to restoring full democracy.

Honduras

Central America
43,277 sq. mi.
Pop: 4.3m.
UN, OAS

Capital: Tegucigalpa (Pop: 604,600)
Official language: Spanish
Religion: Roman Catholic
Political status: Presidential republic
Head of state: José Azcona Hoyo (since
1986)
GNP per capita: $740 (1986)
Currency: lempira ($1 = 1.99)

In July, seven servicemen, part of the 1,200-man U.S. military contingent deployed in Honduras, were injured in a terrorist bomb attack in the north of the country.

Hungary

Central Europe
35,911 sq. mi.
Pop: 10.6m.
UN, CMEA,
Warsaw Pact

Capital: Budapest (Pop: 2.1m.)
Official language: Hungarian
Religions: Roman Catholic 49%, Protestant 23.5%
Political status: Republic
Head of state: Mathias Szuros (since 1989)
Head of government: Miklos Nemeth
(since 1988)
GNP per capita: $2,010 (1986)
Currency: forint ($1 = 59.71)

Barely three months after President Bush visited Budapest, Hungary in October took the historic step of ending 41 years of communist rule. The country declared itself a republic and rejected basic principles of communism such as the dictatorship of the proletariat. The previous month, the government took the unprecedented decision to open its borders with Austria to allow the passage of thousands of East Germans fleeing to the West. In November, the U.S. Congress approved an $81 million aid package, as the EEC also stepped up its assistance. In the country's first free nationwide vote since the Communist takeover in 1948, four opposition parties won a narrow victory in a late November referendum that forced the government to postpone presidential elections scheduled for January 1990. Instead, a new Parliament, to be elected by June 1990, was to choose a president of the republic. The country's economic outlook remained bleak. The government stopped subsidizing staple goods. The cost of food, public transport and heating soared.

Iceland

North Atlantic
39,758 sq. mi.
Pop: 247,357
UN, OECD, NATO, EFTA, NC

Capital: Reykjavik (Pop: 93,245)
Official language: Icelandic
Religion: Evangelical Lutheran
Political status: Parliamentary republic
Head of state: Vigdis Finnbogadottir (since 1980)
Head of government: Steingrimur Hermannsson (since 1988)
GNP per capita: $15,252 (1986)
Currency: krona ($1 = 61.90)

Prime Minister Hermannsson reshuffled her government in September to include members of the moderate-right Bourgeois Party, in a bid to have the majority to push through badly needed economic reforms.

India

Southern Asia
1,222,713 sq. mi.
Pop: 748m.
UN, CW

Capital: New Delhi (Pop: 5,714,000)
Official languages: Hindi, English
Religions: Hindu 82.7%, Muslim 11.2%, Christian 2.6%, Sikh 1.9%, Buddhist, Jain
Political status: Federal parliamentary republic
Head of state: Ramaswamy Venkataraman (since 1987)
Head of government: Vishwanath Pratap Singh (since 1989)
GNP per capita: $270 (1986)
Currency: rupee ($1 = 16.70)

Rajiv Gandhi resigned after suffering a defeat in November elections. He was replaced by 58-year-old Vishwanath Pratap Singh, head of the centrist National Front opposition party, who became the country's seventh prime minister since independence, and was to lead the first minority government in Indian history.

Indonesia

Southeast Asia
741,098 sq. mi.
Pop: 172m.
UN, ASEAN, OPEC

Capital: Jakarta (Pop: 6,503,449)
Official language: Bahasa Indonesian
Religions: Muslim 78%, Christian 11%, Buddhist, Hindu
Political status: Presidential republic
Head of state: Gen. Suharto (since 1968)
GNP per capita: $510 (1986)
Currency: rupiah ($1 = 16.70)

General Suharto, who has been in power for 21 years, indicated in 1989 that his current term, due to end in 1993, may be his last, sparking intense jockeying among opposition and government politicians.

Iran

Middle East
634,724 sq. mi.
Pop: 53.92m.
UN, OPEC

Capital: Tehran (Pop: 6,042,584)
Official language: Farsi (Persian)
Religion: Muslim (Shiite 96%, Sunni 3%)
Political status: Islamic republic
Head of state: Ali Akhbar Hashemi Rafsanjani (since 1989)
Head of government: Ali Akhbar Hashemi Rafsanjani (since 1989)
GNP per capita: $1,690 (1986)
Currency: rial ($1 = 74.22)

The death of Ayatollah Khomeini in June did little to improve relations between Tehran and the West. In August, the country's leaders ruled out the possibility of negotiations with the "hated" U.S. government, accusing the Bush administration of supporting Israel's July abduction of a leading pro-Iranian sheik in Lebanon. President Rafsanjani said in August he would help free Western hostages in Lebanon only when the U.S. proves it is no longer hostile to Iran. In early November, thousands of club-wielding Iranians demonstrated in Tehran to mark the 10th anniversary of the takeover of the U.S. Embassy there. The same month, the U.S. released $567 million in frozen Iranian assets, but this move did little to reduce tensions between the two nations.

Iraq

Middle East
167,925 sq. mi.
Pop: 17.06m.
UN, AL, OPEC

Capital: Baghdad (Pop: 4,648,609)
Official language: Arabic
Religions: Muslim 64%, Christian 2%
Political status: Socialist presidential republic
Head of state: Saddam Hussein at-Takriti (since 1979)
Head of government: Saddam Hussein at-Takriti
GNP per capita: $2,140 (1984)
Currency: Iraqi dinar ($1 = 0.312)

The ending of the war against Iran in August 1988 allowed Iraq's regime to play a far more active role in regional affairs in 1989 and to begin to rebuild its ravaged economy. There was practically no progress in 1989 in negotiations for a lasting settlement of the Gulf War. The arrest in September of a British nurse and an Iranian-born British journalist, who was accused of espionage, caused a major dispute between the two nations.

Ireland

Western Europe
26,600 sq. mi.
Pop: 3.54m.
UN, EEC, OECD

Capital: Dublin (Pop: 920,956)
Official languages: Irish (Gaelic), English
Religions: mostly Roman Catholic; Church of Ireland, Presbyterian, Methodist
Political status: Parliamentary republic
Head of state: Patrick Hillery (since 1976)
Head of government: Charles Haughey (since 1987)
GNP per capita: $5,080 (1986)
Currency: Irish pound ($1 = 0.70)

Basing his decision on a series of highly favorable opinion polls, Ireland's Prime Minister called early parliamentary elections in mid-June, hoping to gain a majority of seats. The gamble did not pay off. Haughey's Fianna Fail Party lost three seats and he was forced to form a coalition government. Despite a slight upturn in the economy in 1989, the government remained faced with a 17 percent unemployment rate, one of the highest in Western Europe, a continued emigration problem and some social unrest. In September, a dispute broke out between Dublin and London over allegations of collusion between police and Protestant extremists in British-controlled Northern Ireland. In early October, the EEC strongly criticized Ireland for allowing excessive urban pollution. However, the year ended on an upbeat note when Ireland qualified for the soccer World Cup in November by beating Malta.

Israel

Near East
8,017 sq. mi.
Pop: 4.44m.
UN

Capital: Jerusalem (Pop: 482,700)
Official languages: Hebrew, Arabic
Religions: Jewish 82%, Muslim 13%
Political status: Parliamentary republic
Head of state: Chaim Herzog (since 1983)
Head of government: Yitzhak Shamir (since 1986)
GNP per capita: $6,350 (1986)
Currency: new shekel ($1 = 2.02)

After nearly two years and more than 600 Palestinian deaths, the intifada, or uprising, showed no sign of abating by year's end. The violent Palestinian protest against Israel's occupation of the West Bank and Gaza weighed heavily on the country's economy and its internal politics. Much-publicized reports of actions undertaken by Israeli security forces to quell the protests drew international criticism. The opening of a dialogue between the U.S. and the PLO as well as PLO chief Yasir Arafat's official visit to France in May, where he was greeted as Palestine's president, caused considerable bitterness in Israel. In July, Israel came under fire for the kidnapping in Lebanon of a pro-Iranian sheik. The year was, however, marked by a warming of relations between Jerusalem and East Bloc nations, most of which had broken ties with Israel after the 1967 Arab-Israeli War. A November visit to the White House by Prime Minister Shamir saw no real progress on implementation of a U.S. peace plan, which Israel refused to accept without guarantees.

Italy

Southern Europe
116,319 sq. mi.
Pop: 57.4m.
UN, EEC, NATO, OECD

Capital: Rome (Pop: 2,817,227)
Official language: Italian
Religion: Roman Catholic
Political status: Parliamentary republic
Head of state: Francesco Cossiga (since 1985)
Head of government: Giulio Andreotti (since 1989)
GNP per capita: $8,570 (1986)
Currency: lira ($1 = 1,373)

Faced with a budget deficit of nearly $50 billion, the coalition government repeatedly attempted to achieve sharp cuts in public spending, notably in the health and education sectors. These moves were greeted by strikes and social unrest. In a late November visit to Rome, Soviet leader Mikhail Gorbachev met with Pope John Paul II at the Vatican.

Ivory Coast

West Africa
124,503 sq. mi.
Pop: 11.63m.
UN, OAU

Capital: Abidjan (Pop: 1.85m.)
Official language: French
Religions: Muslim 24%, Christian 32%, animist 44%
Political status: Presidential republic
Head of state: Félix Houphouët-Boigny (since 1960)
GNP per capita: $740 (1986)
Currency: franc CFA ($1 = 316.90)

The country's aging President in 1989 continued his policy of dialogue with South Africa, much criticized by other African leaders. His costly project to build Christianity's biggest cathedral also came under fire.

Jamaica

Caribbean
4,411 sq. mi.
Pop: 2.3m.
UN, OAS, CW, Caricom

Capital: Kingston (Pop: 524,638)
Official language: English
Religion: mostly Protestant
Political status: Constitutional monarchy
Head of state: Queen Elizabeth II
Head of government: Michael Manley (since 1989)
GNP per capita: $1,068 (1987)
Currency: Jamaican dollar ($1 = 5.78)

Prime Minister Manley traveled widely in 1989, seeking support for Jamaica's ailing economy, burdened by a rising foreign debt, and for his government's plans to set up an armed, international anti-drug force.

Japan

Western Pacific
145,874 sq. mi.
Pop: 122.26m.
UN, OECD

Capital: Tokyo (Pop: 8,209,000)
Official language: Japanese
Religions: Buddhist, Shintoist
Political status: Parliamentary monarchy
Head of state: Emperor Akihito (since 1989)
Head of government: Toshiki Kaifu (since 1989)
GNP per capita: $14,039 (1986)
Currency: yen ($1 = 141.90)

Political scandals rocked Japan in 1989 nearly as often as earth tremors did. Although expected, due to his long illness, Emperor Hirohito's death in January had a profound effect on the people of Japan. The end of the Emperor's long reign was soon followed by the so-called "Recruitgate" scandal, in which leading politicians admitted having received huge payoffs from the Recruit firm. This led to the April resignation of Prime Minister Noboru Takeshita, who was replaced in the following month by Sousuke Uno of the Liberal Democratic Party. In July, Uno became involved in a sex scandal and was forced to resign after his party suffered a crushing defeat in Upper House elections, where the LDP lost its overall majority for the first time since 1955. In August, with the LDP in almost total disarray, Toshiki Kaifu, a former Education Minister, was appointed Prime Minister. However, this constant political turmoil did not harm the country's buoyant economy, which in October marked 46 consecutive months of growth. On the international front, Japan and the Soviet Union were by year's end working on plans to hold a summit meeting in 1991, although this depended on settlement of a dispute over the Soviet-occupied Kurile Islands.

The government said in September that it would forbid marriage for women before the age of 18 as part of a plan to cut down the birth rate, one of the world's highest.

Kiribati

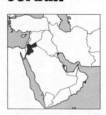

Mid-Pacific
276.9 sq. mi.
Pop: 66,250
CW

Capital: Tarawa (Pop: 24,598)
Official language: English
Religions: Protestant, Roman Catholic
Political status: Presidential republic
Head of state: Ieremia Tabai (since 1979)
GNP per capita: $390 (1985)
Currency: Australian dollar ($1 = 1.33)

The tiny island nation, whose economy relies heavily on the sea, charged in January that South Korean vessels were illegally fishing in its waters.

Jordan

Middle East
34,443 sq. mi.
Pop: 2.97m.
UN, AL

Capital: Amman (Pop: 777,500)
Official language: Arabic
Religion: Sunni Muslim 80%
Political status: Constitutional monarchy
Head of state: King Hussein II (since 1952)
Head of government: Zeid bin Shaker (since 1989)
GNP per capita: $1,540 (1986)
Currency: dinar ($1 = 0.67)

The kingdom's first general elections in 22 years saw a major victory for Muslim fundamentalists, who captured more than 30 seats in the 80-member Parliament. The victory was a setback for King Hussein.

Kenya

East Africa
224,960 sq. mi.
Pop: 22.8m.
UN, CW, OAU

Capital: Nairobi (Pop: 827,775)
Official language: Kiswahili
Religions: Protestant 19%, Roman Catholic 27%, other Christian 27%, Muslim 6%, tribal beliefs 19%
Political status: Presidential republic
Head of state: Daniel arap Moi (since 1978)
GNP per capita: $300 (1986)
Currency: Kenya shilling ($1 = 21.59)

Korea (North)

Northeastern Asia
46,540 sq. mi.
Pop: 21.89m.

Capital: Pyongyang (Pop: 2.64m.)
Official language: Korean
Religions: Buddhist, Chandokyo, Christian
Political status: Democratic people's republic
Head of state: Kim Il Sung (since 1972)
Head of government: Yon Hyong Muk (since 1989)
GNP per capita: $1,180 (1985)
Currency: won ($1 = 0.98)

At year's end, North and South Korea were set for the second exchange of separated families since the end of the Korean War. Tensions remained high between the two nations.

Korea (South)

Northeastern Asia
38,232 sq. mi.
Pop: 42m.

Capital: Seoul (Pop: 9,645,824)
Official language: Korean
Religions: animist, Buddhist, Confucian, Christian
Political status: Presidential republic
Head of state: Roh Tae Woo (since 1988)
Head of government: Kang Young Hoon (since 1988)
GNP per capita: $3,450 (1988)
Currency: won ($1 = 680.89)

In February, Prime Minister Kang Young Hoon, in office since December 1988, promised to hold a national referendum before the end of the year. However, plans to hold the ballot were shelved indefinitely in March after the Prime Minister met with Kim Dae Jung, leader of the opposition Peace and Democracy Party. Kim had earlier supported calls for a full inquiry into the 1980 massacre of demonstrating students and workers at Kwangju. The political climate worsened in April after a leading opposition figure traveled to North Korea to meet with President Kim Il Sung. The government responded by ordering the arrest of scores of people, sparking a wave of violent anti-government demonstrations in several cities. On the economic front, the situation remained bright throughout 1989, despite a slight downturn in the growth rate. In November, President Roh vowed to pursue his policy of working for improved relations with communist North Korea, adding that this process should ultimately lead to the reunification of the two nations.

Kuwait

Middle East
6,880 sq. mi.
Pop: 1.96m.
UN, AL, OPEC, GCC

Capital: Kuwait (Pop: 44,335)
Official language: Arabic
Religions: Sunni Muslim 78%, Shiite Muslim 14%, Christian 6%
Political status: Emirate
Head of state: Shaikh Jabir al-Ahmad al-Jabir as-Sabah (since 1977)
Head of government: Shaikh Saad Abdullah as-Salim as-Sabah (since 1978)
GNP per capita: $13,890 (1986)
Currency: dinar ($1 = 0.30)

The ending of the Iran-Iraq war was hailed with considerable relief in Kuwait, which had feared that the fighting would spill over its borders. In July, Kuwait signed a major trade pact with the Soviet Union.

Laos

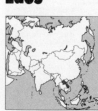

Southeast Asia
91,400 sq. mi.
Pop: 3.83m.
UN

Capital: Vientiane (Pop: 377,409)
Official language: Lao
Religions: mostly Buddhist; tribal 34%
Political status: Democratic people's republic
Head of state: Phoumi Vongvichit
Head of government: Kaysone Phomvihan (since 1975)
GNP per capita: $220 (1984)
Currency: new kip ($1 = 586.70)

Soviet-backed Laos improved its relations with China in 1989, while at the same time stepping up its ties with its non-communist neighbor, Thailand. The regime also sought to establish a more liberal economic system.

Lebanon

Near East
4,036 sq. mi.
Pop: 3.5m.
UN, AL

Capital: Beirut (Pop: 702,000)
Official language: Arabic
Religions: Muslim (Sunni, Shiite, Druze), Christian (mostly Maronite and Greek Orthodox)
Political status: Parliamentary republic
Head of state: Elias Hrawi (since 1989)
Heads of governments: Dr. Selim Hoss (Muslim); Michel Aoun (Christian)
GNP per capita: no reliable figures available
Currency: Lebanese pound ($1 = 459.89)

The year began in a state of political vacuum, due to the existence of two rival governments, a Christian one and a Muslim one. In March, Christian Gen. Michel Aoun launched a "war of liberation" against occupying Syrian forces, who responded by blockading and bombing Christian sectors, killing more than 1,000 civilians over a six-month period. In May, Arab nations asked Morocco, Saudi Arabia and Algeria to seek a lasting solution to the Lebanese crisis. U.S. diplomats were evacuated from Beirut in September after General Aoun accused Washington of having sold out Lebanon to Syria. In November, as a political settlement seemed near, newly appointed President René Moawad was assassinated in Beirut. He was quickly replaced by a Syrian-backed Maronite Christian, Elias Hrawi. Meanwhile, the Muslim Selim Hoss formed a government of national union composed of fourteen cabinet ministers, drawn equally from the Christian and Muslim camps.

Lesotho

Southern Africa
11,720 sq. mi.
Pop: 1.67m.
UN, CW, OAU

Capital: Maseru (Pop: 109,382)
Official languages: Sesotho, English
Religions: Roman Catholic 44%, Protestant 49%
Political status: Constitutional monarchy
Head of state: King Moshoeshoe II (since 1966)
Head of government: Justin Lekhanya (since 1986)
GNP per capita: $410 (1986)
Currency: loti ($1 = 2.67)

In October, General Lekhanya was acquitted of the murder of a student. In May, the Roman Catholic Archbishop of Maseru, Alphonsus Morapeli, died of a heart attack.

Liberia

West Africa
42,989 sq. mi.
Pop: 2.44m.
UN, ECOWAS, OAU

Capital: Monrovia (Pop: 425,000)
Official language: English
Religions: Muslim 26%, Christian, traditional beliefs
Political status: Presidential republic
Head of state: Samuel Kanyon Doe (since 1980)
GNP per capita: $450 (1986)
Currency: Liberian dollar ($1 = 1)

Faced with a major economic crisis, President Doe in November announced an immediate 54 percent increase in the price of rice, the staple food of Liberians, and taxes of up to 100 percent on luxury goods.

Libya

North Africa
679,358 sq. mi.
Pop: 3.96m.
UN, AL, OAU, OPEC

Capital: Tripoli (Pop: 990,697)
Official language: Arabic
Religion: Sunni Muslim 97%
Political status: Socialist people's state
Head of state: Muammar al-Qaddafi (since 1969)
Head of government: Abdessalam Jalloud
GNP per capita: $7,180 (1985)
Currency: dinar ($1 = 0.31)

In June, Colonel Qaddafi hailed the "wisdom and maturity" of the Bush administration, saying he hoped it would not repeat the "errors" of the Reagan era. He added that Libya sought balanced relations with both Washington and Moscow. In September, Libya's leader marked the 20th anniversary of his revolution amid reports that he had ordered the closure of the offices in Tripoli of some 70 "liberation movements."

Liechtenstein

Western Europe
61.8 sq. mi.
Pop: 27,700
EFTA

Capital: Vaduz (Pop: 4,606)
Official language: German
Religions: Roman Catholic 87%, Protestant 8.6%
Political status: Constitutional monarchy
Head of state: Prince Hans Adam II (since 1989)
Head of government: Hans Brunhart (since 1978)
GNP per capita: $15,000 (1984)
Currency: Swiss franc ($1 = 1.63)

In November, Prince Hans Adam II became the ruler of the tiny but wealthy principality following the death of his father, Prince Franz Josef II, who died at the age of 83 after 51 years on the throne. Prince Hans Adam had, in fact, been running the government ever since 1984.

Luxembourg

Western Europe
998 sq. mi.
Pop: 372,100
UN, EEC, NATO, OECD

Capital: Luxembourg (Pop: 76,640)
Official languages: Letzeburgesch, French, German
Religion: Roman Catholic 95%
Political status: Constitutional monarchy
Head of state: Grand Duke Jean (since 1964)
Head of government: Jacques Santer (since 1984)
GNP per capita: $15,680 (1986)
Currency: Luxembourg franc ($1 = 39.14)

In general elections held in June, the ruling coalition lost six parliamentary seats. However, an agreement hammered out the following month between the Socialist and Christian-Democrat parties allowed Santer to remain Prime Minister. He was also appointed Minister of the Treasury and Minister of Culture.

Madagascar

Indian Ocean
226,658 sq. mi.
Pop: 10.92m.
UN, OAU

Capital: Antananarivo (Pop: 703,000)
Languages: Malagasy (official), French
Religions: Christian 50%, Muslim 3%, animist 47%
Political status: Republic
Head of state: Didier Ratsiraka (since 1975)
Head of government: Victor Ramahatra
GNP per capita: $230 (1987)
Currency: Malagasy franc ($1 = 1,443.49)

President Ratsiraka was re-elected in March with 62.7 percent of the vote, although this was 18 percent less than his total in the 1982 presidential elections. The opposition's candidates won upset victories in several major cities, including the capital.

Malawi

Southern Africa
36,325 sq. mi.
Pop: 7.1m.
UN, CW, OAU

Capital: Lilongwe (Pop: 186,800)
Official languages: Chichewa, English
Religions: mostly Christian; Muslim 7%
Political status: Presidential republic
Head of state: H. Kamuzu Banda (since 1966)
GNP per capita: $160 (1986)
Currency: kwacha ($1 = 2.79)

Drought, a poor maize crop, the spread of AIDS and the continued arrival of refugees from the conflict in Mozambique were added burdens on the country's economy.

Malaysia

Southeast Asia
127,317 sq. mi.
Pop: 17m.
UN, ASEAN, CW

Capital: Kuala Lumpur (Pop: 937,875)
Official language: Malay
Religions: mostly Muslim; Buddhist, Hindu, Christian
Political status: Federal constitutional monarchy
Head of state: Sultan Azlan Shah (since 1989)
Head of government: Mahathir Mohamad (since 1981)
GNP per capita: $1,850 (1986)
Currency: ringgit ($1 = 2.71)

Azlan Shah, a British-educated jurist, became Malaysia's ninth King in September, as the government was set to sign an accord to end a decades-long communist insurgency.

Maldives

Indian Ocean
115 sq. mi.
Pop: 200,000
UN, CW

Capital: Malé (Pop: 46,334)
Official language: Divehi
Religion: Muslim
Political status: Presidential republic
Head of state: Maumoon Abdul Gayoom (since 1978)
GNP per capita: $310 (1986)
Currency: rufiyaa ($1 = 9.07)

The last of the 1,200 Indian troops sent in following a bloody 1988 coup attempt left the Indian Ocean island nation in early November.

Mali

West Africa
478,832 sq. mi.
Pop: 7.78m.
UN, OAU

Capital: Bamako (Pop: 404,022)
Official language: French
Religions: Sunni Muslim 90%, animist 9%, Christian 1%
Political status: Presidential republic
Head of state: Moussa Traoré (since 1969)
GNP per capita: $170 (1986)
Currency: franc CFA ($1 = 316.90)

A relatively good 1989 cotton crop and government austerity measures contributed to a slight upturn in the country's economy, which, however, continued to rely heavily on foreign, notably U.S., assistance.

Malta

Southern Europe
121.9 sq. mi.
Pop: 345,636
UN, CW

Capital: Valletta (Pop: 9,239)
Official languages: Maltese, English
Religion: Roman Catholic
Political status: Democratic parliamentary republic
Head of state: Vincent Tabone (since 1989)
Head of government: Eddie Fenech Adami (since 1987)
GNP per capita: $3,470 (1987)
Currency: Maltese lira ($1 = .36)

Malta celebrated its 25th anniversary in September. Its government succeeded in improving relations with the West in 1989, after years of militant socialism and non-alignment.

Mauritania

West Africa
398,000 sq. mi.
Pop: 1.89m.
UN, AL, OAU

Capital: Nouakchott (Pop: 500,000)
Official languages: Arabic, French
Religion: Sunni Muslim 99%
Political status: Republic
Head of state: Maawiya Ould Sidi Ahmed Taya (since 1984)
GNP per capita: $440 (1986)
Currency: ouguiya ($1 = 86.07)

Some 200 people died in May when a border dispute with Senegal erupted into riots. About 100,000 Mauritanians in Senegal and 85,000 Senegalese in Mauritania had to be repatriated.

Mauritius

Indian Ocean
787 sq. mi.
Pop: 1.057m.
UN, CW, OAU

Capital: Port Louis (Pop: 139,038)
Official language: English
Religions: Hindu 53%, Christian 30%, Muslim 13%
Political status: Constitutional monarchy
Head of state: Queen Elizabeth II
Head of government: Anerood Jugnauth (since 1982)
GNP per capita: $1,720 (1987)
Currency: rupee ($1 = 15.65)

Prime Minister Anerood in September asked Indian Ocean states to help him turn the region into a "zone of peace." The government said in October that the drug problem had been brought under control.

Mexico

North America
756,198 sq. mi.
Pop: 82.7m.
UN, OAS, LAIA

Capital: Mexico City (Pop: 12,932,116)
Official language: Spanish
Religion: Roman Catholic 92.6%
Political status: Federal republic
Head of state: Carlos Salinas de Gortari (since 1988)
GNP per capita: $1,850 (1986)
Currency: peso ($1 = 2,575)

Since President Salinas came to power in late 1988, there has been a marked improvement in the oftentense relations between Mexico and the U.S. In early 1989, the Salinas government launched an unprecedented anti-drug effort that won immediate praise from Washington. By September, Mexican police had seized 22 tons of cocaine, the equivalent of all the cocaine seized during the six-year rule of Salinas' predecessor. Mexico's leader, who met with President Bush in July and October, also clamped down on emigrants crossing the U.S.-Mexican border and opened up the country to foreign investors. In October, the two nations signed four important trade and economic accords.

Monaco

Southern Europe
481 acres
Pop: 27,063

Capital: Monaco
Official language: French
Religion: Roman Catholic
Political status: Constitutional principality
Head of state: Prince Rainier III (since 1949)
Head of government: Jean Ausseil (since 1985)
GNP per capita: $10,000
Currency: French franc ($1 = 6.34)

In June, Prince Rainier celebrated his 40 years on the throne as the tiny principality's economy continued its unprecedented boom, due largely to tourism, banking and, to a far lesser degree, gambling.

Mongolia

Eastern Asia
605,022 sq. mi.
Pop: 2m.
UN, CMEA

Capital: Ulan Bator (Pop: 500,000)
Official language: Mongolian
Religion: Lama Buddhism
Political status: People's republic
Head of state: Jambyn Batmonkh (since 1984)
Head of government: Dumaagiyn Sodnom (since 1984)
GNP per capita: $940 (1978)
Currency: tugrik ($1 = 3.38)

Soviet-style reform made its debut in 1989 in Mongolia. Past errors were denounced and schools began teaching a new version of Mongolian history from which the negative Soviet view of Mongol conqueror Genghis Khan had been removed. The regime said it planned to strengthen economic ties with Japan and Europe.

Morocco

North Africa
177,116 sq. mi.
Pop: 23m.
UN, AL

Capital: Rabat (Pop: 518,616)
Official language: Arabic
Religions: Sunni Muslim 98%, Christian 2%
Political status: Constitutional monarchy
Head of state: Hassan II (since 1961)
Head of government: Azeddine Laraki (since 1986)
GNP per capita: $590 (1986)
Currency: dirham ($1 = 8.45)

In July, to mark his 60th birthday, King Hassan released some 300 prisoners. In August, the King made his first trip to Libya since Colonel Qaddafi took power in 1969. This came as relations between the two states were improving after years of tension. In November, the government launched economic reforms, notably the privatization of some of the 700 state-run firms.

Mozambique

Southern Africa
308,642 sq. mi.
Pop: 14.9m.
UN, OAU

Capital: Maputo (Pop: 882,814)
Official language: Portuguese
Religions: animist 60%, Christian 18%, Muslim 16%
Political status: People's republic
Head of state: Joaquim Alberto Chissano (since 1986)
Head of government: Mario da Graça Machungo
GNP per capita: $90 (1986)
Currency: metical ($1 = 813.13)

For Mozambique, 1989 was a year of struggle to put a war-ravaged economy back on its feet. The government followed often-painful IMF economic reform guidelines, including some drastic cuts in social spending. The destruction of schools left more than 500,000 children with no access to education, while poor health care and malnutrition continued to claim lives.

Namibia

Southern Africa
318,261 sq. mi.
Pop: 1.29m.

Capital: Windhoek (Pop: 114,500)
Official languages: Afrikaans, English
Religions: Protestant, traditional beliefs
Political status: South African-controlled territory
Head of state: Louis Pienaar (since 1985)
GNP per capita: $1,020 (1986)
Currency: South African rand ($1 = 2.67)

The last South African soldiers left Namibia in late November, thus ending a 23-year conflict against Marxist SWAPO fighters and Cuban-backed Angolan troops. The South Africans left behind an enemy who had lost virtually every battle but won the war. No official figures have ever been released by South African authorities detailing the cost in manpower and money of its border war in Namibia. Also in November, mineral-rich Namibia, which has lived under South African administration since 1915 and is Africa's last remaining colony, made a giant step toward independence with the holding of U.N.-sponsored elections. The once-outlawed South-West Africa People's Organization, led by Sam Nujoma, won 57.3 percent of the popular vote. The elections were the most danger-fraught phase of the implementation of the U.N. plan for Namibian independence. In December, the new Constituent Assembly began the process of drafting and approving the future nation's first-ever constitution.

Nauru

Western Pacific
8,108 sq. mi.
Pop: 8,042
CW

Capital: Yaren (Pop: 4,000)
Languages: Nauruan, English
Religions: Roman Catholic, Protestant
Political status: Republic
Head of state: Kenas Aroi (since 1989)
GNP per capita: $9,091 (1985)
Currency: Australian dollar
($1 = 1.33)

After 21 years as head of the world's smallest republic, President Hammer DeRoburt was ousted in August by his political ally Kenas Aroi. The former President, however, remained in charge of his nation's trade policy.

Nepal

South Asia
56,827 sq. mi.
Pop: 16.63m.
UN

Capital: Kathmandu (Pop: 235,160)
Official language: Nepali
Religions: Hindu 90%, Buddhist 5%, Muslim 3%
Political status: Constitutional monarchy
Head of state: Birendra Bir Bikram Shah Dev (since 1972)
Head of government: Marich Man Singh Shrestha (since 1986)
GNP per capita: $160 (1986)
Currency: Nepalese rupee ($1 = 24.15)

A trade dispute with India, which threatened to choke Nepal's economy, erupted in March, as India refused to renew bilateral transit and trade agreements. India shut down most of its 15 border posts with Nepal.

Netherlands

Northwestern Europe
16,163 sq. mi.
Pop: 14.71m.
UN, EEC, NATO, OECD

Capital: Amsterdam (Pop: 691,738)
Official language: Dutch
Religions: Roman Catholic 36%, Dutch Reformed 19%
Political status: Constitutional monarchy
Head of state: Queen Beatrix (since 1980)
Head of government: Ruud Lubbers (since 1982)
GNP per capita: $8,500 (1984)
Currency: guilder ($1 = 2.11)

Like many of its European neighbors, the Netherlands spent 1989 gearing up for Europe's single market, scheduled for the end of 1992. European integration and the environment were the chief issues of September general elections, which returned Christian-democrat leader Ruud Lubbers to power at the head of a center-left coalition government.

New Zealand

South Pacific
103,736 sq. mi.
Pop: 3.3m.
UN, CW, OECD

Capital: Wellington (Pop: 325,200)
Official language: English
Religions: Anglican, Presbyterian, Roman Catholic, Methodist
Political status: Constitutional monarchy
Head of state: Queen Elizabeth II
Head of government: Geoffrey Palmer (since 1989)
GNP per capita: $7,110 (1988)
Currency: New Zealand dollar ($1 = 1.72)

The country's vice prime minister Geoffrey Palmer was elected Prime Minister in August following the resignation of David Lange for health reasons. Palmer immediately vowed to continue his predecessor's anti-nuclear policies. These have long been a major source of disagreement between Wellington and Washington and led to New Zealand's withdrawal from the 1951 ANZUS military pact linking Australia, New Zealand and the U.S. However, Palmer, who lived for many years in the U.S., stressed that he would do his utmost to improve relations with Washington. The Palmer government was outspoken in defense of the environment, calling for prompt international action to protect the Antarctic. Relations with France, at an all-time low since the 1985 sinking of the Greenpeace ecological movement's ship Rainbow Warrior by French secret agents, improved considerably.

Nicaragua

Central America
49,363 sq. mi.
Pop: 3.5m.
UN, OAS

Capital: Managua (Pop.: 682,111)
Official language: Spanish
Religion: Roman Catholic 91%
Political status: Republic
Head of state: Daniel Ortega Saavedra (since 1984)
GNP per capita: $790 (1986)
Currency: new cordoba ($1 = 21,239.14)

Nicaragua's leader Daniel Ortega traveled to several West European nations in April, in a bid to raise the $250 million the country urgently needed to stave off economic collapse. By mid-1989, its foreign debt had grown to $7 billion, most of it owed to the Soviet Union and other East Bloc states. On the political front, the Sandinista government and several opposition parties signed an accord in August aimed at guaranteeing that anti-Sandinista candidates would be able to participate in general elections set for February 1990.

Niger

West Africa
458,075 sq. mi.
Pop: 7.19m.
UN, OAU

Capital: Niamey (Pop: 399,100)
Official language: French
Religions: Muslim 97%, animist
Political status: Republic
Head of state: Ali Seybou (since 1987)
Head of government: Mamane Oumarou (since 1988)
GNP per capita: $260 (1986)
Currency: franc CFA ($1 = 316.90)

In a September referendum, 99.3 percent of voters approved a new constitution. At year's end, voters were going back to the polls for presidential elections in which President Seybou stood unopposed.

Nigeria

West Africa
356,667 sq. mi.
Pop: 105m.
UN, ECOWAS, CW, OAU, OPEC

Capital: Lagos (Pop: 1,097,000)
Official language: English
Religions: Muslim 48%, Christian 34%
Political status: Federal republic
Head of state: Gen. Ibrahim Babangida (since 1985)
GNP per capita: $730 (1986)
Currency: Naira ($1 = 7.38)

The Nigerian government was forced to increase fuel prices by a massive 44 percent in early 1989. On the political front, preparations were well under way for a return to a civilian government in 1992.

Norway

N. Europe
125,049 sq. mi.
Pop: 4.2m.
UN, EFTA, NATO, NC, OECD

Capital: Oslo (Pop: 453,730)
Official language: Norwegian
Religions: mostly Evangelical Lutheran; Roman Catholic
Political status: Constitutional monarchy
Head of state: King Olav V
Head of government: Gro Harlem Brundtland (since 1986)
GNP per capita: $16,400 (1986)
Currency: krone ($1 = 6.94)

In May, Prime Minister Brundtland marked her third year in office at the head of a minority labor government. Mrs. Brundtland was still faced with a difficult economic situation and a growing foreign debt.

Oman

Middle East
105,000 sq. mi.
Pop: 1.2m.
UN, AL, GCC

Capital: Muscat (Pop: 250,000)
Official language: Arabic
Religions: Ibadhi Muslim 75%, Sunni Muslim
Political status: Sultanate
Head of state: Qaboos bin Said (since 1970)
Head of government: Qaboos bin Said
GNP per capita: $4,990 (1986)
Currency: rial Omani ($1 = 0.385)

In June, for the first time in Omani history, a woman was elected to the national Chamber of Commerce. In July, visiting U.S. Secretary of State James Baker discussed bilateral cooperation with Oman's ruler.

Pakistan

South Asia
307,293 sq. mi.
Pop: 102.2m.
UN

Capital: Islamabad (Pop: 201,000)
Official languages: Urdu, English
Religions: Muslim 97%, Christian, Hindu
Political status: Federal Islamic republic
Head of state: Ghulam Ishaq Khan (since 1988)
Head of government: Benazir Bhutto (since 1988)
GNP per capita: $350 (1986)
Currency: rupee ($1 = 20.95)

A year after she became the first woman to govern a Muslim country, Prime Minister Bhutto was in December still grappling with the three main problems that face Pakistan: poverty, corruption and violence. In November, she narrowly escaped being ousted, as her political opponents failed by 12 votes to push through a no-confidence vote in the National Assembly. At year's end, the Prime Minister was said to be set for a reshuffle after coming under fire for not fulfilling her electoral promises.

Panama

Central America
29,768 sq. mi.
Pop: 2.32m.
UN, OAS

Capital: Panama City (Pop: 386,393)
Official language: Spanish
Religions: Roman Catholic 85%, Protestant 5%, Muslim 4.5%
Political status: Presidential republic
Head of state: Francisco Rodriguez (since 1989)
GNP per capita: $2,330 (1986)
Currency: balboa ($1 = 1)

The political crisis that had been paralyzing the country ever since the cancellation, amid widespread violence, of the May presidential elections came to a head in October. A group of senior military officers tried to overthrow Panama's strongman, Gen. Manuel Antonio Noriega, the nation's de-facto leader. The coup attempt failed and General Noriega quickly cracked down on his opponents. A few days after the election was declared null by the regime, President Bush called on Panamanians to oust General Noriega and the Pentagon sent in 2,000 troops to reinforce the 10,000 already stationed in the Canal Zone. The wave of political violence led to the recall of the U.S. ambassador and a reduction of embassy staff.

Papua New Guinea

South Pacific
170,702 sq. mi.
Pop: 3.48m.
UN, CW

Capital: Port Moresby (Pop: 152,100)
Official language: English
Religions: Protestant 63%, Roman Catholic 31%, local religions
Political status: Constitutional monarchy
Head of state: Queen Elizabeth II
Head of government: Rabbie Namaliu (since 1988)
GNP per capita: $690 (1986)
Currency: kina ($1 = 0.87)

Prime Minister Namaliu moved to reassure foreign investors in May that his country was overcoming its problems, including of violence that closed the Bougainville copper mine.

Paraguay

South America
157,042 sq. mi.
Pop: 4.01m.
UN, LAIA, OAS, LAES

Capital: Asuncion (Pop: 729,307)
Languages: Spanish, Guarani
Religion: Roman Catholic 97%
Political status: Presidential republic
Head of state: Gen. Andres Rodriguez (since 1989)
GNP per capita: $880 (1986)
Currency: guarani ($1 = 1255.80)

The February overthrow of Gen. Alfredo Stroessner marked the end of Latin America's longest dictatorship. His successor, Gen. Rodriguez, became President in May.

Peru

South America
496,222 sq. mi.
Pop: 21.3m.
UN, LAIA, OAS

Capital: Lima (Pop: 5,258,600)
Official languages: Spanish, Quechua
Religion: Roman Catholic over 90%
Political status: Republic
Head of state: Alan Garcia Perez (since 1985)
Head of government: Luis Alberto Sanchez (since 1989)
GNP per capita: $970 (1985)
Currency: inti ($1 = 5,406.35)

This was a particularly difficult year for President Garcia, who was faced with inflation running at around 2,000 percent annually, a huge and growing foreign debt, growing labor unrest and an active extreme-left guerrilla movement. He vowed in July to spend his final year in office looking for solutions to the country's economic woes. The Shining Path guerrilla group killed a young U.S. journalist in November. The group failed to impose a boycott of a November municipal ballot held as a preliminary to the April 1990 general elections.

Philippines

Southeast Asia
115,830 sq. mi.
Pop: 58.72m.
UN, ASEAN

Capital: Manila (Pop: 1,630,485)
Languages: Filipino, English, Tagalog
Religions: Roman Catholic 83%, Protestant 9%, Muslim 5%
Political status: Republic
Head of state: Corazon C. Aquino (since 1986)
GNP per capita: $614 (1986)
Currency: peso ($1 = 21.21)

The September death in Hawaii of former dictator Ferdinand Marcos was followed in early December by yet another military coup attempt aimed at toppling President Aquino's government. Her regime survived the bloody revolt, believed to have been led by backers of the late President, but the fighting left scores dead or injured. President Bush ordered U.S. Air Force Phantom fighters based near the capital to intervene in support of Mrs. Aquino, although they did not open fire on rebel-held positions.

Poland

Eastern Europe
120,628 sq. mi.
Pop: 37.8m.
UN, CMEA, Warsaw Pact

Capital: Warsaw (Pop: 2,432,000)
Official language: Polish
Religion: Roman Catholic 93%
Political status: Socialist republic
Head of state: Wojciech Jaruzelski (since 1985)
Head of government: Tadeusz Mazowiecki (since 1989)
GNP per capita: $2,070 (1986)
Currency: zloty ($1 = 2,092.06)

Poland this year underwent some of the most profound changes in the country's recent history. In June, Poland held its first semi-democratic elections. In July, the country restored diplomatic relations with the Vatican. These had been broken off in 1945 after the Communist Party came to power. The appointment in August of 62-year-old Tadeusz Mazowiecki as premier, after months of political and social turmoil, marked the end of 40 years of Communist Party domination in Poland. Mazowiecki, a Roman Catholic intellectual and close associate of Solidarity leader Lech Walesa, thus became the first non-communist to head an East Bloc government. This historic event however brought little immediate relief to the country's economic crisis. During a mid-July visit to Warsaw, President Bush announced a major economic assistance plan for Poland, while EEC nations rushed in food assistance in the form of beef, milk products and grain. During a highly successful November visit to the U.S., Walesa, who was awarded the Presidential Medal of Freedom, called for massive and swift Western investment in Poland.

Portugal

Southwestern Europe
35,516 sq. mi.
Pop: 10.29m.
UN, NATO, OECD, EEC

Capital: Lisbon (Pop: 807,937)
Official language: Portuguese
Religion: Roman Catholic 94.5%
Political status: Parliamentary republic
Head of state: Mario Soares (since 1986)
Head of government: Anibal Cavaco Silva (since 1985)
GNP per capita: $2,230 (1986)
Currency: escudo ($1 = 159.43)

Portugal's Premier said in November, after four years in power, that the 13 percent inflation rate, one of the highest in the EEC, was the country's chief problem.

Qatar

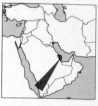

Middle East
4,415 sq. mi.
Pop: 371,863
UN, AL, OPEC, GCC

Capital: Doha (Pop: 217,294)
Official language: Arabic
Religion: Muslim 95%
Political status: Emirate
Head of state: Khalifa bin Hamad ath-Thani (since 1972)
GNP per capita: $22,940 (1984)
Currency: riyal ($1 = 3.65)

The arid Gulf peninsula, which relies heavily on oil revenues, faced some belt-tightening in 1989, but great hopes were pinned on a huge, newly discovered natural gas well.

Romania

Southeastern Europe
91,699 sq. mi.
Pop: 22.8m.
UN, CMEA, Warsaw Pact

Capital: Bucharest (Pop: 2,272,526)
Official language: Romanian
Religions: Orthodox 80%, Roman Catholic 6%
Political status: Socialist republic
Head of state: Nicolae Ceausescu (since 1967)
Head of government: Constantin Dascalescu (since 1982)
GNP per capita: $2,540 (1981)
Currency: leu ($1 = 9.03)

Virtually alone among East Bloc nations, Romania steadfastly rejected any attempts at Soviet-style reforms in 1989. Any open political dissent was crushed, while the government pressed ahead with its widely criticized centralization program, which involves the leveling of an estimated 10,000 rural villages. President Ceausescu, who was unanimously re-elected in November for his sixth term as Communist Party chief and head of state, lashed out against any deviation from his brand of "scientific socialism" and pledged to strengthen the army to "defend revolutionary achievements." Such barbs aimed at Soviet reform policies led to renewed tension between Bucharest and Moscow. Romanians, meanwhile, still faced chronic shortages of food, energy and nearly all consumer goods. The late November defection of former star gymnast Nadia Comaneci was a serious blow to the regime's prestige.

Rwanda

Central Africa
10,169 sq. mi.
Pop: 6.71m.
UN, OAU

Capital: Kigali (Pop: 156,650)
Official languages: French, Kinyarwanda, Kiswhahili
Religions: Christian 68%, traditional 23%, Muslim 9%
Political status: Republic
Head of state: Juvenal Habyarimana (since 1975)
GNP per capita: $290 (1986)
Currency: Rwanda franc ($1 = 80.72)

The presence of more than 60,000 refugees from 1988 massacres in Burundi placed a heavy strain on the economy, also hit in early 1989 by severe flooding. In July, Rwanda signed a five-year aid pact with the U.S.

St. Christopher and Nevis

Caribbean
103 sq. mi.
Pop: 43,700
UN, CW, OAS, Caricom

Capital: Basseterre (Pop: 14,283)
Official language: English
Religions: Protestant 76.4%, Roman Catholic 10.7%
Political status: Constitutional monarchy
Head of state: Queen Elizabeth II
Head of government: Kennedy A. Simmonds (since 1983)
GNP per capita: $1,700 (1986)
Currency: East Caribbean dollar ($1 = 2.72)

The conservative regime, which came to power in 1983 after nearly 30 years of socialist rule, won a third victory in March general elections. The economy was badly hit in 1989 by a worldwide drop in sugar prices.

St. Lucia

Caribbean
238 sq. mi.
Pop: 146,600
UN, CW, OAS, Caricom

Capital: Castries (Pop: 52,868)
Official language: English
Religion: Roman Catholic 86%
Political status: Constitutional monarchy
Head of state: Queen Elizabeth II
Head of government: John Compton (since 1982)
GNP per capita: $1,320 (1986)
Currency: East Caribbean dollar ($1 = 2.72)

St. Lucia marked the 10th anniversary of its independence in February. The economy was boosted by a record banana crop this year.

St. Vincent and the Grenadines

Caribbean
150 sq. mi.
Pop: 112,614
UN, CW, OAS, Caricom

Capital: Kingstown (Pop: 28,942)
Official language: English
Religions: Anglican 47%, Methodist 28%, Roman Catholic 13%
Political status: Constitutional monarchy
Head of state: Queen Elizabeth II
Head of government: James Mitchell (since 1984)
GNP per capita: $960 (1986)
Currency: East Caribbean dollar ($1 = 2.72)

The ruling left-wing New Democratic Party won all 15 seats in the House of Assembly in May elections, the third since independence in 1979.

San Marino

Southern Europe
24.1 sq. mi.
Pop: 22,746

Capital: San Marino (Pop: 4,363)
Official language: Italian
Religion: Roman Catholic 95%
Political status: Republic
Heads of state: Two co-regents appointed every six months
Currency: Italian lira ($1 = 1,373.12)

The tiny republic, founded in 1686, continued to rely heavily on funds sent by its citizens living abroad.

Sao Tome and Principe

Atlantic Ocean
387 sq. mi.
Pop: 115,600
UN, OAU

Capital: Sao Tome (Pop: 34,997)
Official language: Portuguese
Religion: Roman Catholic 80%
Political status: Republic
Head of state: Manuel Pinto da Costa (since 1975)
GNP per capita: $340 (1986)
Currency: dobra ($1 = 107.53)

Saudi Arabia

Middle East
849,400 sq. mi.
Pop: 11.52m.
UN, AL, GCC, OPEC

Capital: Riyadh (Pop: 666,840)
Official language: Arabic
Religion: Sunni Muslim 85%, Shiite 15%
Political status: Kingdom
Head of state: King Fahd ibn Abdul Aziz (since 1982)
Head of government: King Fahd ibn Abdul Aziz (since 1982)
GNP per capita: $6,930 (1986)
Currency: rial ($1 = 3.76)

Saudi Arabia strictly enforced Islamic law in 1989, often applying the death penalty to violators. More than 70 people, 16 of whom were Kuwaiti fundamentalists accused of terrorism, were publicly executed.

Senegal

West Africa
75,750 sq. mi.
Pop: 6.98m.
UN, OAU

Capital: Dakar (Pop: 978,553)
Official language: French
Religions: Muslim 91%, Christian 6%, animist 3%
Political status: Republic
Head of state: Abdou Diouf (since 1981)
GNP per capita: $420 (1986)
Currency: franc CFA ($1 = 316.90)

Senegal and its neighbor Gambia decided in late September to dissolve the confederation the two nations had created in 1981 and which had been called Senegambia.

Seychelles

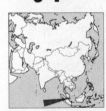

Indian Ocean
175 sq. mi.
Pop: 67,000
UN, CW, OAU

Capital: Victoria (Pop: 23,000)
Languages: Creole, English, French
Religion: Roman Catholic 96%
Political status: Republic
Head of state: France-Albert René (since 1977)
GNP per capita: $3,590 (1988)
Currency: Seychelles rupee ($1 = 5.71)

The year was marked by further democratization of the regime and the economy as the government prepared for general elections in 1990.

President René was elected for a third term in June with 96.1 percent of the vote after running unopposed in general elections. In July, he met President Bush at the White House for the first time.

Sierra Leone

West Africa
27,925 sq. mi.
Pop: 3.88m.
UN, ECOWAS, CW, OAU

Capital: Freetown (Pop: 469,776)
Official language: English
Religions: tribal 52%, Muslim 39%, Christian 8%
Political status: Republic
Head of state: Gen. Joseph Saidu Momoh (since 1985)
GNP per capita: $310 (1986)
Currency: leone ($1 = 62.92)

Tension with neighboring Liberia over the late 1988 expulsion of more than 70 of its citizens from that country decreased in 1989 following mediation efforts by Togolese and Nigerian representatives.

Singapore

Southeast Asia
238.7 sq. mi.
Pop: 2.61m.
UN, ASEAN, CW

Capital: Singapore (Pop: 2,612,800)
Official languages: Chinese, Malay, Tamil, English
Religions: Buddhist, Taoist, Muslim, Hindu, Christian
Political status: Parliamentary republic
Head of state: Wee Kim Wee (since 1985)
Head of government: Lee Kuan Yew (since 1959)
GNP per capita: $7,464 (1987)
Currency: Singapore dollar ($1 = 1.96)

After 30 years in power, Singapore's Prime Minister said in September, on the occasion of his 66th birthday, that he would retire within one year, but only on condition that deputy prime minister Goh Chok Tong was prepared to replace him. Lee added, however, that he planned to remain a member of Singapore's cabinet.

Solomon Islands

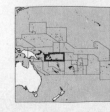

Pacific
10,640 sq. mi.
Pop: 285,796
UN, CW

Capital: Honiara (Pop: 26,000)
Official language: English
Religions: Protestant 76%, Roman Catholic 19%
Political status: Constitutional monarchy
Head of state: Queen Elizabeth II
Head of government: Solomon Mamaloni (since 1989)
GNP per capita: $530 (1986)
Currency: Solomon Island dollar ($1 = 2.40)

In March, Mamaloni, who was Prime Minister from 1981 to 1984, was returned to power. In July, the government said it could not afford to fund a U.N. mission in New York.

Somalia

Northeastern Africa
246,201 sq. mi.
Pop: 6.26m.
UN, AL, OAU

Capital: Mogadishu (Pop: 250,000)
Official languages: Somali, Arabic
Religion: Sunni Muslim 99%
Political status: Republic
Head of state: Mohammed Siad Barre (since 1969)
Head of government: Mohammed Ali Samater
GNP per capita: $280 (1986)
Currency: Somali shilling ($1 = 412.60)

In October, President Barre marked 20 years in office as head of a country ravaged by civil war, ethnic strife and famine. In July, an estimated 1,500 people died in anti-government rioting and the regime was repeatedly criticized by the West for continued human rights violations.

South Africa

Southern Africa
433,678 sq. mi.
Pop: 29.6m.
UN

Capital: Pretoria (Pop: 528,407)
Official languages: Afrikaans, English
Religion: Mainly Christian
Political status: Republic
Head of state: F.W. de Klerk (since 1989)
GNP per capita: $1,800 (1986)
Currency: rand ($1 = 2.70)

Whites-only elections held in September were marred by the bloodiest explosion of anti-government violence in three years, leaving as many as 23 blacks dead and more than 100 injured. On election day, an estimated three million black workers staged a general strike in the country's major cities. Despite this, President de Klerk claimed voters had given him a "mandate for reform." The ballot was far from a whole-hearted endorsement for the President's policies. For the first time since 1953, his ruling Na-

tional Party failed to win the majority of white votes, although it retained control of the government. In the 166-member House of Assembly, the Nationalists lost a quarter of their seats to rivals on both right and left, plummeting from 123 seats to a bare 93. In November, de Klerk promised to put en end to so-called "petty apartheid" as soon as possible. This practice includes the banning of blacks from public places such as beaches.

Spain

Southwestern Europe
194,884 sq. mi.
Pop: 39m.
UN, NATO, EEC, OECD

Capital: Madrid (Pop: 3,123,713)
Official language: Spanish
Religion: Roman Catholic
Political status: Constitutional monarchy
Head of state: King Juan Carlos I
Head of government: Felipe Gonzalez Marquez (since 1982)
GNP per capita: $5,198 (1986)
Currency: peseta ($1 = 118.76)

In January, the Basque separatist group ETA declared a truce in its fight for an independent homeland and talks aimed at reaching a lasting solution got under way with the government. These soon broke down as ETA terrorist attacks spread. Relations with Britain continued to improve despite the long-running dispute over Gibraltar's sovereignty. In October general elections, the ruling Socialist Party lost its overall majority.

Sri Lanka

South Asia
25,332 sq. mi.
Pop: 16.6m.
UN, CW

Capital: Colombo (Pop: 587,647)
Official language: Sinhala
Religions: Buddhist 69%, Hindu 15%, Christian 7%, Muslim 7%
Political status: Republic
Head of state: Ranasinghe Premadasa (since 1989)
Head of government: D.B. Wijeratne (since 1989)
GNP per capita: $400 (1986)
Currency: Sri Lankan rupee ($1 = 40)

The year was marked by continued bloodshed in the vicious, long-running conflict between separatist Tamil guerrillas and the Sinhalese-dominated government. The fighting left an estimated 10,000 dead since the start of the year. During 1989, Indian peace-keeping troops deployed in the north and east since 1987 continued their phased withdrawal, expected to be over by year's end.

Sudan

North Africa
967,500 sq. mi.
Pop: 25.56m.
UN, AL, OAU

Capital: Khartoum (Pop: 476,218)
Official language: Arabic
Religions: Muslim 73%, animist 18%, Christian 9%
Political status: Republic
Head of state: Omar Hassan Ahmed el Beshir (since 1989)
Head of government: Omar Hassan Ahmed el Beshir (since 1989)
GNP per capita: $330 (1987)
Currency: Sudanese pound ($1 = 4.53)

In late June, Prime Minister Sadiq al-Mahdi was overthrown and jailed after a military coup. He and several other former leaders were freed in November by the new military junta. The country remains faced with a desperate economic situation and renewed fighting in the south, where rebels led by Col. John Garang seized several key cities in 1989.

Suriname

South America
63,250 sq. mi.
Pop: 415,000
UN, OAS

Capital: Paramaribo (Pop: 67,905)
Languages: Dutch, English, Creole
Religions: Muslim, Hindu, Christian
Political status: Republic
Head of state: Ramsewak Shankar (since 1988)
GNP per capita: $2,510 (1986)
Currency: Suriname guilder ($1 = 1.80)

In August, a Canadian pilot was seized by Amerindian rebels, who control most of the west of the country. He was held hostage until early October. In November, the government called for urgent peace talks.

Swaziland

Southern Africa
6,705 sq. mi.
Pop: 676,049
UN, OAU, CW

Capital: Mbabane (Pop: 23,290)
Official languages: Siswati, English
Religions: Christian 77%, traditional 23%
Political status: Monarchy
Head of state: King Mswati III
Head of government: Sotsha E. Dlamini (since 1986)
GNP per capita: $730 (1984)
Currency: emalangeni ($1 = 2.67)

Swaziland, which relies almost exclusively on trade with neighboring South Africa, continued throughout the year to extradite to South Africa members of the anti-apartheid African National Congress.

Sweden

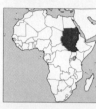

Northern Europe
173,731 sq. mi.
Pop: 8.4m.
UN, EFTA, OECD

Capital: Stockholm (Pop: 663,217)
Official language: Swedish
Religion: Lutheran 95%
Political status: Constitutional monarchy
Head of state: King Carl XVI Gustaf
Head of government: Ingvar Carlsson (since 1986)
GNP per capita: $18,607 (1987)
Currency: Swedish krona ($1 = 6.46)

In July, Christer Pettersson, a 42-year-old Swedish drifter and known drug addict, was found guilty of the February 1986 murder of Prime Minister Olof Palme. However, he was released from jail in mid-October after his conviction was overturned.

Switzerland

Western Europe
15,943 sq. mi.
Pop: 6.6m.
EFTA, OECD

Capital: Bern (Pop: 300,316)
Official languages: German, French, Italian, Romansh
Religions: Roman Catholic 47.6%, Protestant 44.3%
Political status: Federal state
Head of state: Jean-Pascal Delamuraz (since 1989)
GNP per capita: $17,840 (1986)
Currency: franc ($1 = 1.63)

A scandal over charges that her husband was involved in the laundering of drug money, which led to the 1988 resignation of Justice Minister Elisabeth Kopp, continued to rock the country. Mrs. Kopp's parliamentary immunity was lifted in February. In November, 36 percent of the electorate voted for the army's abolition.

Syria

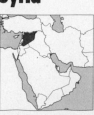

Middle East
71,498 sq. mi.
Pop: 11.4m.
UN, AL

Capital: Damascus (Pop: 1,251,028)
Official language: Arabic
Religion: Sunni Muslim 90%
Political status: Republic
Head of state: Hafez al-Assad (since 1971)
Head of government: Mahmoud Zoubi (1987)
GNP per capita: $2,000 (1984)
Currency: Syrian pound ($1 = 21.13)

The presence of thousands of Syrian troops in Lebanon caused serious tensions with the U.S., which blamed Damascus for much of the bloodshed in that war-torn country. In November, the Soviet Union, for years Syria's main arms supplier, urged President Assad to abandon his quest for military parity with Israel and put more emphasis on defense. Syria has an estimated $15 billion military debt to the Soviet Union.

Taiwan

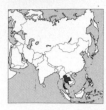

East Asia
13,969 sq. mi.
Pop: 19.7m.

Capital: Taipei (Pop: 2.64m.)
Official language: Chinese
Religions: Buddhist, Taoist, Christian
Political status: Republic
Head of state: Lee Teng-hui (since 1988)
Head of government: Lee Huan (since 1989)
GNP per capita: $5,075 (1987)
Currency: new Taiwan dollar ($1 = 25.84)

Links with China warmed slightly this year and in May Finance Minister Shirley Kuo was able to attend a meeting of the Asian Development Bank in Beijing. In October, all 54 people aboard a China Arlines Boeing 737 were killed when the aircraft hit a mountain in the east of the country. At year's end, Taiwan was set for parliamentary elections.

Tanzania

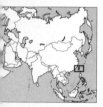

East Africa
364,886 sq. mi.
Pop: 23.2m.
UN, CW, OAU

Capital: Dodoma (Pop: 45,703)
Official languages: Kiswahili, English
Religions: Muslim 33%, Christian 40%
Political status: Republic
Head of state: Ndugu Ali Hassan Mwinyi (since 1985)
Head of government: Joseph S. Warioba (since 1985)
GNP per capita: $240 (1986)
Currency: Tanzanian shilling ($1 = 144.76)

The government said in September that it was launching an all-out war against rampant corruption caused by the drop of government employees' income. Citizens were asked to help stamp out bureaucratic graft.

Thailand

Southeast Asia
198,456 sq. mi.
Pop: 53.9m.
UN, ASEAN

Capital: Bangkok (Pop: 5,609,352)
Official language: Thai
Religions: Buddhist 95%, Muslim 4%
Political status: Constitutional monarchy
Head of state: King Bhumibol Adulyadej (since 1946)
Head of government: Chatichai Choonhavan (since 1988)
GNP per capita: $810 (1986)
Currency: baht ($1 = 25.71)

Following a 42.9 percent cut in U.S. military aid, Thailand turned to China for some of its military requirements. The country played a major role in regional peace efforts undertaken by the Association of South East Asian Nations. In November, Thailand was hit by a typhoon that left more than 300 dead.

Togo

West Africa
21,925 sq. mi.
Pop: 3.25m.
UN, ECOWAS, OAU

Capital: Lome (Pop: 366,476)
Official language: French
Religions: animist 46%, Christian 37%, Muslim 17%
Political status: Republic
Head of state: Gnassingbe Eyadema (since 1967)
GNP per capita: $250 (1986)
Currency: franc CFA ($1 = 316.90)

The country's interior minister, who enjoyed strong popular support, was dismissed for alleged misappropriation of government funds and mismanagement. The economy was boosted by a good harvest and increased production of phosphate.

Tonga

South Pacific
289 sq. mi.
Pop: 95,200
CW

Capital: Nuku'alofa (Pop: 28,899)
Official languages: Tongan, English
Religion: Christian 90%
Political status: Constitutional monarchy
Head of state: King Taufa'ahau Tupou IV (since 1965)
Head of government: Prince Fatafehi Tu'ipelehake (since 1965)
GNP per capita: $580 (1986)
Currency: pa'anga ($1 = 1.33)

International relief aid began arriving in mid-January to help finance reconstruction of vital fishing facilities that were destroyed in December 1988 when Cyclone Gina battered the South Pacific island.

Trinidad and Tobago

Caribbean
1,978 sq. mi.
Pop: 1.24m.
UN, Caricom, CW, OAS

Capital: Port-of-Spain (Pop: 58,400)
Official language: English
Religions: Christian 48.6%, Hindu 25%, Muslim 5.9%
Political status: Republic
Head of state: Noor Hassanali (s. 1986)
Head of government: Arthur Robinson (since 1986)
GNP per capita: $5,120 (1986)
Currency: Trinidad and Tobago dollar ($1 = 4.28)

Unknown assailants tried to assassinate President Hassanali's wife in September, in what the government later said was an attempt to destabilize the regime.

Tunisia

North Africa
59,664 sq. mi.
Pop: 7.32m.
UN, AL, OAU

Capital: Tunis (Pop: 596,654)
Official language: Arabic
Religion: mainly Muslim
Political status: Republic
Head of state: Zine el-Abidine Ben Ali (since 1987)
Head of government: Hamed Karawi (since 1989)
GNP per capita: 1,300 (1986)
Currency: dinar ($1 = 0.96)

April general elections brought added legitimacy to President Ben Ali's government, which seized power in November 1987. In a September government reshuffle, Justice Minister Hamed Karawi was appointed Premier. Ben Ali had his first official meeting with President Bush during a November visit to the White House.

Turkey

Southeastern Europe
300,947 sq. mi.
Pop: 50.67m.
UN, NATO, OECD

Capital: Ankara (Pop: 2,251,533)
Official language: Turkish
Religion: Muslim 98.2%
Political status: Republic
Head of state: Turgut Ozal (since 1989)
Head of government: Yildirim Akbulut (since 1989)
GNP per capita: $1,020 (1986)
Currency: Turkish lira ($1 = 2251.10)

Outgoing liberal Prime Minister Turgut Ozal was elected President for a seven-year term after a late October ballot that was largely boycotted by the left-wing opposition parties. He said he would press ahead with badly needed economic reforms and work so that his country could gain early membership in the EEC. However, French President Francois Mitterrand indicated in November, while he held the EEC's rotating presidency, that Turkey's request to join the 12-nation European Economic Community should be postponed until 1993.

Tuvalu

South Pacific
9.5 sq. mi.
Pop: 8,229
CW

Capital: Funafuti (Pop: 2,620)
Official languages: Tuvaluan, English
Religion: Protestant
Political status: Constitutional monarchy
Head of state: Queen Elizabeth II
Head of government: Tomasi Puapua (since 1981)
GNP per capita: $500 (1984)
Currency: Australian dollar

As part of a multi-million-dollar, three-year development aid project, Japan in early February handed over six brand new vessels to help train Tuvalu's fishermen in the use of modern fishing technology.

Uganda

East Africa
91,343 sq. mi.
Pop: 15.5m.
UN, CW, OAU

Capital: Kampala (Pop: 458,423)
Languages: English, Kiswahili, Luganda
Religions: Christian 62%, Muslim 6%
Political status: Republic
Head of state: Yoweri Museveni (s. 1986)
Head of government: Samson Kisekka (since 1986)
GNP per capita: $230 (1984)
Currency: Uganda shilling ($1 = 200.61)

Local elections held in February, the first fraud-free ballot since 1962, further widened the powers of the ruling National Resistance Council. The following month, tension broke out with neighboring Kenya, which accused Ugandan forces of launching cross-border attacks.

Union of Soviet Socialist Republics

Eurasia
8,649,496 sq. mi.
Pop: 284.5m.
UN, CMEA,
Warsaw Pact

Capital: Moscow (Pop: 8,815,000)
Official languages: Russian, 112 others
Religions: Christian, Muslim, Jewish, Buddhist
Political status: Federal union
Head of state: Mikhail Gorbachev (since 1988)
Head of government: Nikolai Ryzhkov (since 1985)
Head of Communist Party: Mikhail Gorbachev (since 1985)
GNP per capita: $6,000 (1985)
Currency: ruble ($1 = 0.64)

It was a profoundly paradoxical year for Mikhail Gorbachev. His popularity in the West soared to new heights, while at home he was faced with massive strikes, a catastrophic economic situation, soaring crime statistics, bloody ethnic clashes, growing conservative opposition to his reform drive and spreading nationalism. As the Soviet leader traveled to Rome in late November for a historic meeting with Pope John Paul II, and from there to Malta for his first summit conference with President Bush in December, he left behind a nation in a state of turmoil. In the Baltic states, under Soviet control since 1940, millions of Latvians, Lithuanians and Estonians were calling for total political and economic independence from Moscow. In Moldavia, a former province of Romania, there were growing demands for autonomy. Meanwhile, ethnic strife, which left scores of people dead, spread through Uzbekistan, Georgia, Azerbaijan and Kazakhstan. The economic situation worsened dramatically. For the first time since the post-war era, sugar was rationed on a nationwide basis, in addition to butter, meat and other staples. In July, Gorbachev said $16 billion would urgently be spent abroad to buy essential foodstuffs and some badly-needed consumer goods. A mid-year strike by thousands of coal miners, notably in Siberia, further threatened the economy. By late September, there were more than six million people who had no steady employment in the USSR. The authorities admitted that the country had nearly 20 million alcoholics, while overall crime statistics had risen by 35 percent.

United Arab Emirates

Middle East
32,300 sq. mi.
Pop: 1.77m.
UN, AL, GCC, OPEC

Capital: Abu Dhabi (Pop: 670,125)
Official language: Arabic
Religion: Muslim 90%
Political status: Federation of emirates
Head of state: Sheik Zayid ibn Sultan al-Nahayan (since 1971)
Head of government: Sheik Rashid ibn Said al-Maktum (since 1979)
GNP per capita: $14,410 (1986)
Currency: dirham ($1 = 3.68)

In August, Sheik Zayid criticized the U.S. for not doing more to end the war in Lebanon. In June, the government freed two Irishmen who had been arrested for the attempted kidnap of an Arab-Irish girl.

United Kingdom

Northwestern Europe
94,226 sq. mi.
Pop: 55.78m.
UN, CW, EEC, NATO, OECD

Capital: London (Pop: 6,770,400)
Official language: English
Religions: Church of England, Roman Catholic
Political status: Constitutional monarchy
Head of state: Queen Elizabeth II
Head of government: Margaret Thatcher (since 1979)
GNP per capita: $8,920 (1986)
Currency: pound sterling ($1 = .63)

The personality and politics of Margaret Thatcher dominated the year, as they have the decade. Yet her critics believe that the Iron Lady, who in May celebrated 10 years in Downing Street, is finally betraying signs of metal fatigue. She even faced her first challenge for the Conservative Party leadership. During the year she lost a foreign secretary (when she reshuffled Sir Geoffrey Howe) and a chancellor of the exchequer (when Nigel Lawson resigned). Differences over Europe were factors in both changes and Mrs. Thatcher found herself in a minority within the European Community and the Commonwealth. Relations with Mikhail Gorbachev remained warm, but the post-Reagan "special relationship" with the U.S. cooled somewhat, with disagreements over the Vietnamese "boat people."

Europe was also the focus of the Tories' first national defeat in 10 years when a resurgent Labor Party won elections for the European Parliament. The ballot was also bad news for the former Alliance parties, both of which were beaten into third place by the Green Party. Environmental issues played an increasingly important role in politics, but concern over the economy remained paramount. High interest rates, which reached 15 percent in October, failed either to quell fears about the trade deficit or to curb inflation. Privatization, health service reforms and food safety also caused trouble for the government, as did strikes by railwaymen, dockers and ambulance crews. For most people, though, the summer was memorable for its record hours of sunshine rather than its strikes.

Britain was also afflicted by disasters: scores of spectators were crushed to death at the Hillsborough soccer stadium and more than 50 young people on an evening Thames cruise died when their vessel was rammed and sank. The IRA campaign of terrorism continued to claim lives in England and West Germany as well as in Northern Ireland itself.

United States

North America
3,539,289 sq. mi.
Pop: 238.7m.
UN, NATO, OAS, OECD

Capital: Washington D.C. (Pop: 638,333)
Official language: English
Religions: Protestant 56%, Catholic 36.7%, Jewish
Political status: Federal republic
Head of state: George Bush (since 1989)
GNP per capita: $16,710 (1986)
Currency: dollar

As President Bush marked the first anniversary of his election to the White House in November, he could look back on a year marked by improved East-West relations, the fall of the Berlin Wall, rising anti-communist sentiment in East Bloc nations, decreased but still-present trade tensions with Europe and Japan and a well-established peace process in Southern Africa. On the home front, Bush was faced with a devastating drug problem, a growing violent-crime wave, the spread of AIDS and often-acrimonious national debates over abortion and the flag-burning issue. The economic situation remained reasonably stable, despite an October Wall Street panic and a small but worrisome rise in inflation. On the foreign-affairs front, the year saw a crisis in U.S.-China relations after Washington responded to Beijing's anti-democracy crackdown in June by imposing sanctions. In December, Bush held his first summit meeting with Soviet leader Mikhail Gorbachev. This focused on the historic changes sweeping through Eastern Europe's communist states that called into question the post-war partition of Europe. In the Middle East, pro-Iranian terrorists executed a U.S. hostage in July.

The administration in 1989 suffered two foreign policy setbacks: in Nicaragua, where it practically abandoned all hopes of seeing the U.S.-backed contra rebels prevail, and in Panama, where General Noriega continued to openly defy Washington. At home, victory seemed far from assured in the war against drugs, despite a 20-ton September cocaine seizure in Los Angeles. The nation's capital was rocked by an unprecedented crime wave, much of it drug-related. The country was hit by two major natural calamities: the rampage of Hurricane Hugo through South Carolina in September

and the October San Francisco earthquake. In March, a giant crude oil spill caused an unprecedented ecological catastrophe on Alaska's southern shores.

Uruguay

South America
72,172 sq. mi.
Pop: 3.08m.
UN, LAIA, OAS

Capital: Montevideo (Pop: 1,246,500)
Official language: Spanish
Religion: Roman Catholic 66%
Political status: Republic
Head of state: Julio Maria Sanguinetti (since 1985)
GNP per capita: $1,860 (1986)
Currency: nuevo peso ($1 = 692)

Uruguay's first fully democratic elections in 18 years were won in late November by Luis Alberto Lacalle of the opposition National Party. Outgoing President Julio Sanguinetti is to step down in March 1990.

Vanuatu

South Pacific
5,700 sq. mi.
Pop: 149,400
UN, CW

Capital: Vila (Pop: 15,000)
Languages: Bislama, English, French
Religion: Christian 80%
Political status: Republic
Head of state: Fred Timakata (since 1989)
Head of government: Walter Lini (since 1980)
GNP per capita: $350 (1981)
Currency: vatu ($1 = 120)

Former President George Ati Sokomanu was found not guilty in April of having tried in early 1989 to overthrow the government of Prime Minister Lini.

Vatican City

Southern Europe
108.7 acres
Pop: 1,000

Capital: Vatican City
Official languages: Italian, Latin
Religion: Catholic
Head of Roman Catholic Church: Pope John Paul II (since 1978)
Secretary of State: Cardinal Agostino Casaroli (since 1979)
Currency: lira ($1 = 1,373)

The Vatican's finances took a marked turn for the better in 1989, with a budget deficit of $43.5 million. That was approximately $17 million less than had been expected.

Venezuela

South America
352,143 sq. mi.
Pop: 18.77m.
UN, LAIA,
OAS, OPEC

Capital: Caracas (Pop: 1,044,851)
Official language: Spanish
Religion: Roman Catholic
Political status: Republic
Head of state: Carlos Andres Perez (since 1989)
GNP per capita: $2,930 (1986)
Currency: bolivar ($1 = 37.47)

The drug problem worsened considerably for Venezuela in 1989 despite government attempts to fight trafficking. In November, security forces seized more than 4,500 pounds of extremely high grade cocaine.

Vietnam

Southeast Asia
127,245 sq. mi.
Pop: 61.4m.
UN, CMEA

Capital: Hanoi (Pop: 2m.)
Official language: Vietnamese
Religions: Buddhist, Taoist
Political status: Socialist republic
Head of state: Vo Chi Cong (since 1987)
Head of government: Du Muoi (since 1988)
GNP per capita: $200 (1989)
Currency: dong ($1 = 4,528)

For Vietnam's people, 1989 brought hopes that the country, which has been at war for nearly 50 years, would at last enjoy a period of peace. In late September, the last Vietnamese troops sent into Cambodia in 1979 to support the Phnom Penh regime against anti-communist, China-backed guerrillas, left that war-ravaged country. An estimated 60,000 Vietnamese soldiers were killed and many more wounded during the conflict.

Western Samoa

South Pacific
1,093 sq. mi.
Pop: 163,000
UN, CW

Capital: Apia (Pop: 33,170)
Official languages: Samoan, English
Religions: Congregationalist 47%, Roman Catholic 22%, Methodist 16%
Political status: Constitutional monarchy
Head of state: King Malietoa Tanumafili II
Head of government: Tofilau Eti Alesana (since 1988)
GNP per capita: $770 (1985)
Currency: tala ($1 = 2.29)

The small island nation, faced with continued economic woes, invested heavily in tourist facilities, hoping to attract visitors, notably from Australia and the U.S.

Yemen (North)

Middle East
73,300 sq. mi.
Pop: 8.6m.
UN, AL

Capital: San'a (Pop: 427,151)
Official language: Arabic
Religion: Muslim (Sunni 39%, Shiite 59%)
Political status: Republic
Head of state: Ali Abdallah Saleh (since 1978)
Head of government: Abdel Aziz Abdel Ghani (since 1983)
GNP per capita: $550 (1986)
Currency: rial ($1 = 9.81)

North Yemen sought to forge closer ties with Marxist South Yemen. By year's end, the two neighboring states were on the verge of creating a single confederated state.

Yemen (South)

Middle East
130,065 sq. mi.
Pop: 2.3m.
UN, AL

Capital: Aden (Pop: 318,000)
Official language: Arabic
Religions: mostly Muslim, Christian, Hindu
Political status: People's democratic republic
Head of state: Haidar al-Attas (since 1986)
Head of government: Yasin Sa'id Nu'man (since 1986)
GNP per capita: $270 (1987)
Currency: dinar ($1 = 0.35)

Severe April flooding in the central regions caused damage estimated at $75 million, killing thousands of head of cattle and destroying dozens of schools and hospitals.

Yugoslavia

Southern Europe
96,835 sq. mi.
Pop: 23.41m.
UN

Capital: Belgrade (Pop: 1,470,073)
Official languages: Serbo-Croat, Macedonian, Slovene
Religions: Orthodox 41%, Roman Catholic 32%, Muslim 12%
Political status: Federal socialist republic
Head of state: Janez Drnovsek (s. 1989)
Head of government: Ante Markovic (since 1989)
GNP per capita: $2,300 (1986)
Currency: dinar ($1 = 40,876)

In May, Janez Drnovsek, a 38-year-old economist from Slovenia, was appointed President, thus becoming the youngest head of state in Europe. Throughout the year, he battled against the country's worst-ever economic crisis, with inflation nearing 1,000 percent, high unemployment and a spiraling foreign debt. The year was also marked by continued and violent ethnic clashes in the southern Kosovo Province. In November, 92 coal miners died in the country's worst mine disaster.

Zaire

Central Africa
905,365 sq. mi.
Pop: 32.56m.
UN, OAU

Capital: Kinshasa (Pop: 2,653,558)
Official language: French
Religions: mostly Roman Catholic; Protestant, Muslim
Political status: Presidential republic
Head of state: Marshal Mobutu Sésé Séko (since 1965)
Head of government: Pida N'bagui Sambwa (since 1989)
GNP per capita: $160 (1983)
Currency: zaïre ($1 = 414.4)

During a June visit to Washington, President Mobutu rejected charges of human rights violations, saying Zairians supported him 100 percent.

Zambia

Southern Africa
290,586 sq. mi.
Pop: 7.12m.
UN, CW, OAU

Capital: Lusaka (Pop: 818,994)
Official language: English
Religions: Christian 66%, Muslim
Political status: Republic
Head of state: Kenneth David Kaunda (since 1964)
Head of government: Malimba Masheke (since 1989)
GNP per capita: $300 (1987)
Currency: kwacha ($1 = 17.46)

Former Interior Minister Gen. Malimba Masheke was appointed premier in March and said he was committed to sweeping economic reforms.

Zimbabwe

Southern Africa
150,699 sq. mi.
Pop: 8.87m.
UN, CW, OAU

Capital: Harare (Pop: 656,100)
Official language: English
Religions: Animist, Anglican and Roman Catholic
Political status: Republic
Head of state: Robert G. Mugabe (since 1987)
GNP per capita: $780 (1984)
Currency: Zimbabwe dollar ($1 = 2.25)

Despite improved performance by the crucial mining sector, the country is still faced with high unemployment and a heavy debt burden.

Abbreviations

AL	Arab League	
ANZUS	Australia, New-Zealand, U.S.	
ASEAN	Association of South East Asian Nations	
Caricom	Caribbean Community and Common Market	
CFA	African Financial Community currency	
CMEA	(or Comecon) Council for Mutual Economic Assistance	
CW	The Commonwealth	
ECOWAS	Economic Community of West African States	
EEC	European Economic Community	
EFTA	European Free Trade Association	
GCC	Gulf Cooperation Council	
LAES	Latin American Economic System
LAIA	Latin American Integration Association
NATO	North Atlantic Treaty Organization
NC	Nordic Council
OAS	Organization of American States
OAU	Organization of African Unity
OECD	Organization for Economic Cooperation and Development
OPEC	Organization of Petroleum Exporting Countries
UN	United Nations
WP	Warsaw Pact

General Index

Numbers in bold refer to items covered in articles; numbers in italics refer to events listed only in chronologies.

Photo Credit Index

Key for positioning of pictures: B=bottom; T=top; L=left; X=2nd column; Y=3rd column; R=right; M=middle.